D0897494

TAX
INCENTIVES
FOR
HISTORIC
PRESERVATION

A12700 512778

3 1272 00101 5633

TAX INCENTIVES FOR HISTORIC PRESERVATION

BRADLEY UNIVERSITY LIBRARY

Gregory E. Andrews, Editor
National Trust for Historic Preservation

THE PRESERVATION PRESS

THE PRESERVATION PRESS
National Trust for Historic Preservation
1785 Massachusetts Avenue, N.W.
Washington, D.C. 20036

The National Trust for Historic Preservation, chartered by Congress in 1949, is the only national private, nonprofit organization with the responsibility to encourage public participation in the preservation of sites, buildings and objects significant in American history and culture. Support is provided by membership dues, endowment funds and contributions and by matching grants from federal agencies, including the U.S. Department of the Interior, Heritage Conservation and Recreation Service, under provisions of the National Historic Preservation Act of 1966.

National Trust involvement in taxation issues was facilitated by a contribution from the Ella West Freeman Foundation of New Orleans.

Library of Congress Catalogue Card Number 79-93052
ISBN 0-89133-041-0

Copyright © 1980 National Trust for Historic Preservation in the United States. All rights reserved. Printed in the United States of America.

Designed by Gwen Hoelscher & Associates
Drawings by R. David Schaaf

Cover: *The crossroads of The Strand, Galveston, Tex.*

KF
6535
.T39

Contents

JAN 7   1981

3. TAX IMPLICATIONS OF PRESERVATION EASEMENTS

4. TAXATION OF PRIVATE PRESERVATION ORGANIZATIONS

APPENDIXES

Introduction

In 1976 the National Trust for Historic Preservation, joined by the National Park Service, the Advisory Council on Historic Preservation and the National Conference of State Historic Preservation Officers, sponsored a national conference entitled "Public Tax Policy and the Conservation of the Built Environment." This conference, the first of its kind, was called to examine the state of preservation tax law and, in particular, to encourage support for bills then before Congress that later became the historic preservation tax incentive provisions of the Tax Reform Act of 1976. The conference had a significant role in increasing public awareness and discussion of these proposals and in contributing to their enactment, as well as providing a forum for discussing the relationship between tax laws and historic preservation. A generous contribution from the Ella West Freeman Foundation of New Orleans made the conference possible.

Prior to 1976, little had been done to understand, much less mitigate, the often injurious effect most income and property tax laws had on historic properties. Revision of the tax laws was needed to overcome a bias against preservation and in favor of demolition and new construction. This bias created a situation, according to Ada Louise Huxtable of the *New York Times,* whereby "sound business practice [had become] the business of wrecking cities."

Although historic preservation was recognized as a national policy as early as the Antiquities Act of 1906, changing the tax laws to encourage preservation was not suggested until 1964 in a report submitted to President Johnson by the Task Force on the Preservation of Natural Beauty. Then, in 1965, with a Ford Foundation grant, the United States Conference of Mayors formed a Special Committee on Historic Preservation. In its report entitled *With Heritage So Rich* (Random House, 1966), the committee recommended a new national program for historic preservation and concluded that "if the effort to preserve historic and architecturally significant areas as well as individual buildings is to succeed, intensive thought and study must be given to economic conditions and tax policies which will affect our efforts to preserve such areas as living parts of the community." The committee specifically called for legislation providing, in part, for historic preservation as a public, tax-exempt charitable activity; deductibility of gifts of historical easements to proper entities engaged in preservation; and for deductibility of preservation restoration expenditures incurred by private owners of registered historic properties. The recommendations of the committee led to congressional passage of the National Historic Preservation Act of 1966. The 1966 act, however, did not contain any tax incentive provisions.

In 1970, the President's Council on Environmental Quality appointed a Tax

Law Advisory Committee to study the impact of federal tax policy on the environment, including its effect on historic preservation. The study resulted in a joint proposal in 1971 by the council and the U.S. Department of the Treasury for an Environmental Protection Tax Act, whose preservation incentive provisions Congress eventually enacted in October 1976 as part of the Tax Reform Act.

The preservation tax provisions in the Tax Reform Act of 1976 represented a real breakthrough because they established important tax incentives for the preservation and rehabilitation of income-producing historic structures. The act included tax penalties for the demolition of historic buildings and also encouraged the charitable donation of partial property interests, such as facade easements, for historic preservation purposes. In the Revenue Act of 1978, Congress supplemented these important incentives by enacting an investment tax credit for rehabilitating older commercial and other nonresidential income-producing structures.

Despite their relative newness, the tax incentives have generated considerable rehabilitation work on historic structures. The Heritage Conservation and Recreation Service of the U.S. Department of the Interior, which is responsible for certifying the significance and appropriateness of rehabilitation work on buildings benefiting from the 1976 tax incentives, estimates that more than 1,500 structures have been certified "significant" for these purposes and more than 1,150 rehabilitation projects in 45 states, worth more than $640 million, have been given either preliminary or final certification as appropriate.

In enacting the 1976 tax incentives, however, Congress gave them a five-year life. Prior to their expiration in 1981, it is the responsibility of the preservation community to examine carefully the effect of the incentives and to advise Congress as to whether, and in what form, they should be reenacted.

The basic purpose of *Tax Incentives for Historic Preservation* is similar to that of the 1976 conference—to stimulate discussion of, and appreciation for, the significant role that tax laws play in affecting historic properties. The dramatic expansion and improvement in the tax laws since 1976, however, makes the role of this publication different from that of the 1976 conference. *Tax Incentives for Historic Preservation* seeks to explain and evaluate the now numerous laws offering some form of tax relief for historic preservation and, in so doing, to help chart a future course. It is hoped that this publication will, for example, contribute to the discussion already begun about reenactment of the Tax Reform Act of 1976.

Preservationists and the general public should find this book helpful in learning about the many state and local tax relief laws for historic preservation, why they do or do not work and the considerations that should be taken into account in amending them or in enacting other laws. Publication of *Tax Incentives for Historic Preservation* is part of the National Trust's commitment to encourage public participation in the preservation of America's historic and architectural heritage.

James Biddle, President
National Trust for Historic Preservation

2

Editor's Note

A combined citation style has been used in *Tax Incentives for Historic Preservation* in order to facilitate the book's use by laypersons as well as members of the legal community. While based primarily on *A Uniform System of Citation*, 13th Edition (Cambridge: Harvard Law Review Association), the source for citation style in legal publications, *A Manual of Style*, 12th Edition (Chicago: University of Chicago Press) was used as style source for some material cited in this book. The legal writer and layperson are cautioned against using this combined style for footnote or bibliographical reference.

As in legal citations, the volume number is placed before the title of the publication, which is followed immediately by the page number. The legal style for abbreviating publications, statutes and other legal documents is used except where the abbreviation would confuse the layperson. Otherwise, the citations should be self-explanatory.

1. Federal Tax Law

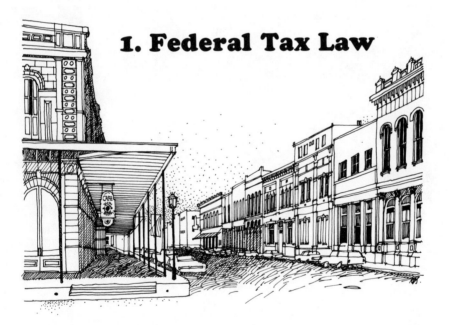

Mortimer Caplin

FEDERAL TAX POLICY AS AN INCENTIVE FOR ENHANCEMENT OF THE BUILT ENVIRONMENT

Discussion of the role of tax policy in the preservation movement should be approached from the viewpoint that U.S. tax laws are fundamentally a mechanism for raising the revenue needed by the government and that this process should be carried out in a fair, rational and straightforward manner. Before complicating the system through use of tax laws for other purposes—whether to regulate conduct or to achieve societal or economic objectives—one should first test the availability of alternative methods for achieving these nonrevenue goals.

However, if Justice Holmes was right in saying that taxes are the price we pay for living in a civilized society, then within this framework perhaps it is appropriate to consider whether the tax system should be used to aid in preserving the structural legacy of our civilization, or at least amended to avoid discrimination against preservation efforts. This article will review the current federal tax policy as it affects the built environment and consider recently enacted tax laws and some other proposals for encouraging preservation efforts. Throughout, any enthusiasm for additional preservationist tax incentives must be tempered by a realistic view of the pitfalls to be faced along the legislative route and by the need to make a sober cost-benefit analysis of each of the alternatives at hand.

Objectives of the Preservation Movement

It is not possible to assess the fairness of current tax law or the need for change without first considering the objectives of preservationists. To the average layperson, the historic preservation movement connotes philanthropic and governmental efforts to restore and preserve well-known and popular historic sites such as Williamsburg, Monticello, Old North Church and Independence Hall. These kinds of efforts—the enhancement and maintenance of historic landmarks for the education and enjoyment of the visiting public—have been the traditional focus of the preservation movement. With the help of the National Trust for Historic Preservation and various state and local agencies and organizations, this basic aspect of historic preservation can continue.

To the preservationists, however, much more is at stake. Our architectural and cultural heritage is not confined to famous old buildings where Thomas Jefferson or George Washington slept or from which Paul Revere received his signals, buildings that have been converted to museums or other tourist attractions. Other categories of property must also be taken into account. The National Register of Historic Places, for example, now lists approximately

---

Mr. Caplin was commissioner, Internal Revenue Service (1961–64), and is currently attorney and partner, Caplin and Drysdale, Washington, D.C.

18,000 properties recognized for their historical or architectural value, and many additional properties have been designated by local government agencies as landmarks or as parts of historic districts. The vast majority of these properties are privately owned and privately occupied and are not supported by public monies or charitable donations. Moreover, beyond this ever-growing list of historically valuable properties, preservationists are increasingly concerned with the fate of old buildings, neighborhoods and districts that may never be officially recognized for their historical value, but which are nonetheless an irreplaceable part of our built environment.

Traditional Focus on Tax Exemptions and Charitable Deductions

U.S. tax laws have long accommodated the traditional part of historic preservation. Groups that operate historic structures as museums on a nonprofit basis may qualify as tax-exempt charitable and educational organizations. As such, they may receive tax-deductible contributions from individuals and corporations as well as grants from other tax-exempt foundations. The Tax Reform Act of 1969, which imposed significant new requirements and restrictions on charitable foundations that are not publicly supported, authorized certain exceptions for "operating foundations." These exemptions were intended, in part, to allow greater freedom in tax-exempt activities to museums and to organizations such as Colonial Williamsburg. Similarly, in 1975 the Internal Revenue Service ruled that a nonprofit organization formed for the purpose of promoting an appreciation of history through the acquisition, restoration and preservation of houses, churches and public buildings having special historical or architectural significance qualifies for tax-exempt status as a charitable organization.[1]

An individual or family that owns a valuable historic property may obtain a tax deduction by contributing the property to a tax-exempt, nonprofit organization or to a governmental unit. Moreover, an outright gift of the property is not always required for a contribution to qualify as a deduction. If the property is a "personal residence" or a "farm," a deduction is allowed for a gift to charity of a remainder interest, which permits the donor to retain the property for life or for a term of years.[2]

Donations of easements may also qualify as deductible contributions. At least since 1964, it has been recognized that a taxpayer's gratuitous conveyance to the United States (or other governmental unit) of a restrictive easement in real property to preserve a scenic view is a charitable contribution, and that a tax deduction may be claimed for the value of the easement.[3] After the enactment of the Tax Reform Act of 1969, there was some concern that deductions for such scenic easements might have been eliminated because the act generally placed restrictions on contributions of less than a taxpayer's entire interest in property. However, the regulations and subsequent rulings made clear that a grant of a perpetual scenic or open space easement would qualify as a charitable contribution.[4]

In 1975, the Internal Revenue Service issued a scenic easement ruling of particular significance to preservationists. The service ruled that an individual who owned a mansion and land declared to be a state landmark because of its unique architectural features, and who granted an easement to the state permanently restricting alteration and further development of the property, could claim a charitable deduction for the value of the easement.[5]

The Tax Reform Act of 1976 further broadened and clarified the deductibility of easements. The act specifically makes deductible the value of contributions of perpetual easements, leases, options or remainder interests in any real property to a government or charitable organization in order to preserve historically important land areas or structures. As amended in 1977, however, this new law applies only to contributions made before June 14, 1981, at which time this law will expire unless extended.[6]

There is much more that can be said about existing laws applicable to tax-exempt organizations and charitable contributions and their impact on preservation efforts. In general, it is fair to say that the existing tax laws are supportive of traditional charitable and public preservation activities.

Broadened Concern for the Built Environment

The more difficult tax policy questions are posed by the broadened concern of preservationists for the built environment, a concern that encompasses neighborhoods, districts and private buildings that will never benefit from public restoration programs or from private charity. The major burden of this aspect of the preservation movement must be borne by private interests—owners of commercial property, real estate developers and individual homeowners. The willingness of private interests to rehabilitate or maintain an older property, rather than allow it to deteriorate or tear it down and build something new, will depend in large measure on economic considerations, including tax considerations. Recent studies indicate that the cost for preservation and reuse of an old building may be substantially lower than that of constructing a new building of similar size.[7] Where preservation is more costly, however, it is unrealistic to expect preservation goals to outweigh economic concerns for cost and return on investment.

Although tax considerations are only a part of the total financial equation, it is evident that the Internal Revenue Code in the past has done little to encourage preservation in the private sector, and some might even say that it has discriminated against private preservation efforts. I do not mean to suggest that those who drafted the code consciously intended to frustrate preservation activities, but some provisions in the code are clearly intended as incentives for new construction and others simply have that effect. Unfortunately, an incentive for new construction is very often a disincentive for preservation.

One such disincentive results from the different rates of tax deductible depreciation for used and new buildings. The code provides that a taxpayer may depreciate the cost of a used commercial building, which includes any part of the cost provided by a mortgage, only on a straight-line basis. That is, the owner may annually deduct a part of the cost, apportioned equally over the years of the building's "useful life." However, if instead a new commercial building had been built or purchased, that same person would have been able to deduct the cost on a "declining balance" method at a rate equal to 150 percent of the straight-line rate.[8]

9

To a limited extent, this result has been altered by the Tax Reform Act of 1976 and the Revenue Act of 1978. First, for buildings constructed on sites formerly occupied by certain historic structures, depreciation may be taken only on a straight-line basis.[9] Second, where the owner of such a historic structure undertakes rehabilitation consistent with its historic character, he or she may either deduct the cost of the rehabilitation through amortization over five years or, if the rehabilitation is substantial, depreciate the cost of the building and the rehabilitation at the same accelerated rate as if the building were new.[10]

Another provision that has operated as a disincentive to preservation is the allowance of a loss deduction when a commercial building is demolished.[11] For many historic buildings this disincentive was removed by the Tax Reform Act of 1976, which disallowed the deduction for the cost of demolition and any loss resulting from it.[12]

The Revenue Act of 1978 added another incentive for rehabilitation. It allows a 10 percent investment tax credit for rehabilitating a qualified building already in use for 20 years or more for income-producing purposes other than residential ones. If the building is a "certified historic structure," then to qualify for this credit the rehabilitation work must be certified by the Secretary of the Interior as consistent with its historic character. A taxpayer cannot take both this credit and the five-year amortization deduction option available under the Tax Reform Act. However, the credit can be taken in addition to the accelerated depreciation option[13] also offered under the Tax Reform Act.

General Observations on Tax Legislation

The significant revisions of the Internal Revenue Code enacted as part of the Tax Reform Act of 1976 and the Revenue Act of 1978 provide a more favorable climate for preservation. However, as many of the new provisions have a limited life, decisions whether to retain them, add to them or cut them back will have to be made in the next few years. Several general observations about tax legislation, both on a policy level and on a practical level, will be useful in making these decisions.

In the first place, there is widespread concern with the many special rules, exceptions and complex statutory provisions that mark a departure from the basic framework of a fair and progressive income tax—often for the purpose of furthering economic and social goals unrelated to the raising of revenue. The complications and inequities created by these provisions have resulted in a series of tax-reform efforts. In these efforts, the provisions attacked have included not only those questioned on their utility in accomplishing their purported goals, but also those that, while working as their original sponsors expected, are now regarded as having created undue tax savings for private interests.

Underlying the concern about the special-purpose tax incentives is the realization that they have a cost, for they are basically an indirect form of government expenditure.[14] And while the cost of tax incentives is difficult to measure and to control, the ultimate tax loss must be paid for by the average taxpayer. Even where a tax incentive does not involve a significant number of revenue dollars, one must consider the intangible cost of further disillusionment over the fairness of the tax laws and the possible adverse impact on the self-assessment tax system.

This problem of public confidence in the fairness of the tax laws is most acute when one considers code provisions that give special tax advantages to particular groups of taxpayers operating in the private sector. An example of this is the low-income rental housing rehabilitation write-offs allowed by section 167(k) of the code. Given the facts that most low-income housing simply does not make money and that depreciation deductions are not available on owner-occupied housing, this provision is valuable only to those with outside taxable income and only to those who rent properties to others. The question is whether the estimated $85 million spent through the tax code on this kind of rehabilitation in 1974 alone, for example, could have helped to rehabilitate more houses if spent directly for that purpose.[15] An indication of the magnitude of this tax expenditure is that from 1966 through fiscal year 1975 federal appropriations for matching grants-in-aid to the states and to the National Trust for preservation purposes totaled only about $50 million.

Apart from the cost and inequity of special-purpose tax provisions, the complexity of the Internal Revenue Code has increasingly led to calls for tax simplification—the curtailment of deductions, credits and special treatment of all kinds—in return for lower tax rates at all levels. In 1963, for example, Sen. Russell Long (D-La.) proposed an optional "Simplified Tax Method" with rates ranging up to a 50 percent maximum.[16] Former Secretary of the Treasury William E. Simon made an even more striking proposal in 1975, suggesting a new mandatory system with rates of 10–12 percent at the low end and 35–40 percent at the high end—an across-the-board cut in personal income tax rates of about 30 percent "without any loss in revenue."[17] This cry was taken up by President Carter during his election campaign, but was significantly weakened in his legislative proposals.

Although every plea for tax simplification seems to be answered by enactment of more complex statutory provisions, U.S. tax policy should aim at doing everything possible to ease the public's burdens of tax compliance and to make the system more administrable by the Internal Revenue Service. It must be plainly recognized that use of the tax system to resolve specific social and economic problems is almost always at cross-purposes with these objectives.

Social Uses of Tax Legislation

Despite competing considerations of fairness, revenue loss and complexity, there are occasions when the use of the tax system to promote nonrevenue ends is justified. Two preconditions should be satisfied: (1) the objective should be of overriding importance to the society and (2) the objective should be one that can be achieved most effectively through the tax system. One must ask whether tax incentives will better achieve the desired results than will alternative governmental programs and whether the tax incentives, when compared with other alternatives, will accomplish this result without substantially higher costs or waste of resources. Some or all of the tax incentives for preservation activities in the 1976 Tax Reform Act and the 1978 Revenue Act may satisfy these stringent criteria. Further, some of this legislation is not intended to provide an artificial stimulus or subsidy for private preservation efforts. Rather, it provides a greater degree of parity, or tax neutrality, between preservation and new construction.

No matter how rational or equitable tax proposals are, however, their fate will ultimately depend on the vagaries of the legislative process. The enactment of tax legislation is a complicated, frustrating and, in the final analysis, highly political process. What is viewed by some as a means of protecting the built environment may, for example, be viewed by others as a serious threat to the construction industry. Powerful contending interests make compromise inevitable. Proposals that start out making good sense may become so riddled with limitations and exceptions that enactment would be of only minimal value to the preservation movement. The Tax Reform Act of 1976's historic structures rehabilitation depreciation provisions mentioned above are almost a classic example of this. As this act shows, if the preservation movement is intent on pursuing its goals through the tax system, it must be prepared to accept imperfect results.

11

Proposals for Additional Tax Incentives

As discussed above, the preservation movement achieved substantial recognition in the Tax Reform Act of 1976 and the Revenue Act of 1978. Other proposals that have been made at various times, primarily in the context of housing rehabilitation but which may be useful in the preservation effort, include:

1. An investment tax credit for investment in the preservation of residential properties.[18]

2. A refundable tax credit for investment in preservation, to be reduced if certain levels of maintenance are not continued.[19]

3. A special maintenance deduction for catch-up repairs that would normally be considered capital improvements.[20]

4. Deferral of taxation of the gain generated by a sale of restored property to the extent that proceeds are used to purchase or restore other similar property.[21]

5. Disallowance of depreciation deduction to the extent that some portion of the amount deductible is not spent o.i maintenance.[22]

These five proposed changes in the tax laws probably would have an immediate positive impact on someone's decision to demolish or to preserve a building. As a matter of overall preservation strategy, however, it is useful to consider whom and what the changes will help. All of the recent depreciation-related changes, denial of the demolition loss deduction and investment tax credit, as the Internal Revenue Code is currently structured, will encourage preservation by owners of commercial property, including in some cases rental houses and apartment buildings. The proposed changes in the tax laws would continue and broaden the incentives. Since encouraging owners of commercial property to maintain and preserve it is an extremely important part of any preservation strategy, particularly in older urban areas, these changes should enhance the entire effort.

However, it must be recognized that owner-occupants of housing will not receive any of those 1976 and 1978 tax law benefits, for they are not allowed to depreciate their property, deduct the cost of maintenance or receive loss deductions for voluntary destruction.[23] Nor do tax-exempt organizations derive any benefits from these provisions for noncommercial properties they own. Therefore, to the extent that a preservation program includes areawide restoration by owner-occupants—such as that in Capitol Hill, Washington, D.C., and the South End, Boston—changes in the structure of depreciation deductions or demolition losses have no incentive effect.

Most of the changes in the Tax Reform Act of 1976 and the Revenue Act of 1978 relate to properties or rehabilitation plans that have been certified by the Secretary of the Interior. This approach is necessary and tends to prevent the use of tax dollars to support projects that preserve or restore in name only. If quality control is to be imposed, it is better that those judgments be made outside the Internal Revenue Service. However, one of the standard arguments in favor of tax incentives, as opposed to direct government expenditures, is that they are cheaper and more efficient than bureaucratically administered programs. To the extent outside certification has been grafted onto the tax law, this argument loses some of its force.[24]

The various tax law changes and proposals discussed here offer only partial solutions to the basic economic problems of preservation and cannot be considered in isolation from nontax approaches. For example, some of the changes may encourage an owner to retain an old building rather than tear it down and construct a comparable new building. But federal tax incentives will not by themselves persuade most owners to forego large new buildings in favor of small old ones. The profits foregone by not constructing a new building may be too great. More direct control through zoning and preservation requirements would appear necessary to overcome this.

Few of the changes or proposals confront the serious problems associated with the high maintenance costs of old buildings. If tax incentives serve only to encourage rehabilitation without encouraging continued maintenance, they may lay the groundwork for new deterioration and a claim that preservation does not work. Yet, to provide continuing tax incentives for maintenance of economically unsound properties would be extremely difficult and costly.

The above mentioned proposal to deny depreciation deductions in order to encourage regular maintenance might be useful in encouraging restoration of deteriorating but not decrepit buildings, although even that plan appears to have serious drawbacks.[25] To be truly effective, an overall preservation program must meet this maintenance problem.

We all have a deep interest in preserving the structural legacy of America. It is far better to live and work where the building heritage of many years is still alive than in the dead monotony that characterizes so much of modern development. As we assist revision of the U.S. tax laws and probe for additional possible solutions, we must recognize that tax incentives by themselves are not sufficient. They can only be a part of an overall preservation strategy, and the development of a total strategy is needed to achieve our ultimate goal.

NOTES

1. Revenue Ruling 75-740, 1975-2 *Cumulative Bulletin* 207.

2. § 170(f)(3)(B)(i) [Statutory references, unless otherwise noted, are to the Internal Revenue code of 1954] and Treasury Reg. § 1.170A-7(b)(3), (4). Code §§ 2055(e)(2) and 2522(c)(2) contain similar provisions for estate and gift tax deductions.

3. Revenue Ruling 64-205, 1964-2 *Cumulative Bulletin* 62.

4. Treasury Reg. §1.170A-7(b)(1)(ii). Revenue Ruling 73-339, 1973-2 *Cumulative Bulletin* 68; Revenue Ruling 75-373, 1975-2 *Cumulative Bulletin* 77.

5. Revenue Ruling 75-358, 1975-2 *Cumulative Bulletin* 76.

6. §§ 170(f)(3), 2055(e)(2), 2522(c)(2).

7. U.S. Dept. of the Interior, *Rehabilitation: An Alternative for Historic Industrial Buildings* (1979); Advisory Council on Historic Preservation, (IV) Report No. 4. *Adaptive Use: A Survey of Construction Costs* (1976); National Trust for Historic Preservation, *Dollars and Sense: Preservation Economics* (Washington, D.C.: National Trust for Historic Preservation, 1971); *Assessing the Energy Conservation Benefits of Historic Preservation: Methods and Examples* and *The Contribution of Historic Preservation to Urban Revitalization,* Washington, D.C. (Prepared for the Advisory Council on Historic Preservation by Booz, Allen & Hamilton, Inc., January 1979.)

8. § 167(j)(1) and (4). The maximum "declining balance" rate for used residential rental property is 125 percent of the straight-line rate, and for new residential rental property, 200 percent of the straight-line rate. Owners of new residential rental property may also use the "sum of the years-digits" method. One study has found that all accelerated depreciation methods result in deductions that are substantially greater in the early years of a building's life than actual depreciation and has suggested that disincentives to preservation caused by the differential rates be solved by limiting all depreciation of real property to the straight-line method. See P. Taubman and R. Rasche, "The Income Tax and Real Estate Investment," 1971 *Tax Incentives* 113, 119–20. To the extent that depreciation deductions for real estate are reduced below the levels available for personal property, there will tend to be a shift of investment dollars away from real estate. However, because real estate transactions are usually more highly leveraged (i.e., financed with a larger percentage of borrowed dollars), a nominal decline in the depreciation rate may still leave a given equity investment in real estate with an after-tax rate of return higher than that for a similar investment in personal property.

9. § 167(n). The structure must have been a "certified historic structure" (generally, one listed in the National Register or located in a registered historic district, which includes those listed in the National Register or designated by a state or local statute and certified by the Secretary of the Interior).

10. § 167(o). The accelerated depreciation or five-year amortization are, however, items of tax preference for purposes of the minimum tax. §§ 56, 57(a)(2).

11. § 165. No deduction is allowed, however, if at the time the property was purchased, the buyer intended to demolish the building. Treasury Reg. § 1.165-3. Under these circumstances, the cost basis of the building plus demolition expenses must be added to the basis of the land and may not be deducted immediately. Treasury Reg. § 1.165-3(a). The effect is to delay any tax benefit from this sort of transaction until sale of the property and to convert the benefit from deduction against ordinary income to a decrease in capital gain.

12. § 280B.

13. Revenue Act of 1978, Public Law No. 95-600, § 315 (Nov. 6, 1978) (codified in §§ 38 and 48).

14. As pointed out in the budget for fiscal year 1977, it is difficult to translate tax incentives into equivalent dollar subsidies. Special Analysis F, Budget of the United States Government, 1977. However, the concept is still useful in overall budget planning.

15. See Staffs of the Treasury Department and Joint Committee on Internal Revenue Taxation, 94th Cong., 1st Sess., *Estimates of Federal Tax Expenditures* 8 (Comm. Print 1975).

16. 109 *Congressional Record* 19706 (1963) (remarks of Senator Long).

17. Address of former Secretary of the Treasury William E. Simon before the Tax Foundation National Conference, December 3, 1975. Also, Dept. of the Treasury, *Blueprints for Basic Tax Reform* (Jan. 17, 1977).

18. This would be a further extension of the current investment tax credit for the rehabilitation of commercial property discussed in the text at note 12, and the credit for machinery and other personal property, §§ 38, 46–50.

19. See, for example, note, "A Federal Strategy for Neighborhood Rehabilitation and Preservation," 11 *Harvard Journal of Legislation* 509 (1974) (hereafter cited as "A Federal Strategy").

20. R.E. Slitor, *The Federal Income Tax in Relation to Housing* 60–68 (National Commission on Urban Problems Research Report No. 5) (Washington, D.C.: United States Government Printing Office, 1968) (hereafter cited as *The Federal Income Tax*).

21. *Cf.* § 1039 (gains on certain sales of low and moderate-income housing may be deferred if proceeds similarly reinvested). It is possible to defer taxation on gains from the sale of income-producing restored property to the extent that the proceeds of sales are used to purchase similar real estate. § 1031. However, this provision does not allow deferral of gain on proceeds that are spent on the rehabilitation of old property rather than on the initial purchase.

22. Address by Edward J. Logue, former development administrator, Boston Redevelopment Authority, March 29, 1967, cited in *The Federal Income Tax,* note 20 above, at 69.

23. Of course, involuntary destruction will give rise to a casualty loss deduction. § 165(c)(3).

24. However, the changes rely to some extent on listing in the National Register and state law, and where they call for a certification by the Secretary of the Interior, they provide standards to be applied. The efficiency loss from requiring an outside judgment therefore may not be as great as it could have been.

25. See *The Federal Income Tax,* note 20 above, at 60–68. Another proposal tries to meet this problem by means of a refundable tax credit for residents of selected areas. See, "A Federal Strategy," note 19 above, at 509, 526-30.

William S. McKee

THE BENEFIT OF ACCELERATED DEPRECIATION: THE IMPACT OF THE TAX REFORM ACT OF 1976

What is the importance, for tax purposes, of the method of depreciation used on a historic building? If I am going to get a million-dollar depreciation deduction over some period of time, why is it so important that I can depreciate more now as opposed to more later? The answer to this question is a key to understanding the accelerated depreciation tax benefits available under the Tax Reform Act of 1976 for rehabilitating commercial and other income-producing historic structures.

The first thing one must understand is the time value of money. If I am able to take depreciation this year and, thus, save taxes this year, the fact that at some point in the future I will not have any more depreciation is not very important to me. Saving dollars today is much more important than saving dollars in the future. In other words, not paying taxes today and putting off the evil day of paying federal income taxes for a period of 15 to 20 years is a valuable opportunity. This is what is known, in the jargon of the trade, as the deferral value of the real estate tax shelter.

A second element of a real estate tax shelter that is created by depreciation deduction is what is known as rate conversion. I am able to deduct depreciation against any ordinary income. If I am a lawyer and I happen to be in a high tax bracket the ability to deduct depreciation against any legal income is valuable to me. But, when I sell a building after purchasing it new and holding it for 15 years, all or a portion of the profit will be taxable at capital gains rates. In other words, if the depreciation deduction does not represent economic reality and is just a paper deduction (that is, the building in fact did not depreciate materially during those 15 years), but during that time I am able to take a deduction against ordinary income, when I sell the building and have to pay a tax, I pay the tax at capital gains rates. This is known as rate conversion, and it is also a valuable element of the real estate tax shelter.

The two combined, deferral and rate conversion, are the essential ingredients for the real estate tax shelter. In many cases there is a tax shelter both in old buildings and new buildings, since straight-line depreciation (applicable to used buildings) can often produce some tax shelter, whereas accelerated depreciation simply produces more. The latter kind of depreciation is now available both to new buildings and to historically or architecturally significant depreciable buildings that qualify under section 2124 of the Tax Reform Act of 1976.

One must understand the nature of the tax shelter provided by accelerated depreciation. The tax shelter, purely and simply, is the ability to take tax depreciation in excess of economic depreciation. If, in fact, my building were to

Mr. McKee is professor of law, University of Virginia Law School, Charlottesville, Va.

wear out quickly, double declining balance depreciation would be of no unwarranted benefit to me. In fact, however, buildings seldom wear out very rapidly. A number of economic studies have indicated that the economic depreciation in the first 10 years of the life of an office building is often less than 1 percent of its value. Nevertheless, the depreciation can often be 30 or 40 percent of the value, or the costs, of the building. The difference between economic and tax depreciation is the tax shelter. Conceptually, it is separate from the building; it is a valuable right that exists almost independently of the economic performance of the building.

The tax shelter behaves in a strange fashion. First, the higher the individual's tax bracket the more valuable the tax shelter. That is why most real estate investors tend to be high bracket taxpayers. Obviously, the higher the tax bracket the more valuable it is not to have to pay taxes on a big portion of your income.

As the tax bracket goes up, the value of the tax shelter increases dramatically both because of deferring more taxes and because of converting more ordinary income into capital gain. As the value of the tax shelter goes up, it becomes more feasible to borrow money to get into that tax shelter, which explains why high bracket taxpayers tend to borrow substantial sums from banks to be able to make these investments.

The most significant thing about the tax shelter is that it is virtually isolated from economic reality. The ability to take depreciation deductions exists whether or not the building is renting well. Thus, there are many real estate investment deals where the only thing that concerns the investor is whether or not the mortgage would be foreclosed on a new apartment project. As long as a project does not go bankrupt, the investor makes a killing. Recent experience has indicated that, unfortunately, a number of developers do go bankrupt and a large number of investors have lost their money. This phenomenon is a product of over-building and of too much aggressiveness in the real estate market; it does not negate the fact that the real estate tax shelter is still present. However, there are people with investments in new property subject to accelerated depreciation rates who are successfully able to weather slumps in the building market. The tax shelter is still extremely valuable to them, even if they do not receive one penny in cash flow from the building. The fact that the tax shelter exists allows them to take tremendous write-offs, to defer the payment of their taxes and to convert ordinary income into capital gain.

16

Gregory E. Andrews, Sally Oldham and *Ward Jandl*

PRESERVATION INCENTIVES IN THE TAX REFORM ACT OF 1976 AND THE REVENUE ACT OF 1978: QUESTIONS AND ANSWERS

Tax Reform Act of 1976

1. *How did the Tax Reform Act of 1976 encourage the preservation of historic structures?*

Section 2124 of the Tax Reform Act, as amended by the Revenue Act of 1978, added new provisions to the Internal Revenue Code that provide major tax incentives for rehabilitation by owners or lessees of commercial or other income-producing historic structures and tax penalties for those who demolish such structures and replace them with new buildings, or substantially alter them.

2. *Which historic structures are affected by the preservation provisions of the Tax Reform Act of 1976?*

Any structure designated a "certified historic structure" by the Secretary of the Interior is covered by these provisions. In general, a certified historic structure is one that is subject to depreciation, as defined by section 167 of the Internal Revenue Code of 1954, and is either listed individually in the National Register of Historic Places or located in a registered historic district and certified by the Secretary of the Interior as being of historical significance to the district. A "registered historic district" means (1) any district listed in the National Register or (2) any district designated under a state or local statute that has been certified by the Secretary of the Interior as containing criteria substantially insuring the preservation and rehabilitation of historic buildings and also certified as substantially meeting all criteria for National Register listing. Section 167 of the Internal Revenue Code limits depreciation deductions to those structures used in a trade or business or held for the production of income, such as commercial or residential rental properties.

For the purposes of the tax penalty provisions in code sections 167(n) and 280B affecting demolition and substantial alteration, any structure located in a registered historic district (defined in section 191(d)(2)) shall be treated as a cer-

Mr. Andrews is an attorney in the Investment Division, Legal Department, Connecticut General Life Insurance Company, Bloomfield, Conn., and was formerly an attorney in the Office of Real Estate and Legal Services, National Trust for Historic Preservation. Ms. Oldham is chief, Tax Reform Act Unit, National Register of Historic Places, Heritage Conservation and Recreation Service, U.S. Department of the Interior. Mr. Jandl is supervisor, Rehabilitation Certification Unit, Technical Preservation Services, HCRS.

tified historic structure unless (1) the Secretary of the Interior has certified that the structure is not a certified historic structure and (2) if certification occurs after the beginning of demolition or substantial alteration, the taxpayer has attested to the Secretary of the Treasury that at the time such work began he or she in good faith was not aware that the structure's lack of significance had to be certified.

3. *Which rehabilitations qualify for these tax benefits?*

For the purposes of the section 191 and 167(o) tax incentives, a rehabilitation must constitute a "certified rehabilitation," which is defined as any rehabilitation of a certified historic structure that the Secretary of the Interior has officially attested to as being consistent with the historic character of the property or of the district in which it is located.

4. *What are the roles of the Heritage Conservation and Recreation Service and the Internal Revenue Service in administering these tax provisions?*

The Secretary of the Interior is responsible for the historical and architectural judgments necessary to decide which properties, districts and rehabilitations may benefit from or be affected by these tax provisions. On behalf of the Secretary, Interior's Heritage Conservation and Recreation Service (HCRS) has promulgated regulations and standards under which it evaluates, for the purposes of certification, the historical significance of certain properties, the effectiveness of the preservation provisions of state and local statutes designating historic districts and the quality and appropriateness of rehabilitation.

On behalf of the Secretary of the Treasury, the Internal Revenue Service (IRS) is responsible for developing and administering all regulations on the tax aspects of these historic preservation tax incentives. For example, the IRS issued proposed regulations on August 30, 1978,* on the section 191 tax incentives. These regulations explain who may claim tax deductions and when under this amortization provision, which historic structures qualify as depreciable for the purposes of this provision and the distinction between new construction and rehabilitation expenses.

TAX INCENTIVES

18

5. *What are the tax incentives for rehabilitation of historic structures that were enacted as part of the Tax Reform Act of 1976?*

Section 191 was added to the Internal Revenue Code and allows an owner or qualified lessee of a certified historic structure to deduct for federal income tax purposes over a 60-month (5-year) period the costs of certified rehabilitation, in lieu of using these costs in computing otherwise allowable depreciation deductions. Under new code section 167(o), the owner of a property qualifying as "substantially rehabilitated historic property" may instead add the rehabilitation expenses to the "basis" or cost in the entire structure and depreciate the basis at a faster rate than would otherwise be possible.

60-Month Amortization Deductions

6. *Can expenses for new construction that is associated with a certified rehabilitation project be deducted under section 191?*

No. Therefore, a taxpayer must carefully apportion project expenses between rehabilitation and new construction.

7. *How does one distinguish rehabilitation expenses deductible under section*

---

*Final regulations were drafted and scheduled to be published in 1980.

191 from new construction costs that are not deductible?

In its August 30, 1978, proposed regulations, the IRS states that it will study all the facts and circumstances to determine whether expenses are attributable to rehabilitation or new construction. The proposed regulations provide that generally expenses will be considered rehabilitation expenses if the foundation and outer walls of the existing building are retained and the costs are attributable to work done within that framework. With few exceptions, any expansion of the existing structure will be considered new construction, such as the addition of a new story or a new garage—even if physically attached to the historic structure. Landscaping, too, is considered new construction.

Costs incurred in structurally modernizing a certified historic structure, if part of a certified rehabilitation, do qualify as deductible rehabilitation expenses, such as expenditures for modern plumbing and electrical wiring and other improvements required by local building or fire codes. A new addition to house an elevator or fire stairs, for example, would be considered rehabilitation work if the HCRS has ruled that placement of these improvements in the historic structure would be destructive of its character. Carpeting, office furniture and draperies would be considered new construction.

8. *Do any indirectly related rehabilitation expenses, such as legal and architectural fees, qualify as tax deductible under the section 191 amortization provision?*

Yes. In proposed regulations issued on August 30, 1978, the IRS explained that architectural and engineering fees, real estate commissions, site survey fees, legal expenses, insurance premiums (including title insurance), developers' fees and other construction-related costs generally may be included as part of those rehabilitation costs deductible under section 191. However, any costs for which a deduction is claimed under any other section of the Internal Revenue Code, or for which specific allowance is made in another section of the code (e.g., section 189 on construction period interest and taxes), cannot be deducted under section 191.

9. *Can section 191 amortization deductions be taken for a certified historic structure that is only in part used for a depreciable purpose?*

Yes. A certified historic structure may be depreciable only in part if, for example, it is a private residence (a non-depreciable use) that contains a separate rental unit, which is depreciable. The August 30, 1978, proposed regulations issued by the IRS specify that in these circumstances the portion of the certified rehabilitation expenses that are attributable to the rental unit may be taken as amortization deductions under section 191. If a taxpayer can prove that all of the costs of a certified rehabilitation were spent on the rental unit, it is possible that the entire amount of expenses may be deducted under section 191.

10. *Must a structure already have been put to a depreciable use following rehabilitation in order to begin taking section 191 tax deductions?*

Yes. The proposed IRS regulations generally require that both the rehabilitation work be completed and the structure put to a depreciable use (commercial or otherwise income-producing) before section 191 tax deductions may be taken. The regulations do permit the taxpayer the option of beginning the 60-month amortization period of deductions after the entire rehabilitation project is completed, or of using separate amortization periods for identifiable separate components of the entire project as these components are put to a depreciable use. However, expenses for completed separate components must not represent only progress payments on partial completion of overall rehabilitation activities.

11. *Can section 191 amortization deductions be taken before obtaining a certification of historical significance or rehabilitation?*

Yes. In its proposed regulations, the IRS provided that a taxpayer may begin the 60-month period allowed under section 191 for taking amortization deductions after a request has been made for, but prior to, issuance of either (or both) a certification of historical significance or rehabilitation by the HCRS. Proofs of certification then must be submitted with the first income tax return filed by the taxpayer after their receipt. If the certifications are not submitted within 30 months of the start of the amortization period, the taxpayer may be asked by the IRS to agree to extend the time period within which the taxpayer will be liable for additional taxes to offset the deductions taken.

12. *May the purchaser of a certified historic structure take the section 191 amortization deductions for certified rehabilitation expenses incurred prior to purchase?*

Normally, no. The proposed IRS regulations establish a general rule that only those expenses incurred after the acquisition of ownership or of a lease may be claimed as deductions under section 191. There is one key exception to this rule: the right of a purchaser of a certified historic structure to claim deductions for certified rehabilitation expenses incurred by the previous owner if the transfer of ownership occurred prior to the building being put into use for a depreciable purpose. The purchaser may begin to take amortization deductions at the time the structure is placed in use or the rehabilitation is completed, whichever comes later. The amount of expenses that the purchaser may deduct is the lesser of the following two amounts: the rehabilitation expenses actually incurred before the date the purchaser acquired ownership, or the portion of the purchaser's cost that is attributable to the rehabilitation expenses incurred before the transfer of ownership.

Accelerated Depreciation

13. *Which properties qualify as substantially rehabilitated historic property and can benefit from accelerated depreciation?*

Section 167(o) of the Internal Revenue Code provides that "substantially rehabilitated historic property" means any certified historic structure for which the cost of certified rehabilitation during the 24-month period ending on the last day of any taxable year, less any amounts allowed as depreciation or amortization, exceeds the greater of $5,000 or the adjusted basis of such property. The adjusted basis is determined at the beginning of the 24-month period and generally refers to the owner's initial cost of the property plus the cost of improvements as of that date less amounts allowed as depreciation.

14. *Can the owner or lessee of a substantially rehabilitated historic property use both the 60-month amortization deductions and accelerated depreciation?*

No. Section 167(o) of the Internal Revenue Code and the proposed regulations issued by the IRS on August 30, 1978, specifically state that a taxpayer who elects to take amortization deductions under section 191 for expenses incurred in a certified rehabilitation may not also take accelerated depreciation deductions under section 167(o), even though the property may qualify as substantially rehabilitated historic property.

TAX PENALTIES

15. *What are the penalties for demolition and replacement with new construc-*

tion that were created by the Tax Reform Act of 1976?

These penalties are found in sections 280B and 167(n) of the Internal Revenue Code. Section 280B provides that an owner or lessee of a certified historic structure cannot use the advantageous tax treatments normally available for any expenditures incurred or loss sustained because of its demolition. For tax purposes, these expenses or losses now must be "capitalized," i.e., added to the cost of the land, rather than deducted along with the remaining undepreciated basis of the demolished building or, in some instances, added to the cost of the replacement structure for depreciation purposes.

New section 167(n) also prohibits accelerated depreciation for any property in whole or in part constructed, reconstructed, erected or used on a site that was occupied by a certified historic structure that has been demolished or substantially altered other than by a certified rehabilitation. The intended effect of these provisions is to discourage the demolition of historic properties.

16. *May structures in registered historic districts be demolished without being subject to the tax penalties?*

Yes. A taxpayer who has received written certification from the HCRS either prior to or after the start of demolition that his or her structure is not of historical significance to its district will not be subject to these tax disincentives affecting demolition and new construction tax deductions. If this certification of nonsignificance occurs after the beginning of demolition, the taxpayer must also certify to the Department of the Treasury that at the time of demolition he or she in good faith was not aware of the certification requirement (see question 2).

CERTIFICATIONS REQUIRED

Certified Historic Structure

17. *How do individually listed National Register properties become certified historic structures for purposes of the Tax Reform Act?*

Individually listed National Register properties automatically are certified historic structures if they are subject to depreciation. To determine whether or not a property is individually listed in the National Register, a property owner should first consult the listing of the National Register properties in the *Federal Register*, which may be found in most large libraries. The list is published the first Tuesday of each February and is updated the first Tuesday of every month. If a *Federal Register* listing is unavailable, the owner should consult the appropriate state historic preservation officer (SHPO).

18. *How do buildings within National Register districts become certified historic structures for purposes of the Tax Reform Act incentives?*

The first step in obtaining certification of a structure not individually listed in the National Register is to obtain a Historic Preservation Certification Application, available from the appropriate SHPO. Part 1 of the application is for certification of historic structures, while Part 2 is for certification of rehabilitations.

The applicant completes Part 1, signs it and submits it to the SHPO, supplying the following: (1) name of applicant and name of property owner, if different; (2) name and address of the structure; (3) name of the historic district; (4) current photographs of the structure; (5) a brief description that includes mention of alterations, distinctive features and spaces, and construction dates; (6) a brief statement of historical and/or architectural significance and (7) a map identifying the location of the structure within the district. The SHPO reviews the application and forwards it with a recommendation to the Heritage Con-

21

servation and Recreation Service, U.S. Department of the Interior, within 45 days after submission of the completed application. (The applicant may submit Part 1 of the form directly to HCRS if the SHPO fails to process the application within the allowed 45 days.) HCRS then reviews the documentation using the Secretary of the Interior's Standards for Evaluating Structures within Historic Districts, which are based on National Register criteria. HCRS notifies the applicant of its determination of the structure's significance within 30 days of receipt of Part 1 of the application by sending either a Certification of Significance or a notice that the structure is not of historical significance to the district.

19. *How do properties within districts created under state or local statutes become certified historic structures for the purposes of these tax incentives?*

Owners or lessees seeking certification of structures within districts designated under state or local statute must follow a three-step process: (1) the state or local statute creating the district must be certified by HCRS (this certification process is described in the answer to question 21); (2) the district in which the structure is located must be certified by HCRS as substantially meeting all of the requirements for National Register listing (this certification may occur as part of the certification of either the state or local statute or that of the individual structure); and (3) the structure itself must be certified using Part 1 of the Historic Preservation Certification Application and following the procedure described in the answer to the preceding question. Many owners and lessees applying for certification of their structures in locally designated districts will find the process expedited by the prior determination of HCRS as to whether or not the statute and local district are certifiable.

20. *Which state or local statutes designating historic districts may be certified?*

Statutes designating (or providing for the designation of) a district or districts, and that contain criteria substantially achieving the purpose of preserving and rehabilitating buildings of historical significance to the district, may be certified. The statute must provide for a duly designated review body, such as a review board or commission, with the power to review proposed alterations to structures within the designated district(s).

22

21. *How are state or local statutes certified?*

Only an authorized representative of the governmental body that enacted the statute may request its certification. The representative applies for certification in writing to the appropriate state historic preservation officer and supplies (1) certification that he or she is authorized by the governing body to make the application; (2) a copy of the statute for which certification is requested, including any bylaws or ordinances for districts already designated under the statute; and (3) a copy of any existing state enabling legislation for historic districts if a local statute is submitted for certification. If possible, documentation for each district designated under the statute, including a description, statement of significance, map with boundaries, inclusive street numbers and noncontributing buildings marked, and representative photographs including streetscapes, should be submitted at the time of request. Documentation on specific districts must, however, be submitted to the SHPO and HCRS before requests may be processed for certification of individual structures within the district.

The SHPO forwards the request to HCRS for review within 45 days of receipt, along with the district documentation and his or her recommendations. The authorized representative may apply directly to HCRS if the SHPO fails to process the request within the allowed 45 days. HCRS reviews the statute (and documentation, if submitted at this time) to determine whether the statute contains criteria that will substantially achieve the purpose of preserving and rehabilitating buildings of historical significance to the district. Written notification of approval or denial of certification of the statute is sent to the applicant and the appropriate SHPO within 45 days of receipt of request.

Certification will have an important impact on the development of local communities having districts designated under state statutes. Therefore, HCRS strongly encourages the authorized representative who requests certification to discuss its impact with affected local governments and citizens prior to submitting a certification request.

Certified Rehabilitation

22. *How is rehabilitation work designated as "certified rehabilitation" for purposes of the Tax Reform Act?*

An applicant seeking certification of rehabilitation work involving a certified historic structure must complete Part 2 of the Historic Preservation Certification Application and submit it to the SHPO; it may be filed at any time during the course of the rehabilitation work. Part 2 requires information on the condition of the structure, a description of the rehabilitation work and its effect on architectural features, and photographs, drawings and sketches illustrating conditions prior to rehabilitation and the proposed, ongoing or completed work.

The SHPO reviews the application and forwards it within 45 days, with recommendations, to HCRS for review and evaluation. HCRS then notifies the property owner in 45 days whether the project is consistent with the Secretary of the Interior's "Standards for Rehabilitation." Upon completion of the rehabilitation work, the owner must notify HCRS, through the SHPO, of the project completion date, state in writing that in his or her opinion the completed work meets the Secretary's "Standards for Rehabilitation" and submit photographs or other materials documenting the completed project. In some cases, inspection of the project may be made by an authorized HCRS representative. If the work meets the Standards, it is certified. These 10 standards are broadly worded to guide the rehabilitation of all historic buildings, such as brewery complexes, warehouses and school and residential structures. The underlying concern articulated in the 10 standards is to prevent the destruction of the historical and architectural integrity of a structure in the process of rehabilitation.

23

23. *What criteria are used in reviewing rehabilitation work?*

All rehabilitation projects that applicants wish certified for purposes of the Tax Reform Act are reviewed and evaluated by the Heritage Conservation and Recreation Service using criteria known as the Secretary of the Interior's "Standards for Rehabilitation," described in question 22, paragraph two.

24. *What portion of the rehabilitation work is reviewed by the Heritage Conservation and Recreation Service?*

HCRS reviews and evaluates the entire rehabilitation project, including temporary and permanent construction on both the exterior and the interior of the structure. Site improvements and new construction adjacent to, or part of, the structure are also reviewed to the extent that they affect the architectural character of the structure.

25. *Must a rehabilitation project be completed before it can be reviewed by the Heritage Conservation and Recreation Service?*

No. An applicant may submit Part 2 of the Historic Preservation Certification Application (see question 18) to the SHPO for certification of rehabilitation work at any time during the course of or before the start of the work, although full certification cannot occur until its completion. Within 90 days (45 days at the state level; 45 days at the federal level), HCRS will notify the applicant in writing of its decision whether the proposed, in process or completed work is consistent with the "Standards for Rehabilitation." Applicants whose proposed or partially completed work does not meet the standards will be advised directly by HCRS, or through the SHPO, of necessary revisions. In some cases, consultations will be made to assist applicants and their architects in developing acceptable design alternatives and utilizing recommended rehabilitation techniques and processes. It is advantageous, therefore, for applications to be submitted early in order to gain preliminary plan approval, thereby lessening the possibility of a later denial of certification for work that cannot easily be corrected.

26. *Will the Heritage Conservation and Recreation Service review the rehabilitation of a structure not yet designated a "certified historic structure"?*

Yes. HCRS will review any rehabilitation proposal for historic structures not yet so designated and will determine whether the work is consistent with its "Standards for Rehabilitation." The rehabilitation work will not be fully approved until the applicant has received a certification of historical significance for the structure.

27. *Can a certification or denial of certification be appealed?*

Yes. Appeals from any certification or its denial may be made in writing to the Chief, Office of Archeology and Historic Preservation, Heritage Conservation and Recreation Service, Department of the Interior, Washington, D.C. 20243, within 30 days of receipt of the certification decision. The Chief, Office of Archeology and Historic Preservation, will review the appeal and written record of the decision in question and advise the property owner or appropriate person of his decision within 30 days of receipt. This decision is final.

LESSEES

28. *Are lessees who undertake certified rehabilitations of historic structures eligible for the tax benefits of sections 191 and 167(o)?*

Yes, in part. Code section 191(f) specifically states that the lessee of a certified historic structure may take amortization deductions for amounts spent in a certified rehabilitation. For a lessee to qualify for these deductions, however, the remaining term of the lease on the date the certified rehabilitation is *completed* must generally be for not less than 30 years, determined without regard to any lease renewal periods. This code section also allows life tenants in certified historic structures to take amortization deductions for their certified rehabilitation expenses.

The section 167(o) tax provision for accelerated depreciation offers a new tax benefit only for *owners* of substantially rehabilitated historic property and not for lessees. However, the Internal Revenue Code has always allowed lessees to take comparable accelerated depreciation deductions for capital improvements to their leasehold premises if the lease term is equal to or longer than the useful life of the improvements. If the lease term is shorter than the useful life, the lessee may still be able to deduct over the lease term the cost of these improvements as business expenses qualifying under section 162 of the code.

TIME AND COST LIMITATIONS

29. *Is there a limited time period within which certified rehabilitation expenses must be incurred to qualify for these tax incentives?*

Yes. The 60-month amortization deduction provision of section 191 applies only to rehabilitation expenses incurred after June 14, 1976, and before June 15, 1981. The accelerated depreciation deductions in section 167(o) available for substantially rehabilitated historic property apply to expenses incurred after June 30, 1976, and before July 1, 1981. Efforts are now under way to seek an extension of these provisions.

30. *Must a taxpayer begin to take deductions under sections 191 or 167(o) within any time limit?*

Yes. Section 191 and the proposed IRS regulations provide that the taxpayer must elect to begin the 60-month (5-year) amortization period for taking deductions with the month following the month in which the amortizable basis is acquired, or with the first month of the succeeding tax year. The amortizable basis is acquired when the expenses for the certified rehabilitation are incurred. The law provides that these expenses must be incurred before June 16, 1981, in order to qualify for section 191 deductions. Therefore, a taxpayer must begin to compute the 60-month amortization period with the month ending July 14, 1981, or with the month ending January 31, 1982. The effect of this requirement is that the taxpayer must choose to begin taking these deductions, at the latest, on his or her 1982 tax return. Since a taxpayer generally cannot begin to take these deductions before the completion of rehabilitation and before the structure is put into service for a depreciable use, these events must also have taken place by 1982 under the current law.

31. *Does use of the 60-month amortization deductions require a minimum amount of rehabilitation expenses?*

No. Unlike the requirements discussed in question 13 for using accelerated depreciation, an owner of a certified historic structure may take amortization deductions for any amount spent in connection with certified rehabilitation.

32. *Is there a limited amount of time during which demolitions of certified historic structures and new construction replacement are subject to the tax penalties?*

Yes. The denial in section 280B of deductions for demolition costs and losses applies to demolitions beginning after June 30, 1976, and before January 1, 1981. The limitation in section 167(n) on depreciation deductions available for new construction replacement applies to construction work occurring after December 31, 1975, and before January 1, 1981.

25

RECAPTURE AND MINIMUM TAX IMPLICATIONS

33. *Are the deductions taken for certified rehabilitation expenses under sections 191 or 167(o) subject to the Internal Revenue Code's recapture rules upon sale of the property?*

Yes. Code section 1250 provides for the recovery, or "recapture," in part upon the sale of a certified historic structure or any depreciation deductions previously taken, including those taken under sections 191 or 167(o). These deductions are subject to recapture to the extent that they exceed the straight-line depreciation deductions that would have been allowable and taken in the alternative. The effect of this recapture rule is that a portion of the gain upon sale equaling this excess recapturable amount will be treated as ordinary income for tax purposes, while the balance of the gain upon sale, if any, will be treated as capital gain for tax purposes.

34. *Are the deductions available under sections 191 and 167(o) for certified historic structures subject to the minimum tax for tax preferences under sections 55-58 of the Internal Revenue Code?*

Yes. These deductions do constitute items of tax preference, as defined in section 57 of the code, and are subject to the minimum tax.

Revenue Act of 1978: Investment Tax Credit

35. *Explain the investment tax credit for rehabilitation provided for in the Revenue Act of 1978.*

The Revenue Act of 1978 added to the Internal Revenue Code a new provision set forth in sections 48(a)(1)(E) and 48(g) that allows taxpayers generally to take an investment tax credit for up to 10 percent of the expenses incurred in rehabilitating many older depreciable buildings. This amount is credited directly against the taxes owed by the taxpayer. Expenses qualifying for this credit must have been incurred after October 31, 1978. The cost of acquiring a structure does not qualify for the credit.

36. *What kinds of buildings qualify for the investment tax credit?*

Any structure that will be used immediately following rehabilitation for a depreciable purpose—i.e., in a trade or business or held for the production of income—generally will qualify for the credit. Buildings to be used for residential rental purposes will not qualify, although hotels and motels used primarily by transients will. Eligible buildings include factories, warehouses, office buildings and retail stores. Prior to rehabilitation, the building may have been used for any purpose, including personal.

The *General Explanation of the Revenue Act of 1978,* prepared by the Joint Committee on Taxation of Congress, which provides guidance to the IRS in preparing its official tax code regulations, discusses additional requirements for qualifying for the tax credit. The *General Explanation* states, ". . . the rehabilitation (expenditure) must be incurred after October 31, 1978, in connection with the rehabilitation or reconstruction of a building which has been in use for a period of at least 20 years before the commencement of the rehabilitation. For this purpose, the determination of the 20-year period would be unaffected by periods during which a building was vacant or devoted to a personal use. In addition, the 20-year test is to be applied to the building without regard to the number of owners. The running of the 20-year period would commence at the earlier of the time depreciation deductions were first allowable with respect to the building or when it was first placed in use for any purpose" (p. 156).

37. *What kind of rehabilitation work qualifies for the investment tax credit?*

Section (48)(g) of the Internal Revenue Code describes only generally the requirements imposed on eligible rehabilitation work. Seventy-five percent or more of the existing external walls of the building being rehabilitated must be retained in place as external walls. Any expenditure for enlargement of the building does not qualify. Additions and improvements to the building must have a useful life or five years or more. The law also provides that qualifying rehabilitation work may include the reconstruction of the building.

The *General Explanation of the Revenue Act of 1978* suggests in greater detail the limits of qualifying expenses (p. 157). Costs must be ones that would be "capitalized" (i.e., added to the "basis" or cost of the building and used in computing allowable depreciation deductions) rather than being taken as immediate business expense tax deductions. Qualifying rehabilitation includes interior or exterior renovation or restoration that materially extends the useful life of the building, significantly upgrades its usefulness or preserves it. Capital expenditures would normally include costs for the replacement of plumbing, electrical wiring, flooring, permanent interior partitions or walls and heating or air-conditioning equipment.

38. *Does the rehabilitation of only a portion of a building qualify for the tax credit?*

In some cases. Rehabilitation costs incurred on part of a building will qualify for the credit only if the rehabilitated part constitutes a "major portion." The *General Explanation of the Revenue Act of 1978* suggests that factors such as volume, floor space and functional differences between the rehabilitated and unrehabilitated parts of the building will be weighed in determining whether rehabilitated space constitutes a "major portion" (p. 156). The *General Explanation* states, for example, that where a substantial part of a building is used for a retail store and another portion is used as a warehouse, each part will usually constitute a major portion of the building for purposes of these provisions.

39. *Can a lessee of qualifying rehabilitated property use the investment tax credit?*

The law does not state clearly whether or not a lessee who incurs qualifying rehabilitation expenses may automatically take the credit. The *General Explanation of the Revenue Act of 1978* states that "if a rehabilitation is undertaken by a lessee, the lessee is eligible for the investment credit for qualified rehabilitation costs incurred by him, to the extent these costs are required to be capitalized by him and are not treated under other provisions of the law as payments in lieu of rent. In determining qualified investment by a lessee, the useful life of a lessee's rehabilitation costs will be the useful life allowed to the lessee for purposes of depreciation or amortization of these costs under code sections 167 and 178" (p. 157). While these comments in the *General Explanation* are not part of the law, they will be given great weight.

The law does allow a lessor who incurs the qualifying expense to consent to the lessee of the property taking the credit. However, code section 48(a)(5) and the IRS regulations specify that any property leased from or leased by a governmental unit is not eligible for this tax credit.

40. *Is there any limit on the amount that may be claimed under this investment tax credit?*

Yes. For the purposes of determining the size of the tax credit, a taxpayer may use up to 10 percent of the total qualifying rehabilitation expenses incurred if the rehabilitation work has a useful life of seven years or more. Ten percent of two-thirds of the expenses may be used for any rehabilitation work having a useful life of the minimum five years allowable or more, but less than seven years. Of this amount, the taxpayer may credit against his or her tax due an amount no greater than the sum of the first $25,000 of tax due plus a percentage of any tax owed above $25,000. This percentage is 60 percent for the tax year 1979, and it rises 10 percent a year until reaching 90 percent for tax year 1982 and years thereafter. If a taxpayer fails during a year to exhaust the full amount of expenses qualifying for this credit, then he or she may use the balance of the qualifying expenses to offset taxes paid during the prior three years, and then as a credit during the succeeding seven tax years for any amount still remaining uncredited, until the amount available as a credit has been used up.

41. *Can the 10 percent investment tax credit be taken together with either of the rehabilitation tax incentives created by the Tax Reform Act of 1976 for certified historic structures?*

The Internal Revenue Code does allow owners of certified historic structures that qualify as substantially rehabilitated historic property under section 167(o) of the code to elect to take both the accelerated depreciated deductions available under section 167(o) and the 10 percent investment tax credit. Section 48(a)(8) of the code, however, specifically prohibits property owners from simultaneously taking the 60-month (5-year) rapid amortization deductions under section 191 and the 10 percent investment tax credit.

42. Does rehabilitation work qualifying for this tax credit have to be approved?

Generally, no. If the rehabilitation expenditures are attributable to a certified historic structure (as defined in section 191(d)(1) of the Internal Revenue Code), however, then the rehabilitation itself must be certified by the Heritage Conservation and Recreation Service according to the standards set forth in code section 191(d)(4) and its accompanying regulations. This means that the owner of a building that has been determined a certified historic structure for the purposes of the tax incentives under the Tax Reform Act of 1976 may take the 10 percent investment tax credit only if the rehabilitation work has been certified.

43. Can nonprofit tax-exempt organizations use the investment tax credit?

Generally, no. There is one exception: nonprofit tax-exempt organizations can use the credit for qualifying rehabilitated property if the property is used predominantly in an unrelated trade or business, the income of which is taxable under section 511 of the Internal Revenue Code.

44. *Is the investment credit taken under section 48(g) subject to the Internal Revenue Code's recapture rules upon sale of the property?*

Although the investment tax credit is not subject to the code's section 1245 and 1250 recapture rules, it is subject to the special recapture rule set forth in section 47 for investment tax credits. This recapture rule does not apply, however, if the property is held by the taxpayer for seven years or more.

45. *Are expenses credited against income tax under the 10 percent tax credit subject to the minimum tax for tax preferences under sections 55–58 of the Internal Revenue Code?*

28

No. Any expenses qualifying for the 10 percent investment tax credit and credited against income tax do not constitute items of tax preference, as defined in section 57 of the code, and therefore are not subject to the minimum tax.

George A. Reigeluth with *Susan Mick* and *Deborah Swift*

FEDERAL TAX POLICY AND HISTORIC PRESERVATION: AN EVALUATION OF THE TAX REFORM ACT OF 1976

During the 1960s and into the 1970s historic preservation benefited greatly from a heightened concern for environmental protection that initially focused on problems of air and water pollution, but subsequently came to encompass the protection of the built environment as well as the natural environment.[1] Similarly, resource conservation and economic concerns have given additional impetus to the historic preservation movement. For example, it is frequently argued that in an era of scarce resources, it makes little economic sense to abandon or demolish vacant portions of the capital stock that could easily be used for other industrial, commercial or residential purposes. Historic buildings, as an especially valuable part of the existing capital stock, present opportunities for such adaptive use.[2]

A related development, the recent burgeoning of neighborhood preservation and rehabilitation efforts, has provided another source of strength for historic preservation. Individuals and groups seeking to maintain or upgrade their neighborhood in the process have often restored buildings of historical or aesthetic significance (even if sometimes using questionable architectural standards).[3] Finally, historic preservation has been pursued as an end in itself, in order to preserve those aspects of our architectural heritage deemed to be of historical significance and value.[4]

As the rationales for promoting historic preservation have multiplied, so too have the techniques used to encourage it. The transfer of development rights, property tax exemptions, legal devices such as easements and covenants and federal tax provisions have all been used to facilitate the preservation of historic structures.[5] This article focuses on one of these techniques—the historic preservation provisions of the federal tax code. The intent of the article is to analyze and quantify the extent to which these provisions and their changes have altered the tax liabilities of an individual who decides to invest in rehabilitating a historic structure and of an investor who decides to demolish the structure and construct a new building on the same site. To the extent that the tax

Mr. Reigeluth is senior urban affairs analyst with Dalton, Dalton and Newport, Washington, D.C., and was formerly research associate for the Public Finance Group of the Urban Institute, Washington, D.C. Susan Mick is a research associate at the Urban Institute and Deborah Swift was an intern with that organization.

This paper was prepared as part of a study of the effects of state, local and federal tax laws on residential rehabilitation, under Contract Number H-2162R to the Urban Institute, Washington, D.C., through the Office of Policy and Development Research of the U.S. Department of Housing and Urban Development. The study was prepared under the direction of George E. Peterson, director, Public Finance Group, Urban Institute.

liabilities of these investors differ, the tax code creates a real financial subsidy for one type of investment activity over the other.

Since the passage of the historic preservation tax provisions in 1976, a relatively large number of investors have attempted to take advantage of the benefits of these provisions. For the period March 1977 to April 1979, the U.S. Department of the Interior's Heritage Conservation and Recreation Service received applications for certification of eligibility for use of the provisions from 900 projects representing about $390 million of rehabilitation investment. Of this number, about 12 percent, if approved, would also involve the use of funds from other federal programs, such as the section 8 housing program, the 312 loan program, the Small Business Administration program or the Economic Development Administration programs.

Similarly, the applications for use of the historic preservation provisions involve a number of different land uses. The applications indicate that 14 percent of the buildings using the provisions will be office buildings after completion of the rehabilitation work; 10 percent, commercial and hotel uses; 14 percent, one to two-family residential purposes; 34 percent, multifamily apartment buildings; and 27 percent, mixed land uses. How much of this investment in the rehabilitation of historic structures has actually been stimulated by the historic preservation provisions of the 1976 Tax Reform Act is largely unknown at this time. Obtaining an answer to this question would require a full model, showing how the historic preservation provisions affect investment decisions within the context of various market conditions. The subsequent analysis, while not undertaking such a modeling effort, does lay the groundwork for such work by focusing on the more limited objective of determining the extent to which the historic preservation provisions have created real tax benefits and financial incentives for investment in rehabilitation of historic structures.

Hypotheses for Analysis

The historic preservation provisions of the tax code came into being in large part because many believed that without these provisions the tax code created a strong financial incentive for investors to demolish historic structures rather than rehabilitate them.[6] The first section of this paper examines this notion by analyzing and measuring the tax liabilities prior to the Tax Reform Act of 1976 of two investors engaging in one or the other of these two investment options—rehabilitation of a historic structure versus its demolition and replacement with new construction. The following sections then examine how the historic preservation provisions of the 1976 Tax Reform Act, and how the subsequent technical corrections to it and other tax changes of the 1978 Revenue Act, have altered these tax liabilities. In each section a two-part analysis follows, with the first part examining how the tax code affects the tax liabilities of the two kinds of investors during the time they *own* their properties; the second part shows how the tax code affects tax liabilities when each investor decides to *sell* his or her property. The article concludes with a discussion of what public policy lessons for the rehabilitation of historic structures flow from this analysis.

Measurement of the tax advantage for one investment activity over the other is carried out by using hypothetical investment and tax liability examples. Before beginning the analysis it is important to lay out the assumptions in back of these examples, which are summarized in table 1. The property in question is presumed to be a medium-sized, income-producing, multifamily structure of historical significance, located in an inner-city neighborhood. Its purchase price is $150,000. For $200,000 it can be fully rehabilitated to maintain its unique architectural and historic features, or for the same amount of money the building can be torn down and a new one built in its place. In each case the amount of rental income flowing from these investments is the same. It is assumed that if rehabilitated, the building will qualify for the certifications by the Secretary of the Interior that are required in order to use the federal tax incentives being investigated. The hypothetical example also assumes two investors, with one opting to rehabilitate while the other chooses to demolish and build anew.

The analysis further shows how the tax liabilities of these alternative investment options differ by changing the assumptions regarding rates of appreciation in property values and lengths of period of ownership. In the first example, it is assumed that the investor sells the property for $525,000 after five years of ownership, which represents a 10 percent uncompounded, annual rate of increase over his original investment of $350,000 ($150,000 purchase price plus $200,000 of rehabilitation or new construction investment). This rate of appreciation in property values, while high for some areas, is not atypical of some urban neighborhoods experiencing rising demand.

The second example of a 5 percent rate of appreciation for 10 years of ownership, resulting in the same sales price of $525,000, demonstrates how varying the rate of return and period of ownership will alter the relative tax liabilities of the two investors.[7] Implicit in these sales prices are the assumptions that the value of the new building ($185,000) will appreciate faster than that of the rehabilitated, old building ($200,000), and that the amount of investment ($200,000) will be fully reflected in the market value of the properties. The

---

Table 1

HYPOTHETICAL EXAMPLES

Category	Assumption
Type of property	Medium sized, multifamily, historic structure located in inner-city neighborhood and held for rental (income-producing) purposes
Purchase price of historic property	$150,000 ($50,000 land; $100,000 building, being the depreciable cost ("basis") of the property[1]
Investment options	
Rehabilitation investment	$200,000
New construction investment	$200,000 ($15,000 demolition; $185,000 new construction)
Undepreciated basis (from original structure)	$100,000
Investors' annual income	$ 60,000
Marginal tax bracket at sale	70 percent
Discount rate	10 percent[2]
Sale price	$525,000
Period of ownership	5 or 10 years
Rate of appreciation	5 percent (if held for 10 years) and 10 percent (if held for 5 years) uncompounded annually

[1] It should be noted that altering the assumptions regarding the portion of the property's value made up by land and improvements will naturally alter the results somewhat. The portions indicated are thought to reflect typical assessment practices.

[2] Throughout the analysis, the various dollar costs and benefits the investor incurs in the future are discounted and expressed in present value terms. This is done to adjust for the fact that overtime money earns interest. To express a future cost or benefit in terms of present-day dollars, therefore, requires that this opportunity factor be taken into account. The present value of these costs or benefits will be less than their future value. Thus, it is necessary to discount these future values and express them in present value terms.

investors are assumed to be earning $60,000 a year, but upon sale of their respective properties, because of their capital gains, they are each in the 70 percent marginal income tax bracket for that year of sale.

Many investors may be able to avoid being in the 70 percent marginal income tax bracket in the year of sale by spreading portions of their income over a number of years and by claiming offsetting tax losses. Thus, this assumption represents a rather atypical situation, but it is used here for two reasons. First, the use of similar tax brackets standardizes the other tax characteristics of the two kinds of investors—that is, their other deductions from and additions to income, which are unrelated to their treatment of the historic property. Second, the highest tax bracket of 70 percent is used because it is often assumed that historic preservation is an investment activity that attracts mainly high-income taxpayers. The following quote from one study indicates that such is the case because, for example, it is only high-income investors who have the resources, interest and expertise to address the administrative concerns of designation and certification of the historic property, which must be followed in order to take advantage of the historic preservation provisions of the 1976 Tax Reform Act.

The National Register designation process [and the resulting rehabilitation investment in historic properties] was not designed to be an upper income phenomenon; it just is. Anyone may propose a neighborhood for designation, but it is perhaps only the well-educated, well-heeled newcomers who can afford to appreciate the fine old architectural features and the invisible quality of the behind-the-walls construction. The old-time neighborhood residents see only the cracks in the plaster, the rotting window sashes, and the peeling paint which their limited incomes (or those of their landlords) cannot repair. The new neighborhood organizations are willing to take the time to research the neighborhood history and fill out (or hire an expert to fill out) the application form which starts the designation [and rehabilitation investment] process rolling.[8]

Assuming similar mortgage situations, rental flows, incomes and tax brackets enables the analysis to hold these factors constant and isolate the marginal impact of changes in the tax law on the tax liabilities and thus rates of return of the two investment options. Where possible, as with the length of ownership and rate of appreciation, the text attempts to indicate how sensitive the results are to fluctuations in the assumptions.

Tax Treatment of Historic Structures Prior to 1976

32

Prior to the 1976 Tax Reform Act it was generally believed that in addition to the market pressures for destruction of historic structures, the federal tax code acted both to discourage their rehabilitation and to encourage their demolition and replacement with new construction. The following quotation is representative of much of what was written about the relationships between the tax code and historic preservation.

Favorable tax treatment for new construction often leads developers to raze attractive older buildings rather than rehabilitate them, thereby destroying significant buildings and changing the character of neighborhoods.[9]

It was specifically in its treatment of demolition expenses and depreciation deductions that the tax code was thought to create financial inducements for investors to demolish historic structures. Prior to the 1976 Tax Reform Act under section 165 of the Internal Revenue Code, an individual who decided to demolish a historic structure rather than rehabilitate it could deduct from taxable income as an ordinary business expense the costs of demolition plus the undepreciated basis of the demolished structure.[10] These deductions were not permitted, however, if the owner acquired the property with the intent to demolish it. Only if the decision to demolish was made after acquisition could the owner take the deductions.[11]

In addition, after constructing a new building on the site formerly occupied by the historic structure, the property owner could depreciate the costs of the new building at an accelerated rate. The use of the 150 percent declining balance methods was (and still is) allowed on the costs of new commercial structures and the 200 percent declining balance method for new residential rental structures. For the owner deciding to rehabilitate, the tax code was considerably less generous. The owner could only add the costs of rehabilitation to the remaining basis of the existing property and depreciate the total amount using the 125 percent declining balance method for residential rental property, or the straight-line method for commercial property.[12] The implications of these tax laws were that even though they invested similar amounts of money and generated the same amount of before-tax income, the after-tax income and thus annual rate of return for the investor in new construction, using the 200 percent declining balance method of depreciation, was considerably higher than that of the investor in rehabilitation using the 125 percent method.

Table 2, which shows the allowable depreciation deductions under the two hypothetical pre-1976 investment situations, illustrates this point quite clearly. For the individual who decided to tear down the historic structure and invest in new construction, the present value of the sum of the depreciation deductions over the 20-year useful life of the property came to $194,760 (column 2), which is $66,540 or 52 percent greater than the $128,220 of depreciation

---

Table 2

PRE-1976 TAX REFORM ACT DEPRECIATION DEDUCTIONS:
NEW CONSTRUCTION vs. REHABILITATION

Year	New Construction[1]		Rehabilitation[2]	
	Accounting	Present Value[3]	Accounting	Present Value[3]
1	$ 9,200 + 100,000[4] + 15,000[5]	$112,955	$ 9,375	$ 8,523
2	17,575	12,978	18,164	15,012
3	15,818	11,884	17,029	12,794
4	14,232	9,723	15,965	10,904
5	12,312	7,955	14,967	9,293
6	11,531	6,507	14,967	8,448
7	10,378	5,326	14,967	7.680
8	9,340	4,357	14,967	6,982
9	8,406	3,565	14,967	6,347
10	7,565	2,917	14.967	5,770
11	6,809	2,387	14,967	5,246
12	6,809	2,170	14,967	4,769
13	6,809	1,972	14,967	4,335
14	6,809	1,913	14,967	3,941
15	6,809	1,630	14,967	3,583
16	6,809	1,482	14,967	3,257
17	6,809	1,347	14,967	2,961
18	6,809	1,225	14,967	2,692
19	6,809	1,113	14,967	2,447
20	6,809	1,012	14,967	2,225
21[6]	3,405	460	7,483	1,011
Total		$194,760		$128,220

[1] *$185,000 of new construction investment depreciated at 200 percent declining balance.*
[2] *Both the $100,000 of remaining basis + $200,000 of rehabilitation investment are depreciated at 125 percent declining balance method.*
[3] *10 percent discount rate used.*
[4] *Remaining basis of former property.*
[5] *Demolition costs.*
[6] *Half-year convention is observed.*

deductions (column 4) allowed for the investor who rehabilitated the property instead. The differences are much more pronounced if one looks just at the earlier years of ownership. For the new construction investment scenario, the present value of the depreciation deductions allowed in the first five years was $155,495 which is almost three times greater than the $56,526 of depreciation deductions allowed for rehabilitation.

After 10 years the present value of the depreciation deductions for new construction was $178,169, which is almost twice as much as the $91,753 of depreciation deductions allowed for rehabilitation.[13] These figures provide an interesting insight into the impact that variations in the length of ownership have on the relative tax liabilities of these different investments. The largest differences in the amounts of depreciation that may be deducted from current income occur in the early years of ownership.

In assuming a 10 percent discount rate to compute the present value of depreciation deductions, this analysis follows the assumptions of previous studies.[14] One study of the impact on corporate investors of the historic preservation provisions found that changing the discount rate from 10 percent to 15 percent did not significantly alter the results of the analysis.[15]

These differences in allowable depreciation deductions again were due to the fact that the tax code used to allow the investor in new residential construction to deduct demolition costs and the remaining basis of the old property and to calculate his annual depreciation on the new investment at the 200 percent declining balance rate instead of the 125 percent rate used by the investor in rehabilitation. Given that these investors were both in the 70 percent marginal income tax bracket, the present value of $98,969 more in depreciation deductions in the first five years for the investor in new construction meant that amount more in income escaped taxation. Expressed another way, the hypothetical investor in new construction paid $69,278 ($98,969 × .70) less in taxes during the first five years and $60,491 less in taxes during the first 10 years than the investor in rehabilitation. It is for this reason that the tax code was said to create a financial incentive for new construction over rehabilitation.

But this analysis covers only part of the tax provisions that determine whether or not the tax code formerly discouraged rehabilitation of historic structures. If one looks at how the tax code treated the capital gains realized from the sale of these different investments, quite a different picture from the one just presented emerges. Using the assumptions presented at the outset and the depreciation figures just discussed, it is possible to compare the tax liabilities resulting from the sale of the two investments. After five and 10 years of ownership, each investor is presumed to have been able to sell his or her property at the same price of $525,000. The sales prices were the same despite the difference in holding periods, because it is assumed that the investor selling after five years of ownership realized a 10 percent uncompounded annual rate of appreciation, whereas the investor selling after 10 years experienced only a 5 percent annual rate of appreciation. Tables 3 and 4 show how each investor would have computed his or her tax liability in the year of sale.

For the individual who demolished the historic structure and constructed a new building, line 1 in section A of table 3 indicates that he realized a gross capital gain at sale after five years of ownership of $259,691. To compute the tax on this gain the tax code required the individual first to subtract the amount of excess depreciation (lines 2 through 6) taken while owning the property (in this case five years). The resulting net capital gain (line 7) of $231,625 was then divided in half into an excluded portion (line 9), which was a tax preference item subject to minimum tax, and a portion subject to normal income tax rates. The minimum tax on tax preference items was added to the tax code in 1969 to assure that income that had previously gone untaxed would at least be taxed at the minimum rate of 10 percent of the tax preference items.

The untaxed portion of the net capital gain is an example of a tax preference item.

Prior to 1976, however, the tax code allowed the taxpayer to exclude from the amount of tax preference items $30,000 plus the amount of income tax due. Thus, line 16 shows that no minimum tax was owed in the year of sale because the individual's income tax liability of $124,265 (line 15) plus $30,000

Table 3

TAX LIABILITY FROM SALE OF NEW BUILDING
AFTER 5 AND 10 YEARS OF OWNERSHIP

A. After 5 Years:

	Sales Price	Purchase Price	Improvements	Depreciation[1]	Gross Capital Gain
(1)	$525,000	− ($150,000	+ $185,000	− $69,691)	= $259,691
(2)	69,691	Accelerated depreciation deductions for 5 years (200% declining balance)			
(3)	− 41,625	Straight-line depreciation deductions for 5 years			
(4)	28,066	Excess depreciation subject to recapture as ordinary income			
(5)	259,691	Gross capital gain			
(6)	− 28,066	Excess depreciation			
(7)	231,625	Net capital gain			
(8)	× .5	Portion of capital gain excluded			
(9)	115,813	Tax preference item subject to minimum tax			
(10)	115,813	Portion of capital gain subject to income tax			
(11)	60,000	Annual income			
(12)	28,066	Excess depreciation			
(13)	203,879	Taxable income			
(14)	× .7	Marginal tax rate			
(15)	124,265	Tax liability (53,090 + 70% of amount over $102,200)			
(16)	115,813 — (30,000 + 124,265) < 0: Thus, no minimum tax on tax preference items in year of sale				

B. After 10 Years:

	Sales Price	Purchase Price	Improvements	Depreciation[1]	Gross Capital Gain
(1)	$525,000	− ($150,000	+ $185,000	− $116,911)	= $306,911
(2)	116,911	Accelerated depreciation deductions for 10 years (200% declining balance)			
(3)	− 87,875	Straight-line depreciation deductions for 10 years.			
(4)	29,036	Excess depreciation subject to recapture as ordinary income			
(5)	306,911	Gross capital gain			
(6)	− 29,036	Excess depreciation			
(7)	277,875	Net capital gain			
(8)	× .5	Portion of capital gain excluded			
(9)	138,938	Tax preference item subject to minimum tax			
(10)	138,938	Portion of capital gain subject to income tax			
(11)	60,000	Annual income			
(12)	29,036	Excess depreciation			
(13)	127,974	Taxable income			
(14)	× .7	Marginal tax rate			
(15)	141,132	Tax liability (53,090 + 70% of amount over $102,200)			
(16)	138,938 — (30,000 + 141,132) < 0: Thus, no minimum tax on tax preference items in year of sale.				

---

[1] *Does not include first year demolition or undepreciated basis deduction specified in table 2, as this has already been deducted as a cost.*

was large enough to offset completely the amount of tax preference items ($115,813). To compute his tax liability, section 1250 of the IRS code required the investor to claim the amount of excess depreciation taken while owning the property (line 4) as ordinary income. This (line 12) plus his annual income (line 11) and the portion of capital gain subject to income tax (line 10) constituted his taxable income in the year of sale ($203,879). In this way the excess depreciation deductions that lowered the individual's tax liability while he owned the property were recaptured at the time of sale by increasing the tax liability for that year.

Section B of table 3 shows how lengthening the period of ownership to 10 years increased the investor's tax liability at the time of sale to $141,132, which was $16,867, or 14 percent, greater than the $124,265 tax liability due after five years of ownership. This increase reflected the $47,220 more in depreciation deductions the owner had to claim in computing his capital gain realized from sale of his property after 10 years of ownership. The five additional years had the effect of increasing both the portion of the larger capital gain subject to income taxes (line 10), and the amount of excess depreciation subject to income taxes (line 12).

Table 4 shows that the individual who invested in rehabilitation instead of new construction went throught the same set of steps to calculate his tax liability at the time of sale. But as line 15 in section A of table 4 indicates, upon sale of the property after five years his tax liability was only $114,025, or $10,240 less than the tax liability of the individual who invested in new construction. The difference is due to the fact that while he owned the residential property the investor in rehabilitation was only able to use the 125 percent declining balance method of depreciation. Thus, his annual depreciation deductions were considerably less than the investor in new construction who was able to use the 200 percent declining balance method (see table 2). As a result, at sale the investor in rehabilitation only had to claim $8,000 in excess depreciation as ordinary income under the code's recapture rules, while the investor in new construction had to claim more than three times this amount, or $28,066, in excess depreciation.

For the investor in historic preservation who sold a property after 10 years of ownership, section B of table 4 shows that this tax liability was $140,160 or $972 less than the tax liability of the investor in new construction who also sold a property after 10 years. Thus, changing the period of ownership from five to 10 years diminished the absolute difference in the tax liabilities of the investors in new construction versus historic preservation from $10,240 to $972.

However, while the tax liabilities at sale of the investors in new construction were greater than those of the investors in rehabilitation, the differences were not large enough to offset the tax savings from the depreciation deductions the investors in new construction realized while owning their properties for five and 10 years respectively. Pulling together data from the previous tables, table 5, section A shows that when the net tax aspects of both the period of ownership and time of sale of the two investors who sold after five years are considered, the investor in new construction paid in present value terms $62,920 less in taxes (line 11) than did the person who decided to rehabilitate the historic structure. With sale after 10 years of ownership and an annual rate of return of 5 percent instead of 10 percent, table 5, section B indicates that the present value of the net tax savings for the investor in new construction decreased slightly to $60,116. In other words, consistent with the popular opinion expressed above and before the Tax Reform Act of 1976, when the necessary aspects of the tax code are considered, it does appear that the tax code prior to 1976 created substantial financial incentives for demolition of historic structures and for the construction of new buildings in their place. The important point still remains, however, that the present value of the net tax gains from new construction of $62,920 and $60,116 for five and 10 years of ownership respectively were less than the $69,278 and $60,491 of tax savings realized during the period of ownership as a result of investing in new construction instead of rehabilitation—that is, the operation of the tax laws at the time of sale acted to erode somewhat the tax gains realized during the period of ownership.

Another study[16] has arrived at similar conclusions with respect to the tax code's pre-Tax Reform Act treatment of historic preservation versus demolition and new construction. This study finds that prior to the Tax Reform Act the after-tax life-cycle costs were 4.8 percent greater for the corporation that in-

---

Table 4

TAX LIABILITY FROM SALE OF RENOVATED HISTORIC STRUCTURE AFTER 5 AND 10 YEARS OF OWNERSHIP

A. After 5 Years:

	Sales Price	Purchase Price	Improvements	Depreciation	Gross Capital Gain
(1)	$525,000	– ($150,000	+ $200,000	– $75,500)	= $250,500
(2)	75,500	Accelerated depreciation deductions for 5 years (125% declining balance)			
(3)	– 67,500	Straight-line depreciation deductions for 5 years			
(4)	8,000	Excess depreciation			
(5)	250,500	Gross capital gain			
(6)	– 8,000	Excess depreciation			
(7)	242,500	Net capital gain			
(8)	× .5	Portion of capital gain excluded			
(9)	121,250	Tax preference subject to minimum tax			
(10)	121,250	Portion of capital gain subject to income tax			
(11)	60,000	Annual income			
(12)	8,000	Excess depreciation			
(13)	189,250	Taxable income			
(14)	× .7	Marginal tax rate			
(15)	114,025	Tax liability (53,090 + 70% of amount over $102,200)			
(16)	121,250 — (30,000 + 114,025) < 0: Thus, no minimum tax on tax preference items in year of sale.				

B. After 10 Years:

	Sales Price	Purchase Price	Improvements	Depreciation	Gross Capital Gain
(1)	$525,000	– ($150,000	+ $200,000	– $150,335)	= $325,335
(2)	150,335	Accelerated depreciation deductions for 10 years (125% declining balance)			
(3)	– 142,500	Straight-line depreciation deductions for 10 years			
(4)	7,835	Excess depreciation			
(5)	325,335	Gross capital gain			
(6)	– 7,835	Excess depreciation			
(7)	317,500	Net capital gain			
(8)	× .5	Portion of capital gain excluded			
(9)	158,750	Tax preference item subject to minimum tax			
(10)	158,750	Portion of capital gain subject to income tax			
(11)	60,000	Annual income			
(12)	7,835	Excess depreciation			
(13)	226,585	Taxable income			
(14)	× .7	Marginal tax rate			
(15)	140,160	Tax liability (53,090 + 70% of amount over $102,200)			
(16)	158,750 — (30,000 + 140,025) < 0: Thus, no minimum tax on tax preference items in year of sale.				

vested $1 million to rehabilitate a historic structure than for the corporation that invested a similar amount to demolish it and build a new structure. Because the study analyzes the corporate tax liabilities of these competing investment options for a historic, nonresidential building, it has to use the 150 percent declining balance method of depreciation (instead of the 200 percent method used in the earlier discussion) in computing the annual depreciation deductions for the new construction investment option; but other than that the underlying assumptions of the two studies are quite similar.

Of course, several objections can be raised to conclusions based on this kind of hypothetical analysis. The first is that not all investors sell their properties after five or 10 years, preferring to hold onto them for a longer period. Some investors who own low-income housing may do so in part to avoid the sting of the recapture provisions. For example, if low-income housing is held for more than 8⅓ years (100 months), section 1250 of the tax code permits a gradual phasing out of the recapture of excess depreciation as ordinary income at the rate of 1 percent per month.[17] At the end of 16⅔ years (200 months) the recapture provisions no longer apply and the entire gain on the sale of the property qualifies for capital gains treatment. Thus, the operation of these phaseout provisions provides increasingly more favorable tax treatment of new construction relative to rehabilitation, for with progressively longer periods of ownership the amount of excess depreciation that is recaptured declines. But given that much of the investment that takes place on the site of a historic structure (whether it is new construction or rehabilitation) is unlikely to involve the provision of housing for low-income tenants, the phaseout of recapture will not be germane to investors trying to decide between new construction and historic preservation.

Even if low-income housing were involved and the phaseout provisions did have relevance, it is not clear whether it will benefit investors to retain ownership of property to take advantage of the phaseout of the recapture provisions. The following example taken from a study of the financial incentives created by accelerated depreciation for rehabilitation supports this skepticism:

Consider investors in the 50 percent bracket who use discount rates of from 10 to 15 percent. If we make the further assumption that the cost of rehabilitation results in exactly an equal increase in value at the time the property is sold, the present value of depreciation deductions plus the after-tax proceeds at sale attributable to rehabilitation are greater if the property is sold after five years than if held to take advantage of the recapture phaseout. The benefits of capital gains treatment are overshadowed by postponement of receipt of the proceeds of sale. In order for it to be worthwhile to hold the real estate past five years, there must be an increase in capital value attributable to rehabilitation cost during the additional period of hold and/or the taxpayer must increase his net rental income during that period through rent increases or reductions in operating costs.[18]

Other questions can also be raised about the validity of the above conclusions that prior to the 1976 Tax Reform Act the recapture provisions of the tax code reduced substantially at the time of sale the tax benefits it extended to the investor in new construction during his period of ownership. Some would argue, for example, that while the tax code does recapture at the time of sale much of the excess depreciation deductions it extends during the period of ownership, for many investors their "time horizon" is sufficiently short as to make the benefits of the depreciation deductions more important than concerns about eventual capital gains and recapture of those benefits.[19] Furthermore, this recovery of foregone taxes takes place only if the taxpayer sells his or her real estate investment and realizes a capital gain. According to this line of argument, some investors who are involved in real estate for tax shelters may not behave in this manner; that is, they may make their initial investment, use the high depreciation deductions available in the early years of ownership to shelter other income and then carry out some form of "like-kind" exchange to avoid capital gains and to take advantage of another round of depreciation deductions.

Section 1031 of the IRS code allows investors to defer payment of capital gain on their property if they exchange it for property "of a like kind." For these investors, the high depreciation deductions possible through the use of the 200 percent declining balance method of depreciation with new residential construction may have been worth more than the higher tax liability at the time of sale, because the latter could be postponed indefinitely by exchanging one property for another of a similar kind. While "like-kind" exchanges no doubt occur, it is not clear how widespread the practice was or continues to be.

The previous analysis has shown that prior to 1976 the tax laws did create a substantially more favorable net tax situation for the investor in new construction than for the investor in rehabilitation of a historic structure. This

---

Table 5

COMPARATIVE NET TAX TREATMENT OF NEW CONSTRUCTION AND HISTORIC PRESERVATION WITH SALE AFTER 5 AND 10 YEARS

A. After 5 Years:

	Accounting		Present Value[1]
(1)	$184,137	Depreciation deductions with new construction (200%)	$155,495
(2)	− 75,500	Depreciation deductions with historic preservation (125%)	− 56,526
(3)	108,637		98,969
(4)	× .70		× .70
(5)	76,046	Tax savings during 5 years of ownership as a result of investing in new construction instead of rehabilitation	69,278
(6)	124,265	Tax liability on sale of new structure	77,159
(7)	− 114,025	Tax liability on sale of historic structure	− 70,801
(8)	10,240	Tax loss as a result of doing new construction instead of rehabilitation	6,358
(9)	76,046	Tax gain from new construction during ownership	69,278
(10)	− 10,240	Tax loss from new construction at sale	− 6,358
(11)	65,806	Net tax gain from new construction	62,920

B. After 10 Years:

	Accounting		Present Value[1]
(1)	$231,831[2]	Depreciation deductions with new construction (200%)	$178,169
(2)	− 150,335	Depreciation deductions with historic preservation (125%)	− 91,753
(3)	81,496		86,416
(4)	× .70		× .70
(5)	57,047	Tax savings during 10 years of ownership as a result of investing in new construction instead of rehabilitation	60,491
(6)	141,132	Tax liability on sale of new structure	54,413
(7)	− 140,160	Tax liability on sale of historic structure	− 54,038
(8)	972	Tax loss as a result of doing new construction instead of rehabilitation	375
(9)	57,047	Tax gain from new construction during ownership	60,491
(10)	− 972	Tax loss from new construction at sale	− 375
(11)	56,075	Net tax gain from new construction	60,116

---

[1] *10 percent discount rate.*
[2] *In addition to depreciation these figures include deductions for the costs of demolition and for the remaining basis of the former structure.*

finding holds even when the assumptions regarding annual rates of appreciation and period of ownership were altered. To address this unfavorable tax situation Congress enacted the historic preservation provisions of the Tax Reform Act of 1976. In the next section an analysis is made of the impact these provisions have had on this tax situation.

Historic Preservation Provisions of the 1976 Tax Reform Act

To eliminate the tax incentives for demolishing historic structures and replacing them with new buildings, Congress enacted section 2124 of the Tax Reform Act of 1976.[20] Changes resulting from the act cover four major areas of tax law: (1) demolition costs and losses, (2) depreciation of property, (3) depreciation and amortization deduction of rehabilitation expenses and (4) deduction of charitable contributions of interests in property.

According to the act, only investors owning "certified historic structures" are eligible to use the historic preservation provisions of section 2124. The building qualifies as a "certified historic structure" if it is income producing and (1) is listed in the National Register and (2) is located in a registered historic district and is certified by the Secretary of the Interior as being of historical significance to the district.[21]

The term "registered historic district" means (1) any district listed in the National Register and (2) any district that has been designated under a state or local statute certified by the Secretary of the Interior as containing criteria assuring the protection of buildings historically significant to the district and that has been certified as meeting substantially all requirements for National Register listing.

As indicated in the previous section, prior to these reforms the tax code contained two provisions that increased the amount of annual business losses and depreciation deductions that an investor demolishing a historic structure and building a new one could take over those allowed for an investor deciding to rehabilitate the historic structure. The first deduction allowed the investor to take as an ordinary business loss the sum of the cost of demolishing the historic structure and the undepreciated investment (or remaining basis) in the building.[22] The second incentive permitted the investor to use the 200 percent declining balance method of depreciation for the new residential rental structure built on the site of the demolished historic building and the unrecovered investment (or remaining basis) in the building.

Section 2124 of the Tax Reform Act of 1976 changes both of these provisions. Investors are no longer permitted to deduct as business expenses the costs of demolishing certified historic structures and the remaining undepreciated interest (basis) in the demolished building. These amounts must be added to the owner's original basis in the land on which the demolished structure stood.[23] According to one account "this change reduces the tax benefit from (demolition and new construction) since it disallows deductions of these costs as an ordinary business expense, postpones realization of any benefit until the time of sale of the property, and reduces the relative benefit of the transaction."[24] Section 2124 also abolishes the incentive of accelerated depreciation on all new construction on a site formerly occupied by a certified historic structure.[25] Thus, the investor has to use the straight-line method to depreciate the costs of new construction.[26] For the purposes of each of these tax penalties, all structures located in registered historic districts are presumed to be certified.

In addition to providing these deterrents to demolition and new construction, the Tax Reform Act of 1976 established two incentives that enable individuals who rehabilitate "certified historic structures" to use more accelerated methods of deducting their rehabilitation costs than were available before. Two alternative methods were made available: The owner can either deduct the rehabilitation costs through amortization over a five-year period or can add the rehabilitation costs to the original cost or "basis" of the structure and depreciate the entire basis amount over the building's useful life by using, for a residential building, the 200 percent declining balance method. In both instances the rehabilitation work must meet certain architectural standards and be certified, and for those electing to use the five-year write-off the remaining basis of the existing structure continues to be depreciated at the old 125 percent declining balance. To use five-year amortization, the law does not require spending a certain minimum amount on rehabilitation,[27] while accelerated depreciation is permitted only on a "substantially rehabilitated historic structure,"[28] which is defined as one whose improvements generally exceed the greater of the adjusted basis of the property, or $5,000.

Another tax incentive provided by the Tax Reform Act that is not directly related to rehabilitation is a charitable deduction for the donation to qualifying public and private nonprofit organizations of a perpetual partial interest in property, such as "limited term conservation easements or remainder interests in real property granted exclusively for conservation purposes."[29]

The 1976 Tax Reform Act also changed the provisions dealing with the minimum tax. Prior to the 1976 Tax Reform Act the IRS code allowed $30,000 plus an amount equal to the regular income tax owed to be excluded from tax preference items for the purposes of computing the minimum tax. The 1976 act cut the annual preference income exclusion for individuals to $10,000, or one-half the regular income taxes, whichever amount is greater. The minimum tax rate was also raised from 10 percent to 15 percent.

Revenue Act of 1978

Because of certain unforeseen difficulties with the historic preservation provisions as originally enacted, the Revenue Act of 1978 made several necessary changes. One of the most serious difficulties in the original 1976 law in terms of its financial implications involved the provisions for recapturing upon sale differences in the five-year amortization deductions taken by the investor in historic preservation. Section 1245 of the Internal Revenue Code was amended to require that all amortization deductions of rehabilitation costs would be fully recaptured and taxed as ordinary income at the time of sale and not treated as capital gains.[30] For the investor in a "substantially rehabilitated" historic structure, however, who used accelerated depreciation (i.e., 200 percent declining balance) instead of the five-year amortization, section 1250 imposed the traditional recapture rule: that only accelerated depreciation in excess of otherwise allowable straight-line depreciation is subject to recapture as ordinary income at sale.

This discrepancy created some perverse financial implications in that in some instances the investor in historic preservation who amortized rehabilitation expenses over five years was left worse off by the historic preservation provisions in terms of the net after sale tax liabilities than were either the investor in historic preservation who used accelerated depreciation *or* the investor who demolished the historic structure and put up a new building. According to Lifton:

this disparity between the recapture methods . . . appears to be contrary to congressional intent and has resulted from a drafting error. Recent legislative history indicates that Congress intended that amortization deductions be recaptured only to the extent that they exceeded the depreciation deductions otherwise allowable.[31]

This discrepancy was one of the problems that the technical corrections of the 1978 Revenue Act corrected by making the recapture treatment of amortization deductions the same as that for accelerated depreciation deductions.[32] The Heritage Conservation and Recreation Service of the U.S. Department of the Interior explains this change as follows:

41

The recapture treatment for the amortization provision governing the sale of real property is changed by the Revenue Act to provide the same tax treatment upon sale of a property as exists for accelerated depreciation. The taxpayer will apply capital gains on the portion of the amortized amount that instead could have been straight line depreciated in the period of ownership and will pay full income tax rates on the amortized amount beyond straight line.[33]

The corrections also clarified the fact that investors may not take advantage of amortization and accelerated depreciation tax benefits simultaneously and standardized application of certification requirements to local, state and national historic districts.[34]

Several other recent tax changes have further altered the tax environment for investors in new construction and rehabilitation, as well as for other types of investors and taxpayers. For example, the Revenue Act of 1978 changed the tax provisions affecting capital gains to require that only 40 percent of capital gains be taxed as ordinary income, rather than the prior level of 50 percent. The remaining 60 percent of capital gains is a tax preference item.[35] In addition, the 1978 Revenue Act created the alternative minimum tax, which becomes payable only if the amount of the alternative minimum tax is greater than the total of the investor's regular income tax plus his regular minimum tax. The alternative minimum tax is levied on such tax perference items as the excluded portion of capital gains and excess itemized deductions.[36] The alternative tax provides a graduated scale of tax—i.e., the first $20,000 of preference items is exempt. There is a 10 percent tax on the next $40,000, or a tax liability of $4,000; a 20 percent tax on the next $40,000 of preference items—i.e., on preference income from $60,000–$100,000, or an $8,000 tax liability on this portion; and a 25 percent tax on preference income over $100,000.

Finally, the Revenue Act also created a 10 percent investment tax credit for certain rehabilitation expenses. This credit can be used alone, in conjunction with the Tax Reform Act's accelerated depreciation benefit for rehabilitated historic structures, and/or in conjunction with deductions for charitable contributions of perpetual partial interests in the property. It cannot be used with the five-year amortization deduction option and, more importantly for the examples thus far discussed, the investment credit applies only to rehabilitation of income-producing *commercial* or *industrial* structures that have been in use for at least 20 years before the start of rehabilitation. Therefore, it does not apply to most residential structures. In addition, the property does not have to be historically designated. However, if it has been declared a certified historic structure for the purpose of the 1976 Tax Reform Act's incentives, the rehabilitation work for which the tax credit is being taken must be certified by the Secretary of the Interior.[37]

As is evident, the Revenue Act did not alter the tax benefits provided by the 1976 Tax Reform Act to the investor rehabilitating a residential historic structure. The costs of such rehabilitation can still be amortized over a five-year period or depreciated at the accelerated 200 percent rate.

To determine how these reforms have altered the tax treatment of the investor in demolition and new construction compared to the investor who rehabilitates the historic structure, the following analysis, using the same assumptions as before, computes both the period of ownership and the year of sale tax differences between the two investment situations. Table 6 summarizes the differences in the amounts of depreciation allowed during ownership under the new provisions for new construction and rehabilitation. Column 2 of table 6 shows that if the investor in new construction holds onto a property for its full 20-year useful life, he or she will be able to deduct in present value terms $75,171 worth of depreciation deductions. This figure is less than half the amount ($194,760) that could be deducted prior to 1976 with a similar amount of new construction investment (see table 2), and is only half the amount ($148,805) that can be deducted by rehabilitating the historic structure instead

Table 6

1976 TAX REFORM ACT DEPRECIATION DEDUCTIONS:
NEW CONSTRUCTION vs. REHABILITATION

| Year | New Construction[1] | | Rehabilitation | | | |
| | Accounting | Present Value[2] | Amortization[3] | | Accelerated Depreciation[4] | |
			Accounting	Present Value	Accounting	Present Value
1	$4,625[5]	$ 4,205	$23,125	$ 21,023	$15,000	$ 13,636
2	9,250	7,645	46,055	38,062	28,500	23,554
3	9,250	6,950	45,676	34,317	25,650	19,271
4	9,250	6,318	45,322	30,956	23,085	15,767
5	9,250	5,744	44,989	27,935	20,777	12,901
6	9,250	5,221	24,989	14,106	18,699	10,555
7	9,250	4,747	4,989	2,560	16,829	8,636
8	9,250	4,315	4,989	2,327	15,146	7,772
9	9,250	3,923	4,989	2,116	13,631	6,359
10	9,250	3,566	4,989	1,923	12,268	4,730
11	9,250	3,242	4,989	1,749	10,516	3,686
12	9,250	2,947	4,989	1,590	10,516	3,351
13	9,250	2,679	4,989	1,445	10,516	3,046
14	9,250	2,436	4,989	1,314	10,516	2,769
15	9,250	2,214	4,989	1,194	10,516	2,517
16	9,250	2,013	4,989	1,086	10,516	2,290
17	9,250	1,830	4,989	987	10,516	2,081
18	9,250	1,664	4,989	897	10,516	1,891
19	9,250	1,512	4,989	816	10,516	1,719
20	9,250	1,375	4,989	742	10,516	1,563
21	4,625	625	2,494	337	5,258	711
Total		$75,171		$187,472		$148,805

[1] $185,000 at straight line; excludes old basis and demolition costs.
[2] 10 percent discount rate used.
[3] Includes $200,000 in rehabilitation amortized in 5 years; + $100,000 of remaining basis depreciated at 125 percent declining balance.
[4] Includes $200,000 in rehabilitation costs, plus $100,000 of remaining basis, both of which are depreciated at 200 percent declining basis.
[5] Half-year convention is observed.

of tearing the structure down (see columns 4 and 6, table 6).

These pronounced differences flow from the historic preservation provisions whereby the investor in new construction is no longer allowed to deduct from income as a business expense the demolition costs and the remaining undepreciated basis in the demolished property, nor is the investor allowed to use the 200 percent declining balance method of accelerated depreciation. Thus, he or she can depreciate only $185,000 of investment in new construction using the straight-line method, whereas before it was possible to deduct the $100,000 of remaining basis and the $15,000 of demolition costs and depreciate the $185,000 of new construction investment at the 200 percent declining balance rate. The investor in rehabilitation, on the other hand, can now deduct $187,482 in expenses if using five-year amortization and $148,805 with the 200 percent rather than with the formerly allowed less accelerated 125 percent declining balance method of depreciation under which schedule the investor could deduct only $128,220 (see table 2).

The differences are even more pronounced if one looks just at the earlier years of ownership. For demolition and new construction, only $30,862 in present value of depreciation deductions are permitted in the first five years of ownership, which is $121,431 less than, or only 20 percent of, the $152,293 of deductions in present value terms allowed for the individual who depreciates rehabilitation expenses using the five-year amortization schedule. For the investor using the 200 percent declining balance method, the first five years of depreciation deductions total $85,129, which is $54,267 larger than, or almost three times the amount allowed for, new construction. For the investor in rehabilitation using amortization, the $121,431 more in deductions means that amount more in income escapes taxation. The same sort of tax avoidance is true with the investor in rehabilitation using 200 percent declining balance who has $54,267 more in depreciation deductions. Given that these investors are in the 70 percent marginal income tax bracket, the investor using amortization will thus pay $85,000 less in taxes ($121,431 × .70) and the person using 200 percent declining balance will pay $37,987 less in taxes ($54,267 × .70) during the first five years than the investor in demolition and new construction. This situation is the exact opposite of the one existing prior to the 1976 Tax Reform Act presented in the first section, where the investor in new construction was paying, in present value terms, $69,278 less in taxes than the investor in rehabilitation.

If these investors hold onto their properties for 10 years instead of five, then the investor in new construction is able to take, in present value terms, $52,634 in depreciation deductions, which is $122,691 less than or only 30 percent of the $175,325 of allowable deductions for the investor who amortizes rehabilitation expenses. For the investor using the 200 percent declining balance method, the first 10 years of depreciation deductions total $123,181, which is $70,547 larger than, or almost four times, the amount allowed for new construction. Thus, the investor in new construction will pay $85,884 ($122,691 × .70) more in taxes than the investor who amortizes and $49,383 ($70,547 × .70) more in taxes than the investor who uses accelerated depreciation.

Table 7, which summarizes these results, makes clear that for the investor in historic preservation who amortizes rehabilitation costs there is little additional tax savings to be gained in present value terms from holding onto the property for more than five years. The individual who uses accelerated depreciation, however, experiences a steady gain in period-of-ownership tax savings the longer the property is held.

But again this analysis treats only one of many parts of the tax code that determines whether or not the historic preservation provisions create the incentives they are intended to. If one looks at how the tax code treats the capital gains realized from the sale of these different investments, a different picture

44

from the one just presented emerges. Using the same assumptions presented earlier and the depreciation figures just discussed, it is possible to compare the tax liabilities resulting from the sale of these investments. Again it is assumed that after five and 10 years of ownership each investor is able to sell a property at the same price of $525,000. Tables 8, 9 and 10 compare the tax liabilities of each investor at the time of sale.

For the individual who decides to demolish the historic structure and construct a new building, table 8, section A shows that after five years the total tax liability at sale is $84,205, which is $40,060 or 32 percent less than was the $124,265 tax liability after five years upon sale before the 1976 Tax Reform Act and 1978 Revenue Act (see table 3, section A). Table 8, section B shows that after 10 years of ownership the tax liability at sale of the investor in new construction increases to $97,155, reflecting the greater amount of capital gain realized, even though the annual rate of appreciation is 5 percent in table 8, section B instead of the 10 percent rate used in table 8, section A. This increased tax of $97,155 is still $43,977 or 31 percent less than was the $141,132 tax liability at sale before the tax reforms (see table 3, section B). The main reason for these differences is that before the 1976 Tax Reform Act, the investor in new construction could claim a much larger amount of depreciation deductions than is now possible, which served to increase both the capital gain and the amount of excess depreciation subject to recapture as ordinary income. As a result of the act the investor in new construction is now allowed to use only straight-line depreciation.

Tables 9 and 10 show how the provisions of the 1976 Tax Reform Act as amended by the 1978 Revenue Act have affected the tax liability at sale of investors in historic preservation. Table 9, section A indicates that for the investor in historic preservation who amortizes rehabilitation costs and sells his or her property after five years the new tax provisions have increased the tax liability at the time of sale to $187,817, which is $73,792 or 65 percent over the level of $114,025 prior to the 1976 Tax Reform Act (see section A, table 4, line 15). More importantly, this tax liability of $187,817 is over $100,000 more than the $84,205 liability of the investor in new construction, shown in section A, table 8. Both of these results are due to the larger amount of depreciation deductions that the investor who amortizes rehabilitation costs now can claim over the level that was previously allowed and to the resulting increase in capital gain upon sale.

45

Table 7

DEPRECIATION DEDUCTIONS AND TAX SAVINGS:
NEW CONSTRUCTION vs. HISTORIC PRESERVATION
(Present Value)

Sale	New Construction	Historic Preservation	
		Amortization	Accelerated Depreciation
After 5 years:			
Deductions	$30,862	$152,293	$ 85,129
Tax savings		85,002	37,987
After 10 years:			
Deductions	52,634	175,325	123,181
Tax savings		85,884	49,383
After 20 years:			
Deductions	75,171	187,482	148,805
Tax savings		78,617	51,544

Comparing the results of table 9, section B with those in table 8, section B indicates that increasing the period of ownership to 10 years only marginally enhances the tax effects at time of sale for the investor in historic preservation who uses amortization compared to the position of the investor in new construction. It is also important to note that thus far none of the investors in this analysis has had to pay either the minimum tax or the alternative minimum tax. With respect to the minimum tax, exclusions have always been large enough to offset the value of the tax preference items; whereas with the alternative minimum tax, it has not been big enough to be larger than the sum of the regular income tax and the minimum tax. Thus, it has not been operative in these examples.

Because of the considerably smaller amount of depreciation deductions taken, table 10 shows that investors in historic preservation who use accelerated depreciation have much smaller tax liabilities at sale than those investors who use the five-year amortization. But these liabilities are still considerably greater than those for investors in new construction (see table 8). From a public policy perspective, the interesting and important question is whether these larger amounts of tax liabilities at sale for investors in historic preservation are so large as to offset the tax savings they realized from the greater depreciation deductions while owning the properties.

Bringing together data from the previous tables on tax liabilities both during

---

Table 8

TAX LIABILITY FROM SALE OF NEW BUILDING WITH SALE AFTER 5 AND 10 YEARS

A. After 5 Years:

	Sales Price	Purchase Price	Improvements	Depreciation	Gross Capital Gain
(1)	$525,000	− ($150,000 + 15,000[1]	+ 185,000	− $41,625)	= $216,625
(2)	216,625	Gross capital gain			
(3)	× .6	New portion of capital gain excluded			
(4)	129,975	Tax preference item subject to alternative minimum tax			
(5)	86,650	Remainder of capital gain subject to income tax			
(6)	+ 60,000	Annual income			
(7)	146,650	Taxable income			
(8)	× .7	Marginal tax rate			
(9)	$ 84,205	Tax liability ($53,090 + 70% of amount over $102,200)			

No minimum tax on tax preference items in year of sale.

B. After 10 Years:

	Sales Price	Purchase Price	Improvements	Depreciation	Gross Capital Gain
(1)	$525,000	− ($150,000 + 15,000[1]	+ 185,000	− 87,875)	= $262,875
(2)	262,875	Gross capital gain			
(3)	× .6	New portion of capital gain excluded			
(4)	157,725	Tax preference item subject to alternative minimum tax			
(5)	105,150	Remainder of capital gain subject to income tax			
(6)	+ 60,000	Annual income			
(7)	165,150	Taxable income			
(8)	× .7	Marginal tax rate			
(9)	$ 97,155	Tax liability ($53,090 + 70% of amount over $102,200)			

No minimum tax on tax preference items in year of sale.

---

[1] Demolition costs.

ownership and at the time of sale, tables 11 and 12 summarize the net tax positions of the two types of investors. For investors selling their properties after five years with 10 percent rates of annual appreciation, table 11 shows that both investors in historic preservation realize net tax gains by deciding to do rehabilitation instead of new construction—that is, in both instances of amortization and accelerated depreciation the tax savings realized by the investor in historic preservation during the period of ownership are large enough to offset completely the tax losses experienced at sale and to be greater than the tax savings from new construction.

While both investors in historic preservation realize sizable net tax gains, it is clear that the investor who amortizes rehabilitation costs and sells after five years generates $6,960, or 51 percent, more in tax savings ($20,677) in present value terms than the investor who uses accelerated depreciation ($13,707).

Table 9

TAX LIABILITY FROM SALE OF HISTORIC STRUCTURE
AFTER 5 AND 10 YEARS
(Having Used Amortization)

A. After 5 Years:

	Sales Price	Purchase Price		Improvements	Depreciation	Gross Capital Gain
(1)	$525,000	− ($150,000	+	200,000	− 205,167)	= $380,167
(2)	205,167	Amortization deductions				
(3)	− 67,500	Straight-line depreciation deductions				
(4)	137,667	Excess depreciation subject to recapture as ordinary income				
(5)	380,167	Gross capital gain				
(6)	− 137,667	Excess depreciation				
(7)	242,500	Net capital gain				
(8)	× .6	New portion of capital gain excluded				
(9)	145,500	Tax preference item subject to alternative tax				
(10)	97,000	Remainder of capital gain subject to marginal tax rate				
(11)	137,667	Excess depreciation				
(12)	60,000	Annual income				
(13)	294,667	Taxable income				
(14)	× .7	Marginal tax rate				
(15)	$187,817	Tax liability ($53,090 + 70% of amount over $102,200)				

B. After 10 Years:

	Sales Price	Purchase Price		Improvements	Depreciation	Gross Capital Gain
(1)	$525,000	− ($150,000	+	200,000	− 250,113)	= $425,113
(2)	250,113	Amortization deductions				
(3)	− 142,500	Straight-line depreciation deductions				
(4)	107,500	Excess depreciation subject to recapture as ordinary income				
(5)	425,113	Gross capital gain				
(6)	107,500	Excess depreciation				
(7)	317,613	Net capital gain				
(8)	× .6	New portion of capital gain excluded				
(9)	190,568	Tax preference item subject to alternative tax				
(10)	127,045	Remainder of capital gain subject to marginal tax rate				
(11)	107,500	Excess depreciation				
(12)	60,000	Annual income				
(13)	294,545	Taxable income				
(14)	× .7	Marginal tax rate				
(15)	$187,732	Tax liability ($53,090 + 70% of amount over $120,200)				

Table 12 demonstrates that changing the underlying assumptions to sale after 10 years and a 5 percent annual appreciation rate increases these differences and the net tax savings from investing in historic preservation as opposed to new construction. The investor using amortization now realizes a net tax savings of $50,963 in present value terms, while the investor using accelerated depreciation garners a $30,779 savings, both of which are more than double the savings realized under the other set of assumptions.

In comparing tables 11 and 12 to table 5 it is clear that the historic preservation provisions have improved considerably the net tax position of investors in historic preservation relative to that which existed prior to the provisions. A summary of these changes is presented in the following section.

Table 10

TAX LIABILITY FROM SALE OF HISTORIC STRUCTURE
AFTER 5 AND 10 YEARS
(With Accelerated Depreciation)

A. After 5 Years:

	Sales Price	Purchase Price	Improvements	Depreciation	Gross Capital Gain
(1)	$525,000 –	(150,000 +	200,000 –	113,012) =	$288,013
(2)	113,012	Accelerated depreciation			
		(200% on $200,000 + $100,000, basis of original building)			
(3)	– 67,500	Straight-depreciation deductions			
(4)	45,512	Excess depreciation			
(5)	288,013	Gross capital gain			
(6)	– 45,512	Excess depreciation			
(7)	242,500	Net capital gain			
(8)	× .6	Portion of capital gain excluded			
(9)	145,500	Tax preference item subject to alternative minimum tax			
(10)	97,000	Portion of capital gain subject to marginal tax rate			
(11)	60,000	Annual income			
(12)	45,512	Excess depreciation			
(13)	202,512	Taxable income			
(14)	× .7	Marginal tax rate			
(15)	$123,308	Tax liability ($53,090 + 70% of amount over $102,200)			

B. After 10 Years:

	Sales Price	Purchase Price	Improvements	Depreciation	Gross Capital Gain
(1)	$525,000 –	(150,000 +	200,000 –	189,585) =	$364,585
(2)	189,585	Accelerated depreciation			
		(200% on $200,000 + $100,000, basis of original building)			
(3)	– 142,500	Straight-line depreciation deductions			
(4)	47,085	Excess depreciation			
(5)	364,585	Gross capital gain			
(6)	– 47,085	Excess depreciation			
(7)	317,500	Net capital gain			
(8)	× .6	Portion of capital gain excluded			
(9)	190,500	Tax preference item subject to alternative minimum tax			
(10)	127,000	Portion of capital gain subject to marginal tax rate			
(11)	60,000	Annual income			
(12)	47,085	Excess depreciation			
(13)	234,085	Taxable income			
(14)	× .7	Marginal tax rate			
(15)	$145,410	Tax liability ($53,090 + 70% of amount over $102,200)			

Conclusions and Policy Implications

In order to determine the net tax impact of a particular tax incentive such as the historic preservation provisions of the Internal Revenue Code, each section of this article has underscored the importance of examining the tax implications both during the period of ownership and at the time of sale. The provisions of the tax code represent a highly interdependent system: When a new provision is inserted or an old one changed, a chain reaction of tax consequences is often set in motion, which makes it difficult to determine the final effect of the initial change on an investor's tax liability. That the historic preservation provisions have had this effect is clearly demonstrated in table 13, which summarizes the findings of the previous sections by showing how the tax position of an investor in residential historic preservation has changed over time in response to changes in the code.

Under the pre-1976 Tax Reform Act situation, row 1 of table 13 shows that during a five-year ownership period the individual who decided to invest $200,000 to rehabilitate a depreciable, residential historic structure had to pay in present value terms $73,350 more in taxes than did the person who decided

Table 11

COMPARATIVE NET TAX TREATMENT OF NEW CONSTRUCTION AND HISTORIC PRESERVATION
(With Sale After 5 Years)

	Accounting	Amortization	Present Value
(1)	$205,165	Depreciation deductions with rehabilitation (amortization)	$152,293
(2)	− 41,625	Depreciation deductions with new construction (straight-line)	− 30,862
(3)	163,540		121,431
(4)	× .7		× .7
(5)	114,478	Tax savings during 5 years of ownership from doing rehabilitation instead of new construction	85,002
(6)	187,817	Tax liability on sale of historic structure (amortization)	116,620
(7)	− 84,205	Tax liability on sale of new structure (straight-line)	− 52,285
(8)	103,612	Tax loss from doing historic preservation instead of new construction	64,335
(9)	114,478	Tax gain from historic preservation (line 5)	85,002
(10)	− 103,612	Tax loss from historic preservation (line 8)	− 64,335
(11)	$ 10,886	Net tax gain from doing rehabilitation instead of new construction	$ 20,667
		Accelerated Depreciation	
(12)	113,012	Depreciation deductions with rehabilitation (200% declining balance	$ 85,129
(13)	− 41,625	Depreciation deductions with new construction (straight-line)	− 30,862
(14)	71,387		54,267
(15)	× .7		× .7
(16)	49,971	Tax savings during 5 years of ownership from doing rehabilitation instead of new construction	37,987
(17)	123,308	Tax liability on sale of historic structure (200%)	76,565
(18)	− 84,205	Tax liability on sale of new structure (straight-line)	52,285
(19)	39,103	Tax loss from doing rehabilitation instead of new construction	24,280
(20)	49,971	Tax savings from rehabilitation	37,987
(21)	39,103	Tax loss from rehabilitation	24,280
(22)	$ 10,868	Net tax gain from doing rehabilitation instead of new construction	$ 13,707

to demolish the structure and construct a new one. This tax difference reflects the fact that the investor in new construction used to be able to deduct his or her remaining interest (basis) in the old property plus demolition costs as ordinary business expenses. In addition the investor could depreciate new construction costs at a more accelerated rate (200 percent declining balance) than could the investor in rehabilitation, who could use only the 125 percent declining balance method of depreciation.

Row 1 also shows, however, that upon sale of their respective properties after five years of ownership the investor in rehabilitation had a tax liability that was, in present value terms, $6,358 less than that of the investor in new construction. The investor in new construction had a higher tax liability because of the larger capital gains at sale and larger excess depreciation deductions subject to recapture and taxation as ordinary income. For the investor in new construction, however, the higher tax liability at sale than that for the investor in rehabilitation is not large enough to offset the lower taxes during ownership, with the result that the investor who rehabilitates the historic structure ends up with a net tax loss of $62,920 if selling after five years or $60,116 if selling property after 10 years and realizes a 5 percent instead of a 10 percent annual

Table 12

COMPARATIVE NET TAX TREATMENT OF NEW CONSTRUCTION AND HISTORIC PRESERVATION
(With Sale After 10 Years)

	Accounting	Amortization	Present Value
(1)	$250,110	Depreciation deductions with rehabilitation (amortization)	$175,325
(2)	− 87,875	Depreciation deductions with new construction (straight-line)	− 52,634
(3)	162,235		122,691
(4)	× .7		× .7
(5)	113,564	Tax savings during 10 years of ownership as a result of investing in rehabilitation instead of new construction	85,884
(6)	187,732	Tax liability on sale of historic structure (amortization)	72,379
(7)	− 97,155	Tax liability on sale of new structure (straight-line)	− 37,458
(8)	90,577	Tax loss as a result of doing historic preservation instead of new construction	34,921
(9)	113,564	Tax savings from historic preservation (line 5)	85,884
(10)	− 90,577	Tax loss from historic preservation (line 8)	− 34,921
(11)	$ 22,987	Net tax gain from doing rehabilitation instead of new construction	$ 50,963
		Accelerated Depreciation	
(12)	$189,585	Depreciation deductions with rehabilitation (200% declining balance)	$123,181
(13)	− 87,875	Depreciation deductions with new construction (straight-line)	− 52,634
(14)	101,710		70,547
(15)	× .7		× .7
(16)	71,197	Tax savings during 10 years of ownership from doing rehabilitation instead of new construction	49,383
(17)	145,410	Tax liability on sale of historic structure (200%)	56,062
(18)	− 97,155	Tax liability on sale of new structure (straight-line)	− 37,458
(19)	48,255	Tax loss from doing rehabilitation instead of new construction	18,604
(20)	71,197	Tax savings from rehabilitation	49,383
(21)	− 48,255	Tax loss from rehabilitation	− 18,604
(22)	$ 22,943	Net tax gain from doing rehabilitation instead of new construction	$ 30,779

Table 13

SUMMARY OF CHANGES IN TAX SITUATION OF INVESTORS IN HISTORIC PRESERVATION

(Relative to Investor in New Construction)
(Present Value)[1]

	(1) Tax loss (−) or gain (+) during ownership				(2) Tax loss (−) or gain (+) at sale				(3) Net tax loss (−) or gain (+)			
	Amortization		Depreciation		Amortization		Depreciation		Amortization		Depreciation	
	5 yrs.	10 yrs.	5 yrs.	10 yrs.	5 yrs.	10 yrs.	5 yrs.	10 yrs.	5 yrs.	10 yrs.	5 yrs.	10 yrs.
(1) Pre-1976 Tax Reform Act	−69,278	−60,488			+6,358	+375			−62,920	−60,116		
(2) Post-1976 Tax Reform Act and 1978 Revenue Act	+85,002	+85,884	+37,987	+49,383	−64,335	−34,921	−24,280	−18,604	+20,667	+50,963	+13,707	+30,779

[1] *10 percent discount rate used.*

rate of appreciation (row 1, column 3). Thus, before the 1976 Tax Reform Act the tax code created substantial tax benefits for the investor who tore down historic structures and put new buildings in their place rather than rehabilitating the structures. It is important to point out that the net benefits are not so large as those realized just during the period of ownership.

The historic preservation provisions of the 1976 Tax Reform Act dramatically altered the tax treatment of investments in new construction and historic preservation. Row 2 of table 13 shows that in present value terms the investor in historic preservation who amortized rehabilitation expenses under section 191 paid $85,002 less in taxes than the investor in new construction during the five years they owned their properties and $85,884 less for 10 years. In comparison, the investor who depreciated rehabilitation expenses under section 167(o) paid $37,987 less in taxes during five years' ownership than did the investor in new construction. The two accelerated deduction options for rehabilitation and the limitation to straight-line depreciation for new construction explain most of these tax differences. The historic preservation provisions that prevent the investor in new construction from deducting demolition costs and the remaining basis of the original property as ordinary business expenses account for the remainder of the difference.

Because investors in rehabilitation have to pay recapture taxes on their excess depreciation deductions at the time of sale, their tax liabilities at this time are considerably higher than those of investors in new construction, who have no excess depreciation to claim because of the Tax Reform Act's limitations. Row 2, column 2 of table 13 shows that at sale after five years the person who has amortized rehabilitation expenses pays $64,335 more in taxes than the investor in new construction, which gives the investor in historic preservation a net tax gain of $20,667 (row 2, column 3). (Immediately following the 1976 Tax Reform Act and prior to its correcting amendments, however, the investor who used amortization was actually worse off from a tax perspective than before passage of the act, because the full amount of the amortization deductions was recaptured at sale. It is only by standardizing the recapture treatment of excess depreciation resulting from amortization or depreciation that the 1978 Revenue Act has been able to create the positive net tax situation shown in table 13 for investors who use amortization.)

For the investor who uses accelerated depreciation, table 13 also shows that a net tax gain of $13,707 is realized if the property is sold after five years and $30,779 if sold after 10 years. Both of these figures are substantially lower than the tax gains of the investor using amortization. But it is clear from this table that the net tax position of investors in historic preservation has improved substantially over the negative tax climate that prevailed prior to the 1976 Tax Reform Act and 1978 Revenue Act. Under similar sets of assumptions the tax reforms have bestowed the largest net tax benefits on the investor who prior to the acts was investing in historic preservation and sold after 10 years. This investor sustained a $60,113 net tax loss in present value terms (table 13, row 1, column 3), whereas after passage of the acts with similar rates of appreciation and ownership periods a net tax gain of $50,963 is realized if amortization is used or $30,779 if accelerated depreciation is used.

An important point still remains, however. Because of the recapture of excess depreciation at sale, the net tax benefits of investing in historic preservation instead of new construction are much less than are the initial tax benefits favoring preservation that are realized during the period of ownership. The fact that the historic preservation provisions act as somewhat of a two-edged sword raises questions about how effective they are as public policy instruments in stimulating additional historic preservation.

To determine how much additional rehabilitation the historic preservation provisions have or are likely to stimulate would require additional analysis. But it is clear from this analysis that the provisions with their amendments have achieved their more limited objective of creating a more favorable tax situation for historic preservation. The role these tax considerations play in influencing investment decisions depends in large part on the characteristics of the housing markets involved, the possibilities for realizing capital appreciation and on the behavior of real estate investors and financiers and what sorts of tax incentives are important to them.

For some investors, the substantial tax reductions provided by the historic preservation provisions in the early years of ownership may be the most attractive aspect of these incentives. For others the longer term net tax benefits of the provisions may be a more important consideration. For those investors who want to avoid higher tax liabilities at sale, actual avoidance of the historic preservation provisions through the use of straight-line depreciation may be preferable. Or they might favor an investment tax credit similar to the one now in place for older commercial structures. This approach has the benefit of producing a dollar reduction in taxes for each dollar invested (up to a certain limit) and of not involving the investor in considerations of recapture provisions. Others have argued that property tax exemptions are needed to stimulate historic preservation.[38] Whatever public policy tools are used, it is clear from this analysis that in the future prior to implementation of specific policies a more thorough understanding of their consequences is needed than existed with respect to the historic preservation provisions.

NOTES

1. On this point see the President's Council on Environmental Quality, *Second, Third and Fourth Annual Reports* (1971–73) (Washington, D.C.: United States Government Printing Office); and R. Roddewig and M. Young, "New Shelters in Old Properties: The Tax Reform Act of 1976," 3 *Real Estate Issues* No. 2 (Winter 1978) (hereafter cited as "New Shelters in Old Properties").

2. The adaptive use of historic properties has been discussed by C. Page, "Reusing History," in *Nation's Cities* (April 1978).

3. For an interesting account of the role historic preservation plays in neighborhood revitalization see P. Meyers and G. Binder, *Neighborhood Conservation: Lessons from Three Cities* (1977) (Washington, D.C.: Conservation Foundation).

4. For a good account of traditional rationales for historic preservation see National Trust for Historic Preservation, T. Wrenn and E. Mulloy, *America's Forgotten Architecture* (1976) (New York: Pantheon Books).

5. For different proposals to promote historic preservation, see J. Costonis, *Space Adrift* (1974) (Urbana: University of Illinois Press); *The Transfer of Development Rights* (G. Rose, ed.) (1975) (New Brunswick, N.J.: Center for Urban Policy Research); "New Shelters in Old Properties," note 1 above; Maryland Environmental Trust, *Conservation Easements* (1974); and R. Brenneman, "Historic Preservation Restrictions: A Sampling of State Statutes," 8 *Conn. Law Review* No. 2 (1976).

6. See the "Environmental Protection Tax Act and the Historic Structures Tax Act, an Analysis for the Advisory Council on Historic Preservation," reprinted in 121 *Congressional Record* S1831 (1975).

7. See Touche Ross & Co., *Study on Tax Considerations in Multi-Family Housing Investments* (1972) (prepared for the U.S. Department of Housing and Urban Development under Contract H-1227, Washington, D.C.: U.S. Government Printing Office) (hereafter cited as "Study on Tax Considerations").

8. "New Shelters in Old Properties," note 1 above. Material within brackets [] has been added.

9. President's Council on Environmental Quality, *Third Annual Report* at 134 (1972) (Washington, D.C.: U.S. Government Printing Office).

10. The original "basis" of a property refers to the original cost of the property, which is usually its fair market value. The original basis thereafter may be adjusted through additions for improvements and/or subtractions for depreciation. The remaining basis is the amount of the

original basis that remains at a given period in time after these adjustments have been made. See § 1.165-3 of the *Treasury Regulations* for further detail on this question.

11. For a more detailed explanation, see Lifton, "Historic Preservation and the Tax Reform Act," XI *San Francisco Law Review* 463-4 (1977) (hereafter cited as "Historic Preservation").

12. The IRS has ruled that even in cases involving substantial rehabilitation as in this example, the investment must be added to the existing basis and depreciated at the 125 percent declining balance rate. However, many real estate developers indicate that the IRS has not questioned their treatment of rehabilitation as new construction for tax purposes and their use of the 200 percent declining balance method in computing their annual depreciation deductions.

13. These figures for the present value of the depreciation deductions taken during the period of ownership are not the same as those presented in tables 3 and 4. The reason for the difference is that in computing capital gains at sale, the investor is not allowed to use the present value of his or her depreciation deductions, but rather must use their actual accounting value.

14. For justification of the use of a 10 percent discount rate, see I. Lowry, C.P. Rydell and D. de Ferrante, "Testing the Supply Response to Housing Allowances: An Experimental Design" 79-87 (1971) (The Rand Corporation) (WN-7711-UI); P. Taubman and R. Rasche, "Subsidies, Tax Law, and Real Estate Investment," Joint Economic Committee of the U.S. Congress, *The Economics of Federal Subsidy Programs, Part 3—Tax Subsidies* (1972) (Washington, D.C.: U.S. Government Printing Office).

15. S. Weber, *Historic Preservation Incentives of the 1976 Tax Reform Act: An Economic Analysis* (1979) (National Bureau of Standards, Technical Note No. 980) (Washington, D.C.: U.S. Government Printing Office) (hereafter cited as "Historic Preservation Incentives").

16. *Id.* at 11.

17. Internal Revenue Code § 1250(a)(1)(c)(iv).

18. J. Heinberg, "Tax Incentives and Housing Rehabilitation: A Policy Analysis," 6 (1971) (Working Paper No. 112–37, Washington, D.C.: Urban Institute).

19. "Study on Tax Considerations," note 7 above, at 19.

20. The Tax Reform Act of 1976, Public Law No. 94-455, § 2124, 90 Stat. 1916 (codified in scattered sections of 42 United States Code).

21. Internal Revenue Code § 191 (d)(1). A good deal of discussion and debate has taken place concerning the process of certification of historical significance. The technical corrections of the Revenue Act of 1978 address some of the issues. For more detail see "Historic Preservation," note 11 above, at 461.

22. Internal Revenue Code, §§ 165(a) and 165(c). The deductions are available only if the owner did not intend to demolish the structure upon buying it.

23. Internal Revenue Code, § 280B.

24. "Historic Preservation," note 11 above, at 465.

25. Internal Revenue Code, § 167(n).

26. Apparently a number of aspects of the initial legislation dealing with the designation of historic structures made it possible for investors to avoid in some instances this provision. For more details, see "Historic Preservation," note 11 above, at 469.

27. Internal Revenue Code, § 191.

28. Internal Revenue Code, § 167(o).

29. See § 170(f)(3)(B)(iii), Internal Revenue Code. "New Shelters in Old Properties," note 1 above, at 10.

30. Section 1245 was amended in this manner by § 2124(a)(2) of the Tax Reform Act of 1976.

31. "Historic Preservation," note 11 above, at 479. *Senate Report No. 1236*, 94th Cong., 2nd Sess. 505.

32. The Revenue Act of 1978, Public Law No. 95-600, § 701(f), 92 Stat. 2901 ("Clarification of Provisions Providing Tax Incentives to Encourage the Preservation of Historic Structures").

33. Heritage Conservation and Recreation Service, U.S. Department of the Interior, "Technical Corrections to the Tax Reform Act of 1976" (Nov. 20, 1978).

34. Section 309 of the Tax Reduction and Simplification Act of 1977, Public Law No. 94-30, provided that charitable donations for historic preservation must now be granted permanently instead of for only 30 years as originally specified by § 2124 of the Tax Reform Act of 1976.

35. See the Revenue Act of 1978, Public Law No. 95-600, § 1202(a).

36. *Id.* at § 421 (codified in § 55 of the Internal Revenue Code).

37. Revenue Act of 1978, Public Law No. 95-600, § 311. The use of a building following a rehabilitation determines whether or not it qualifies as a commercial or industrial structure for purposes of the tax credit.

38. "New Shelters in Old Properties," note 1 above, at 27.

REHABILITATION UNDER THE TAX REFORM ACT OF 1976: CASE STUDIES

Part One

Gregory E. Andrews

Academy Hill, Jonesboro, Tenn.

Old Use: Jonesboro High School. Abandoned by Washington County School Board in 1972. Home of the Sourwood Regional Arts Center and Appalachian Theatre Ensemble 1974-77 as part of effort to find suitable adaptive use. All alternatives for public use of this building were explored and found impractical.

New Use: Academy Hill, a 13-unit luxury residential condominium association.

Description: Two-story brick structure (1926); central wooden portico with Doric columns. Located in the Jonesboro Historic District, which is listed in the National Register of Historic Places.

Tax Reform Act Certifications: Certified by U.S. Department of the Interior on November 22, 1977, as contributing to significance of Jonesboro Historic District; occupies a key and commanding position in the district. Proposed rehabilitation work given preliminary approval on February 10, 1978.

Rehabilitation Work: Exterior required only minor tuck pointing, cleaning selected areas with water and reconstructing cupola based on original design from old photographs and recovered fragments of the original. Roof and exterior architectural details repaired. Two-story brick stair/elevator tower and one-story covered parking structure added at rear. New clustered wiring, plumbing and mechanical services installed in original school corridors and ceilings lowered to eight feet. Classrooms converted to living areas and bedrooms, and ceilings there retained at original height to accommodate large windows. Existing walls retained where possible; all new interior partitions covered with smoothly finished sheet rock to match repaired original plaster walls. All new materials will match the original style of the building as closely as possible. Interior woodwork retained and repaired. New double-hung, six-over-six windows installed.

U.S. Department of the Interior assured on compatibility of new rear parking structure and treatment of stamped metal ceiling in former auditorium; ceiling being left exposed in major rooms of residential units on new second-floor level in auditorium. Owners found Interior Department's "Standards for Rehabilitation" to be clear and fair. No changes in project required to comply with standards. Jonesboro Historic Zoning Commission approved proposed changes to building prior to start of work.

Mr. Andrews is an attorney in the Investment Division, Legal Department, Connecticut General Life Insurance Company, Bloomfield, Conn., and was formerly an attorney in the Office of Real Estate and Legal Services, National Trust for Historic Preservation.

Academy Hill, Jonesboro, Tennessee

Rehabilitation Schedule: Building acquired January 1978; construction begun April 1978; completion expected November 1979.

Site Area: 52,600 square feet, of which building occupies 10,000 square feet.

Gross Building Area: 29,760 square feet (before rehabilitation, 26,000 square feet).

Costs:

Acquisition: $34,400.

Rehabilitation (direct and indirect): approximately $1,056,000. Rehabilitation costs include the following:

(1)	materials and labor	$927,913	(approximately $36 per square foot of living area—e.g., elevator and public areas not included)
(2)	architect's fee	23,450	
(3)	legal fee (not including condominium conversion legal work)	2,000	
(4)	insurance (as of 4/1/79)	5,270	
(5)	permits	316	
(6)	Tax Reform Act certifications	0	(done by one of owner's stockholders)
(7)	financing (includes loan interest payments)	65,000	

Financing: $500,000 mortgage loan from First Tennessee Bank and Trust Company at 9.5 percent interest, payable two years, eight months after date of contract. Mortgage guaranteed by Small Business Administration (SBA) under Contractor Loan Program. Balance of rehabilitation cost contributed by owner's two stockholders through combination of cash equity and personal loans.

Financing package took eight months to put together after preparation of preliminary specifications and feasibility studies because of financial community's skepticism. Five lending institutions refused to finance until assurances obtained of stockholders' credit worthiness, SBA loan guarantee and consumer interest in project. Preliminary certification of rehabilitation prior to start of project also helped attract financing.

Company owning project is also the prime contractor. Innovative agreement between company and its two stockholders, who are the project developers, provides that upon project completion, stockholders will buy out company's interest in the project and company will purchase stockholders' shares in it.

Post-Rehabilitation Space and Rates: 13 condominium units created, ranging from 1,440 to 2,440 square feet in size and with from one to three bedrooms. Eight units were committed for sale by oral agreement before completion of project despite lack of firm price.

Appraised Value:

Not yet determined; pending project completion.

Total sales price: $1,285,650.

Tax Aspects: Owner-developer plans to sell most condominium units created by the rehabilitation. Initial purchasers of units who lease them for income-producing purposes may take tax deductions under the Tax Reform Act of 1976 for the rehabilitation costs so long as the owner-developer has not previously done so. Owner-developer would not have undertaken this project without availability of these tax deductions. Investors in this project probably will rehabilitate other properties in Jonesboro Historic District in order to take these tax deductions.

Comments: Adaptive use of this school facility will yield many benefits besides structural preservation, including a substantial property tax payment from this formerly tax-exempt property. Project will also help stabilize the surrounding residential neighborhood containing many historic homes threatened by neglect or development pressures.

Participants:

Owner-developer—Sutphin Construction Company, Inc., Jonesboro, Tenn. (Contact: William E. Kennedy, 400 West Main Street, Jonesboro, Tenn. 37659).

Architect—Eugene E. Burr, 619½ Gay Street, Knoxville, Tenn. 37902.

Old Use: Hotel, in gradual decline.

New Use: 121 apartment units for low and moderate-income elderly.

Description: Four-story, brick, Greek Revival structure (1833), with several late 19th-century changes, including addition of fifth floor and five-story wing and kitchen. The only remaining example of the luxury "palace" hotels constructed in the 1830s and patterned after Boston's famed Tremont House; listed individually in the National Register of Historic Places.

Tax Reform Act Certifications: Automatically a certified historic structure because individually listed in National Register. Proposed rehabilitation work received preliminary approval from the U.S. Department of the Interior on December 28, 1977.

Rehabilitation Work: Restoration of original rooflines and chimneys by removal of fifth floor. Demolition of late 19th-century wing and kitchen additions and construction of two contemporary, six-story brick wings, with glass connections to original structure. Removal of exterior paint by chemical wash. Exterior brickwork and Greek Revival ornamentation restored. Interior work included necessary modifications and renovations for conversion of hotel rooms to apartments. Second-floor ballroom, with high coffered ceiling and 10-foot windows; adjoining English Room restored to original appearance for public viewing and use. Facilities created for residents include arts and crafts room, dining room, library, laundry and lounges.

After a careful review, U.S. Department of the Interior decided that major demolition work would not impair significance of entire structure; however, testing was required of chemical methods for paint removal on facade. Owner was comfortable with Interior Department's "Standards for Rehabilitation" and found the required governmental review to be informative and smooth.

Rehabilitation Schedule: Building acquired in September 1977; work begun March 1978; completed May 1979.

Site Area: 38,906 square feet, of which building occupies 30,276 square feet.

Gross Building Area: 49,600 square feet.

59

Costs:

Acquisition: $350,00.

Rehabilitation (direct and indirect): $4,100,000, approximately $41 per square foot based on entire cost and $31 per square foot based only on direct construction costs. Rehabilitation costs include the following:

(1)	direct construction costs (materials and contractor's fee)	$3,325,000
(2)	architect's fee	140,000
(3)	legal fee	20,000
(4)	insurance	10,000
(5)	Tax Reform Act certifications	10,000
(6)	financing	1 percent of construction loan; 4 percent of permanent loan

Financing: $350,000 mortgage loan for six months at 12 percent interest rate, held by an investor in project, financed initial acquisition. $4,475,000 construction loan for 18 months at 12 percent interest rate from Northern National Bank of Bangor and Industrial National Bank of Providence, R.I., supplemented by a $4,475,000 permanent loan for 40 years at 8.5 percent interest rate provided by Maine State Housing Authority from proceeds of bond sale.

Bangor House, Bangor, Maine

Federal subsidy of rental payments made under section 8 of the National Housing Act, under which tenants pay no more than 25 percent of their monthly income in rent. Government pays the balance necessary for owner to recover expenses.

Post-Rehabilitation Space and Rates: Net rentable area: 85,270 square feet (includes apartments and community facilities)

Rental units and rates: 95 one-bedroom units, each 625 square feet, rent at $472 a month; 26 two-bedroom units, each 750 square feet, rent at $508 a month.

More than 300 applications for apartments were received.

Property Taxes:
Before rehabilitation: approximately $2,000.
After rehabilitation: $50,000.

Tax Aspects: Owner expects to amortize and deduct all rehabilitation costs, to the maximum extent allowable, over the 60-month (5-year) period provided under section 191 of the Internal Revenue Code. Had this tax incentive been unavailable, owner would have used the similar, but less advantageous, tax deduction available under section 167(k) for the rehabilitation of low-income rental housing. Owner plans to seek certifications under section 191 for other rehabilitation projects now under way.

Participants:
Owner—Bangor House Proprietary (Morton Myerson and John Allen, general partners), Box 1484, Manchester, Mass. 01944.
Contractor—Salter Corporation, Arsenal Street, Augusta, Maine 04330.
Architect—Childs Bertman Tseckares Associates, Inc., 306 Dartmouth Street, Boston, Mass. 02116.

Bush/Breyman Bldg., Salem, Oregon

Old Use: Retail and office building.

New Use: Rehabilitated for same purpose.

Description: Two-story Queen Anne building (1889). Brick on stone foundation with cast-iron front and cast-iron interior columns. Single-story rear addition added in 1926. Located on city's historic business thoroughfare. Listed individually in the National Register of Historic Places. Owned by same family since construction.

Tax Reform Act Certifications: Automatically a certified historic structure because individually listed in National Register. Completed rehabilitation work certified May 26, 1978, following preliminary approval April 10, 1978.

Rehabilitation Work: Exterior doors and walls repainted; windows and doors repaired. Main stairway braced and woodwork repaired. Interior doors, wainscoting and walls repaired. Partitions (1965) removed and ceilings lowered. New elevator and rest rooms installed; two skylights fitted with new glass. No changes in project required in order to comply with U.S. Department of the Interior's "Standards for Rehabilitation."

Rehabilitation Schedule: Construction begun June 1977; completed June 1978.

Site Area: 9,570 square feet, of which building occupies 6,500 square feet.

Gross Building Area: 16,720 square feet (basement, 5,000 square feet; first floor, 6,500 square feet (with small mezzanine); second floor, 5,220 square feet).

Costs:

Construction: $36,000 in 1889.

Rehabilitation (direct and indirect): $151,000, or approximately $9.03 a square foot. (Note: $125,000 of the total cost was spent on the second floor, at a rate of $23.95 a square foot. A modern building of comparable size in Salem today would cost $40-$50 a square foot to build.) Rehabilitation costs include the following:

(1)	materials and labor (supplied by contractor)	$96,390
(2)	contractor's fee	10,167
(3)	additional construction	27,213
(4)	architect's fee	1,176
(5)	insurance and taxes	4,992
(6)	permits	286
(7)	Tax Reform Act certification	200
(8)	financing (includes construction loan interest)	9,541

63

Financing: $145,000 construction loan for one year at 9¾ percent interest rate from American Federal Savings and Loan (Salem) supplemented by a $145,000 mortgage loan for 25 years at 9¾ percent interest rate from the same bank. Owner contributed $6,000 and obtained financing easily because of building's location in central business area and because of success of earlier rehabilitation projects that had allayed skepticism in the local financial community.

Post-Rehabilitation Space and Rates: Net rentable area: 10,850 square feet (first floor, 6,500 square feet; second floor, 4,350 square feet).

Rental units and rates: First floor rents as a single unit of commercial space at 28 cents a square foot, or approximately $1,845 a month (note: tenant allowed free use of the 5,000-square-foot basement); second floor rents as a single unit of office space at 55 cents a square foot, or approximately $2,400 a month (includes eight off-street parking spaces). Both floors are rented.

Owner pays all taxes, utilities, heat, air-conditioning, janitorial service and exterior and elevator maintenance costs. Comparable new office space rents for 65-70 cents a square foot. State property tax relief for historic structures enables owner to delete from leases the usual clause passing on to renters any increases in property tax.

Post-Rehabilitation Profitability:

Annual gross income (less expected 5 percent vacancy and credit loss)	$48,393
Annual operating expenses	18,555
Annual mortgage interest	14,075
Total annual expenses	32,630
Annual net income	15,763
Return on investment	10.2 percent on equity ($155,000); 9.9 percent on total investment

Appraised Value:
Before rehabilitation: $85,000.
After rehabilitation: $300,000.

Tax Aspects: *Federal:* Owner plans to amortize and deduct all rehabilitation costs, to the maximum extent allowable, over the 60-month (5-year) period provided under section 191 of the Internal Revenue Code. Owner believes that this tax incentive will "make a good deal of difference" in the economics of this rehabilitation project and in his spendable income.

State: Under Oregon Revised Statutes sections 358.475-358.565, assessment on this historic property has been frozen for 15 years, at $81,800, in return for owner's promise to maintain the property according to certain preservation standards. High property taxes in Oregon (assessments at 100 percent of cash value, 1979 tax rate of 24.77 mills) make this tax relief attractive. Owner now pays approximately $2,045 in property taxes, $5,386 less than would be owed without tax relief (based on present fair market value). (Note: A bill before Oregon's legislature would allow assessors to increase *all* property assessments annually to reflect inflation. Historic properties would still be exempt from general reassessments.)

Participants:

Owner-developer—Evan B. Boise, 147 Commercial Street, N.E., Salem, Ore. 97301.
Contractor—Jensen-Ritchie Construction, Inc., 2245 Judson Street, S.E., Salem, Ore. 97302.
Architect—Charles Hawkes, 1110 Saginaw Street South, Salem, Ore. 97302.

Old Use: St. Clare High School and Convent. The school was closed in 1973 and the property was sold to developers. A planned $2 million renovation and conversion to 60 condominiums failed to materialize.

New Use: Chateau Clare, a complex of 88 apartment units for the elderly and handicapped.

Description: Gothic Revival structure (1889) with polychrome brickwork, slate roof, copper cornice and a chapel with stained glass windows. Building is part of l'Eglise du Precieux Sang church and parish complex, constituting Rhode Island's first French national church. Listed in the National Register of Historic Places.

Tax Reform Act Certifications: Application made April 1, 1978, for certification of historical significance; building certified April 15, 1978, as contributing to the significance of the l'Eglise du Precieux Sang National Register historic district. Rehabilitation work certified April 27, 1978, following application April 20, 1978. Owner reports that certification process went smoothly.

Rehabilitation Work: Exterior cleaned and mortar repaired as necessary; wooden facade ornamentation and window sashes repaired or replaced; storm windows installed; 6 stained glass windows cleaned; deteriorated sections of slate roof replaced. Iron roof cresting retained and copper cornice repaired. Tower with 2 elevators constructed. Exterior fire escapes removed.

Significant architectural and artistic details of interior retained, such as high ceilings and extensive detail work. Carpeting installed throughout except where retention of bare hardwood floors requested by tenants. Security system added, and electrical and plumbing systems modernized.

Rehabilitation Schedule: Building acquired February 1976; rehabilitation begun immediately; completed January 1977.

Site Area: 81,058 square feet, of which building occupies 21,120 square feet.

Gross Building Area: 76,600 square feet (unchanged by rehabilitation).

Costs:

Acquisition: $300,000.

Rehabilitation (direct and indirect: $2,100,000, or approximately $33.33 per square foot for entire cost and $25 per square foot for direct construction cost. Rehabilitation costs include the following:

(1) direct construction costs (materials and contractor's fee)	$1,800,000
(2) architect's fee	80,000
(3) legal fee	25,000
(4) insurance	12,000
(5) Tax Reform Act certification	10,000
(6) financing	10 percent of construction loan; 4.25 percent of permanent loan

Financing: $2,400,000 construction loan for 18 months at 9 percent interest rate from Rhode Island Hospital Trust Company (Providence), supplemented by a $2,400,000 permanent mortgage loan for 40 years at 7.5 percent interest rate obtained from Government National Mortgage Association (GNMA). Federal insurance of mortgage required and obtained from the Federal Housing Administration (FHA).

Federal subsidy of rental payments made under section 8 of the National Housing Act. Under this program, tenants pay no more than 25 percent of their

65

Chateau Clare, Woonsocket, Rhode Island

monthly income in rent. Government pays the balance necessary for owner to recover expenses.

Post-Rehabilitation Space and Rates:
Net rentable area: 57,450 square feet.
Rental units and rates: 8 efficiency units, 400 square feet each, rent at $254 a month; 61 one-bedroom units, 540 square feet each, rent at $338 a month; 19 rented.

Post-Rehabilitation Profitability:

Annual gross income	$375,540
Annual operating expenses (including debt service)	309,900
Annual net income	52,400
Return on investment (equity)	6 percent

Property Taxes:
Before rehabilitation: none (a public institution).
After rehabilitation: $23,000 (annually).

Tax Aspects: Owner has begun to amortize and deduct all rehabilitation costs, to the maximum extent allowable, over the 60-month (5-year) period provided under section 191 of the Internal Revenue Code. Owner finds this tax provision useful because the higher tax shelter it provides makes the project more profitable. Had this tax incentive been unavailable, owner would have used the similar, but less advantageous, tax deduction allowable under section 167(k) for the rehabilitation of low-income rental housing. Owner plans to seek certifications under section 191 for other rehabilitation projects now under way.

Participants:
Owner—Chateau Clare Company (Morton Myerson and John Allen, General partners), c/o Myerson/Allen and Company, 306 Dartmouth Street, Boston, Mass. 02116.
Contractor—Cayer Construction Company, Providence, R.I.
Architects—C.E. Maguire, 31 Canal Street, Providence, R.I. 02903; Ira Rakatausky and Associates, 15 Meeting Street, Providence, R.I. 02903.

Old Use: Mill.

New Use: Restaurant and health-care facility.

Description: Three-story brick structure (1882), with wooden interior frame and trussed gable roof; 1910 addition has wooden beams and iron columns. Originally known as the Bay State Mill, it was part of the American Screw Company Mills complex. Following a series of fires in 1971, the present owner rehabilitated the structure in 1974-75 by replacing the windows, sandblasting the exterior and interior and removing modern interior partitions. It is located in the Moshassuck Square Historic District, which is listed in the National Register of Historic Places.

Tax Reform Act Certifications: Certified by U.S. Department of the Interior May 1977 as contributing to the significance of the Moshassuck Square Historic District. Completed rehabilitation work certified by U.S. Department of the Interior January 1978.

Rehabilitation Work: Sprinkler system installed; three internal fire stairs constructed; concrete floors laid and two hydraulic elevators installed; new boiler room constructed; masonry surfaces, wood beams and cast-iron columns will remain exposed in public areas and in some tenant spaces for aesthetic reasons. A central decorative stairway, opening onto an atrium, was constructed under a new barrel-vaulted skylight. A deluge sprinkler system assures fire safety in the stairwell area. An adjoining parking garage was constructed.

The U.S. Department of the Interior required retention of the remaining original doors. Despite reservations about architectural compatibility, Interior approved the adjacent parking garage, the skylight and a new entrance to the restaurant on the grounds that all the changes are reversible and do not damage the integrity of the original structure. (Note: Interior would have found the 1974 sandblasting and window replacement unacceptable had they been called upon to certify the rehabilitation work done at that time.)

Rehabilitation Schedule: Building acquired 1972; rehabilitation work begun 1972 and stopped 1974; present project begun 1976; completed September 1978.

Site Area: 107,119 square feet, of which structure occupies approximately 12,000 square feet.

Gross Building Area: Approximately 64,000 square feet.

Costs:

Acquisition: $139,929.

Rehabilitation (direct and indirect): $3,700,000, or approximately $58 per square foot.

City of Providence purchased this property with a grant from the U.S. Department of Housing and Urban Development and then resold it in 1972 at a discount to the present owner.

Financing:

Acquisition and construction financed by equity contributions of owner and by $2,800,000 mortgage loan from a commercial bank for one year at an interest rate of 2.5 percent above prime rate. Permanent $2,800,000 mortgage loan obtained from an insurance company for 15 years at 9¾ percent interest.

Construction lender was unwilling to make a loan on this project until permanent financing was obtained. Permanent lender wanted assurances of continued quality development and rehabilitation work in the surrounding area.

Post-Rehabilitation Space and Rates: Net rentable area: 61,206 square feet. Rental units and rates: One commercial unit of 53,091 square feet rents at

Moshassuck Arcade,   Providence,   Rhode Island

$9.64 a square foot; a restaurant occupies the remaining 8,115 square feet and pays $8.48 a square foot.

Appraised Value:
Before rehabilitation: $139,929.
After rehabilitation: $3,800,000.

Tax Aspects: Owner plans to amortize and deduct all rehabilitation costs, to the maximum extent allowable, over the 60-month (5-year) period provided under section 191 of the Internal Revenue Code. If owner had not already chosen to deduct these costs under section 191, he would have utilized the 10 percent investment tax credit for rehabilitation that was created by the Revenue Act of 1978.

Participants:
Owner—Moshassuck Arcade Company (George Macomber, general partner), 89 Brighton Avenue, Brighton, Mass. 02134.
Contractor—George B. H. Macomber Company, 89 Brighton Avenue, Brighton, Mass. 02134.
Architect—Steffian-Bradley Associates, Inc., 19 Temple Place, Boston, Mass. 02111.

2304-2306 South 11th Street, St. Louis, Mo.
(Soulard Neighborhood Historic District)

Old Use: Two town houses containing a total of four apartment units, all of which had been gutted by fire.

New Use: Rehabilitated for continued use as apartment units.

Description: Two detached brick town houses (1880), each two stories with a full attic and a slate mansard roof with dormers. Located in the Soulard Neighborhood Historic District, which is listed in the National Register of Historic Places.

Tax Reform Act Certifications: Certified by U.S. Department of the Interior October 18, 1977, as contributing to the significance of the Soulard Neighborhood Historic District. Following notification of project completion by owner December 23, 1977, rehabilitation work was certified by U.S. Department of the Interior February 10, 1978.

Rehabilitation Work: Exteriors restored as closely as possible to original appearance. New windows installed with wood frame sashes identical to original ones; dormers rebuilt; slate replaced as needed; some brickwork in rear replaced. Interiors given contemporary treatment because no significant features remained after the fire. No problems encountered in meeting U.S. Department of the Interior's "Standards for Rehabilitation."

Project received required approval May 1977 from the St. Louis Landmarks and Urban Design Commission because of its location in a locally designated historic district. No conditions imposed or changes required to secure this approval.

Rehabilitation Schedule: Building acquired June 1977; work began immediately; completed October 1977.

Site Area: 4,305 square feet of which townhouses occupy 1,447 square feet.

Gross Building Area: 4,000 square feet total for the two town houses.

Costs:
Acquisition: $1,500.
Rehabilitation (direct and indirect): approximately $82,000 or about $20.50 per square foot. Rehabilitation costs include the following:

(1) direct construction costs (materials and contractor's fee)	$74,600
(2) architect's fee	2,000
(3) legal fee	0
(4) insurance	3,000
(5) Tax Reform Act certifications	500
(6) licenses, permits, etc., required (other than Tax Reform Act certifications)	500
(7) financing	0

Property was purchased from a rehabilitation contractor who, as part of transaction, received contract to rehabilitate.

Financing: $75,000 mortgage loan, in form of deed of trust, for 25 years at 9 percent interest rate from City Bank in St. Louis. Personal guarantees of owner-partners required as additional collateral. Equity contributions of owners covered the balance of the costs.

Property tax rate in St. Louis, which has been kept low to help fight urban exodus, has contributed to the feasibility of this project.

Post-Rehabilitation Space and Rates:
Net rentable area: 2,932 square feet. Rental units and rates: Two residential

Soulard Historic District Town Houses, St. Louis

units, each 600 square feet, rent at $180 a month; two residential units, each 800 square feet, rent at $235 a month. All units are rented.

These rents are typical for rehabilitated units in the area. Unrehabilitated units of approximately the same size in a nearby building owned by these same developers each rent at about $60 a month.

Post-Rehabilitation Profitability:

Annual gross income	$10,600
Annual operating costs and debt service	$9,700
Net cash flow before taxes	$900
Return on equity investment	22 percent

Property Taxes:
Before rehabilitation: $180 a year
After rehabilitation: $300 a year

Tax Aspects: Owners expect to amortize and deduct all rehabilitation costs, to the maximum extent allowable over the 60-month (5-year) period provided under section 191 of the Internal Revenue Code. Owners chose this tax provision, rather than the tax incentive in section 167 for substantially rehabilitated historic structures, because of the larger deductions available during the first several years of ownership.

Participants:
Owner—WNW Venture (partnership of an attorney, accountant and banker), c/o W. Stanley Walch, Esq., Thompson & Mitchell, One Mercantile Center, St. Louis, Mo. 63101.
Contractor—Guy McClellan, Mead-McClellan Partnership, 9435 Workbench Drive, Kirkwood, Mo. 63127.
Architect—Charles T. Berger, 608 North Spring, St. Louis, Mo. 63108.

Part Two

Peter H. Brink

Projects in The Strand, Galveston, Tex.

Section 191 of the Internal Revenue Code, created by the Tax Reform Act of 1976 and amended by the Revenue Act of 1978, allows a taxpayer to deduct by amortization over a period of 60 months the cost of certified rehabilitation work on a certified historic structure.

The impact of the 60-month amortization deductions may be seen in the figures for a representative Strand rehabilitation project. The building is a three-story, 13,500-square-foot brick structure with heavy timber beams and joists, handsome cast-iron colums and trim on the facade. Prior to rehabilitation, the interior was a large open space, used for wholesaling and storage. Rehabilitation has adapted the first floor to retail shops and the upper two floors to apartments.

Major Project Costs:

Acquisition	$ 35,000
Construction	198,500
Architect's fee	8,000
Financing	13,000
Administration (including legal)	9,500
Total	$264,000

(13,500 square feet gross; $19.56 per gross square foot cost)

Annual Operating Statement Pro Forma:

A. *Income*

Total gross income	$ 35,500
Less vacancy allowance	2,700
Effective gross income	$ 32,800

B. *Operating expenses*

Utilities	$ 1,200
Taxes	3,000
Insurance	2,200
Miscellaneous	2,200
Total	$ 8,600

C. *Net income* — $ 24,200

D. *Debt service* (K = .098664, the constant for annual computation of debt service)

(Annual interest and principal repayment) — $ 20,200

E. *Cash flow after debt service* — $ 4,000

F. *Mortgage amount* — $204,500

G. *Equity* — $ 59,500

H. *Project cost* — $264,000

I. *Return on investment* ($24,200 ÷ $264,000) — 9.2 percent

Mr. Brink is executive director of the Galveston Historical Foundation and has lectured and written widely about historic preservation. He is a graduate of Harvard Law School and admitted to practice in New York and Washington, D.C. Special thanks are expressed to James L. Foutch and Michael J. Fieglein, attorneys with the firm of Dibrell, Dibrell, Greer, and Brown of Galveston, who reviewed drafts of this article.

Mensing Brothers Bldg.,
The Strand, Galveston, Texas

Assuming the owner is in a 40 percent tax bracket and has sufficient income to utilize the Tax Reform Act's incentives, the tax deduction based on 60-month amortization deductions is:

Rehabilitation cost (project cost less acquisition)	$229,000
Deduction available for each of five years (rehabilitation cost divided by 5, assuming all costs qualify for the amortization deductions)	$ 45,800
Tax saving based on 40 percent bracket	$ 18,320

Although the 9.2 percent return on investment is not high for a real estate project, the owner may be able to realize a tax saving of $18,320 in each of the first five years of the project, although he will have used up any deductions regarding these rehabilitation costs for years subsequent to these five. Thus, a very attractive cash benefit to the owner of $4,000 plus $18,320, or a total of $22,320, results in each of these five years. In addition, the owner is slowly building up his equity in the property by using $20,200 of the proceeds of the project annually to service the debt. Assuming 25-year amortization on the financing, repayment of principal goes very slowly, however: 7.2 percent, or $14,700, is repaid at the end of five years; 18.3 percent, or $37,400, at the end of 10 years. The cash benefit derived from these additional rehabilitation tax deductions allows the owner to reduce his debt by that extra $22,320 a year, which in itself equals a debt reduction of $111,600 over the five years. This figure would dramatically reduce the amount needed for debt service each year, and further illustrates the attractiveness of the tax saving resulting from the 60-month amortization provision. The net effect of these tax provisions will vary depending on when the property is sold and the effect of recapture at that time.

The Importance of the Section 191 Amortization Deductions

In talking with eight owners who have undertaken rehabilitation of buildings within The Strand, a historic district listed in the National Register of Historic Places as a National Historic Landmark, since the effective date of the 60-month amortization deductions, the following responses regarding the importance of the incentive were received:

76

Building 1: The incentive was a factor, although not determinative, in the owner's rehabilitation of the 1859 building for artists' studios and retail shops. Nearly $100,000 has been spent to date; certification of the structure as contributing to The Strand and approval of rehabilitation plans were obtained in April 1978. Final certification of rehabilitation will occur once photographs, and possibly a field-inspection, confirm that the work has been completed as proposed. The owner began taking deductions based on the 60-month amortization allowance in her 1977 tax return.

Building 2: The incentive did not exist when the owner bought the 1871 building and invested $100,000 to rehabilitate the first floor for offices. It was "a very significant factor," however, in his later decision to proceed with the $60,000 conversion of the second floor to apartments. The owner applied for certification of the structure and both phases of rehabilitation in April 1978, and within a few weeks the state historic preservation officer recommended certification to the Secretary of the Interior, who approved the certifications shortly thereafter.

Building 3: The incentive was "decisive" in the decision to commit more than $1,000,000 to the rehabilitation of a 30,000-square-foot building constructed in 1871 for a large restaurant, shops and offices. The owner, an independent oil producer, states that "the project could not have been done without the accelerated amortization; it did not make economic sense without it. The 60-month amortization is a fine vehicle to enable me to carry out a civic duty and to make sense of the project." The owner obtained certification of the structure and of rehabilitation plans in March 1978.

Building 4: The incentive did not exist when the owners purchased the 30,000-square-foot building (1882). At the time, they "were committed to spending $300,000 for basic rehabilitation with some space rented as storage or for tenants to develop. The tax incentive was a significant factor in our deciding to proceed instead with rehabilitation costing $700,000. The tax incentive tipped the scale when we were close on this decision, and it provides a cushion against hidden costs." Certifications of the structure and rehabilitation plans have been approved, and the building is now occupied by restaurants, shops and offices.

Building 5: The incentive was a minor factor in the decision to invest $200,000 in rehabilitating the first floor of an 1871 building into shops and the third floor into apartments. When the owner tried to use the incentive, he did not then have sufficient income to offset the deduction available, so has not applied for certification.

Building 6: The owner views the incentive as crucial in his efforts to proceed with rehabilitation work ranging in estimated cost from $500,000 to $900,000 on a 30,000-square-foot structure (1895). After two years the owner has not, however, been able to develop the project to the point where rehabilitation work can begin.

Building 7: The owner has begun rehabilitation with an estimated cost of $200,000 to convert three floors of a modified 1890 building into apartments and offices. The owner is aware of the 60-month incentive and is considering utilizing it. The incentive was not, however, a significant factor in his decision to proceed with the project.

Building 8: The owner was unaware of the incentive when he proceeded with a $100,000 conversion of the first floor of an 1871 building to retail uses. He is now checking into the provisions and will consider them in deciding whether to rehabilitate the two upper floors of the building.

These responses indicate that the 60-month amortization tax deductions, although rarely the controlling factor in decisions to rehabilitate structures, are generally a positive factor of some significance. Originally a problem with the incentive arose from the inequitable tax recapture provision. Indeed, some Strand owners would probably not have utilized the incentive had they realized the meaning of this recapture provision. Fortunately, the Revenue Act of 1978 corrected this inequity by limiting the recapture of deductions taken by virtue of the 60-month amortization provision to the amount by which these deductions exceed the straight-line depreciation deductions that would otherwise have been taken.

Surprisingly, no owner volunteered an objection to the requirement that rehabilitation work be approved by the U.S. Department of the Interior as a condition to obtaining these tax breaks. At least one owner who was unwilling to apply for a matching restoration grant from the Texas Historical Commission because he did not want a deed restriction on his building plans to pursue certification even though this means his rehabilitation plans must be approved. All in all, the Galveston Historical Foundation (GHF) sees this control of rehabilitation as a positive factor. GHF has been unable to obtain deed restrictions on some Strand buildings charted for development and, in any case, design controls in the GHF's deed restrictions do not extend to interior rehabilitation. (In these cases, only persuasion can be used and it may not work.) Similarly, developers intent on cutting up residential structures for rental apartments are strongly interested in the 60-month incentive and, often for the first time, are considering the architectural character of the structure in their planning in order to qualify for this tax benefit. In these instances the lure of the tax incentive to persuade owners not to abuse buildings with improper rehabilitation is most important. Naturally, if the potency of this lure could be augmented through additional incentives, the certainty of acceptance of such review and prevention of abuse would be increased.

Basic to the effectiveness of this tax incentive is, of course, the ability of the owner or investor to use the substantial deductions for accelerated amortization to offset both income generated by the building and other personal income. At the same time, it is important that this tax break be obtained by use of a legal structure for ownership that still assures the investors that their liability is limited to their actual investment and to specific undertakings by them with regard to loans to finance the project. Thus, Strand owners are invariably utilizing either corporations qualifying under subchapter S of the code or limited partnerships in order to assure that they can "pass through" these deductions for use against other income while still limiting their liability (except for the general partner in the limited partnership). Any change in the tax laws that would disallow this pass through with regard to these legal structures would have a disastrous effect on rehabilitation activities. Such a change would not only greatly diminish the value of the 60-month amortization provision, but would also remove the cushion of setting operating losses that may be incurred on the rehabilitation project against other personal income of the owner or investor. A third legal structure that provides many of the same pass-through and limited liability advantages is the Real Estate Investment Trust. To date, however, no Strand project has utilized this format, although several prospective buyers are investigating it.

Disincentives to Demolition of Historic Structures

The Tax Reform Act of 1976 provides two disincentives regarding demolition of historic structures: Deductions normally available for the cost of demolishing a historic structure and accelerated methods of depreciation tax deductions usually available for a new structure erected on its site are disallowed if the structure is a "certified historic structure" or, if located in a "registered historic district," has not been certified prior to or following demolition as not of historical significance to the district.

Although these disincentives seem a promising aid to preservationists, they were ineffective in the one situation so far in Galveston in which they were applicable. For several years, GHF had been trying to convince a local bank not to demolish an 1860 structure within The Strand National Register district for additional bank parking. As demolition became more likely in the spring of 1977, we tactfully sent a summary of the new tax provisions to the bank officials. These provisions would clearly disallow any deduction for the estimated $15,000 cost of demolishing the structure. Insofar as we can ascertain, however, this disallowance had no effect on the thinking of the bank officials. The second disincentive, in addition, was inapplicable because the bank planned to use the site for a surface parking lot, for which only straight-line depreciation could be used in any case. Indeed, the building finally burned down in February 1978 while subject to a court injunction barring demolition until specified historical investigation and documentation had been completed. Ironically, the bank will in all likelihood be able to deduct demolition costs incurred to complete destruction of the building and site clearance.

This experience suggests that when a local business strongly believes it must demolish a historic structure to obtain parking or other space for expansion, the additional costs incurred by disallowance of these deductions will not be a significant factor in the thinking of the business. On the other hand, these disincentives would seem to hold good promise as one of the factors influencing an owner of a historic structure who is simply trying to determine the most financially advantageous use of or development for his property.

Blum Bldg., The Strand, Galveston, Texas

Stanley L. Blend

STRENGTHS AND WEAKNESSES OF FEDERAL TAX INCENTIVES FOR THE PRESERVATION OF HISTORIC PROPERTIES

Donations of Partial Interests in Property

The Tax Reform Act of 1976 added subsection (iii) to Internal Revenue Code section 170(f)(3)(B). This provides a tax deduction for a contribution of either a lease on, option to purchase, easement with respect to or a remainder interest in real property that is granted exclusively for conservation purposes to a charitable organization. As originally adopted, the subsection required that the lease, option or easement be for a duration of not less than 30 years. However, the Tax Reduction and Simplification Act of 1977 amended this provision to provide that the lease, option or easement must be in perpetuity. The "in perpetuity" limitation of this section substantially limits its potential use. In my negotiations to obtain funds for rehabilitation, potential lenders have expressed hesitance to make loans where the gift of an easement in perpetuity has been made. Apparently, others have met similar resistance. The concern of the lenders is that the gift limits the utility of the structure or property to its present use, which may not be the highest and best use in the future. Furthermore, lenders are most concerned that the statute does not identify definite rights and powers that must be granted to the donee of the easement. The lack of explanatory governmental regulations in this area has substantially limited the utility of this section.

Another problem with subsection (iii) concerns the valuation of the property interest transferred. Generally, "the difference between the fair market value of the total property before the granting of the easement and the fair market value of the property after the grant is the fair market of the easement given up" (Revenue Ruling 73-339, 1973-2 Cumulative Bulletin 68). It is difficult, however, to determine the nature of the property interest given up in the case of a gift of an easement to a charitable organization. Generally, the gift takes the form of a facade easement with the donor retaining the use of the facade. The value of this gift is made up of two parts: (1) the decrease in value of the underlying property resulting from the limitation on its use and (2) the physical value of the actual property interest transferred to the donee. Again, the lack of Internal Revenue Service guidelines concerning the valuation of such easements could create substantial hardship for taxpayers on subsequent audit and review of their returns.

Demolition Disincentives

The Tax Reform Act of 1976, as amended by the Revenue Act of 1978, created certain disincentives to demolishing a historic structure and building

---

Mr. Blend is a shareholder in the San Antonio, Tex., law firm of Oppenheimer, Rosenberg, Kelleher and Wheatley, Inc.

a new structure on the site. These disincentives are contained in Internal Revenue Code sections 167(n) and 280B. Generally, section 167(n) provides that accelerated methods of depreciation will not be allowed to real property constructed, reconstructed, erected or used on a site formerly occupied, on or after June 30, 1976, by a certified historic structure or any structure in a National Register historic district or certified local historic district if the structure was demolished or substantially altered other than by a certified rehabilitation. It is unclear whether this disincentive would apply to new construction on a site in a historic district that was listed in the National Register or certified *following* demolition. In addition, there is a question whether this penalty would apply in a situation in which a new building is constructed on a tract of land that includes within it a smaller parcel on which a certified historic property was located and then demolished.

The effect of this disincentive depends to a great extent on the economic situation of the area of the country where the property is located. It depends heavily on the difference in cost between new construction and rehabilitation. This disincentive likely will not prevent the demolition of a historic structure if the net cost of new construction is still much cheaper. The disincentive's effect also depends substantially on the purpose of the new construction. For example, many landowners who construct a new building for their own account no longer use any form of accelerated depreciation but, instead, use component straight-line depreciation as the form of recovering their capital in the new construction. Denial of accelerated depreciation, therefore, would not affect their demolition plans for a historic building. Component straight-line depreciation is a method by which each component part of the structure (e.g., roof, electrical and mechnical) is separately depreciated over its individual useful life. This form of depreciation differs from composite depreciation, in which the cost of the entire structure is recovered over the composite life of the structure. Component straight-line depreciation avoids the applicability of the recapture rules of code section 1250 on the gain from the sale of a structure if the structure has been held in excess of one year. Recapture under section 1250 would usually apply to depreciation taken on an accelerated basis. Accordingly, this particular disincentive generally would have its greatest impact on an investor wanting to use accelerated depreciation as a tax shelter, because rapid depreciation creates noncash tax "losses" that a taxpayer can offset against his or her other income.

The other disincentive is code section 280B, which provides that an owner or lessee of a certified historic structure, or of a structure located in a registered historic district, will not be allowed a deduction for the amount expended for its demolition, or for any loss resulting from the demolition. These costs must be added to the cost of the land and may not be added to the cost of the replacement structure, which prevents the owner from getting certain tax deductions during the period of ownership. This disincentive would not apply to a structure located in a registered historic district if the Secretary of the Interior certified to the Internal Revenue Service that the structure was not of historical significance to the district. The certification of the Secretary of the Interior may occur after the beginning of the demolition, but if so the taxpayer must certify that prior to demolition he or she was not aware of the requirement to obtain a certification of nonsignificance from the Secretary of the Interior. Generally, the effect of this disincentive depends on the nature of the property and the cost of demolition. if the demolition cost is low, and the new structure will be very expensive, this provision will have little impact upon a taxpayer's decision.

If this disincentive is to be retained the law must be clarified. As presently drafted, a taxpayer can avoid the negative effect of this particular section only by obtaining the clearance of the Secretary of the Interior before the demolition and, if after demolition, by also certifying that he was unaware of the provision. Generally, the tax law imposes knowledge of all tax provisions on taxpayers. It is practically impossible for any taxpayer to certify lack of knowledge of this particular law prior to undertaking any demolition. The law should be changed to allow taxpayers more freely to receive retroactive approval of the demolition. For example, assume a taxpayer owns a historic property that is substantially damaged by fire and the city requires that it be demolished for safety reasons. In this instance, the taxpayer could not deduct the demolition cost since he or she would be required to demolish the structure before being able to get permission from the Secretary of the Interior, and the taxpayer may be ineligible for retroactive approval if he or she was aware of this disincentive. This is unfair and should be changed.

Rehabilitation Incentives

The Tax Reform Act of 1976, as amended by the Revenue Act of 1978, adopted special incentives for recovering the rehabilitation costs of certified historic properties through special depreciation and amortization tax deductions enacted as code sections 167(o) and 191. Generally, section 167(o) applies to capital expenditures incurred in the certified rehabilitation of a certified historic property if the expenditures incurred during the 24-month period ending on the last day of any taxable year exceed the greater of (1) the taxpayer's adjusted basis in the structure on the first day of the 24-month period or (2) $5,000. If these tests are satisfied, the property is considered "substantially rehabilitated," which will allow the taxpayer to treat the property as though it were new and as though the taxpayer were the first user of it. Thus, the taxpayer would be entitled to 150 percent declining balance accelerated depreciation on commercial property and 200 percent declining balance accelerated depreciation on residential rental property. As a result of the Revenue Act of 1978's creation of a limited investment credit for rehabilitation and the right to combine this credit with section 167(o) accelerated depreciation, this incentive should have more application than the amortization deduction provision set forth in section 191.

Code section 191 allows a taxpayer to deduct, by amortizing over a 60-month period, any capital expenditure incurred in a certified rehabilitation of a certified historic structure. Amortization deductions for this purpose shall be partly "recaptured" under section 1250 and taxed at ordinary income rates in the same manner as excess accelerated depreciation. The advantage of these deductions is that they allow a taxpayer to recover rapidly his capital investment in the project. Furthermore, in some instances they may make a project economical that would otherwise be considered uneconomical because for tax purposes the substantial noncash "losses" created by rapid amortization can offset other income. However, the use of this particular incentive has been adversely affected by the introduction in 1978 of the 10 percent investment tax credit for rehabilitation expenditures and the fact that the credit will not be available to a taxpayer electing rapid amortization under section 191.

In discussions with landowners and their representatives around the country, it appears that the use of sections 167(o) and 191 is not as extensive as it would otherwise be as a result of the sometimes cumbersome certification process. Some landowners have complained that it has taken more than six months to have a property certified. Such delays only hurt the utility of these sections.

There are several matters that must be defined in order to further encourage taxpayers to use these tax incentives for historic preservation. While it is clear that a taxpayer may not use both section 167(o) and section 191 with regard to the same structure, it is unclear whether this rule would apply with regard to one property containing different structures and whether a taxpayer could elect to use section 167(o) on one structure and section 191 on another. The most serious question involves what constitutes a "rehabilitation" for tax purposes. In August 1978, the Internal Revenue Service issued proposed regulations, but they do not adequately define a rehabilitation and appear to adopt a restrictive rather than a liberal approach in making a definition. Inadequate definition creates a hardship for taxpayers involved in large projects because it necessitates obtaining a private ruling (if one can be obtained) prior to packaging the rehabilitation of a historic property under these tax incentive provisions. This problem could be corrected by better defining the jurisdiction of the Secretary of the Interior and that of the Internal Revenue Service. The author suggests that the Secretary should determine what constitutes a qualified rehabilitation and that such determination should be binding on the Internal Revenue Service.

Investment Tax Credit

The Revenue Act of 1978 has had a significant impact on the tax incentives adopted in the Tax Reform Act of 1976 by adding subsection (E) to code section 48(a)(1), which extends the investment tax credit provisions to certain qualified rehabilitated buildings. In several important respects the tax credit may be more effective in preserving and rehabilitating old buildings and historic ones in particular than the Tax Reform Act's incentives. First, it is important to note that this new section applies to any income-producing building that has been in use for at least 20 years, except—generally—ones used for residential purposes. No determination of historical significance is necessary to qualify a building for the tax credit. Second, this section also specifically provides that for its purposes rehabilitation shall include reconstruction. It can be argued, therefore, that rehabilitation for purposes of sections 167(o) and 191's preservation incentives does not include reconstruction because of its omission from these sections. Third, the investment tax credit applies in the case of the rehabilitation of a certified historic structure only if the rehabilitation has been certified by the Secretary of the Interior. This will act as a disincentive for the public to have properties listed in the National Register or certified as being of historical significance because without either the owner would have complete discretion over the rehabilitation of the property and would still be entitled to the investment tax credit. Fourth, it is important to note that the investment tax credit is a true incentive because it is a dollar for dollar offset against an individual's tax bill and does not in any way lessen the taxpayer's capital investment in the property for depreciation purposes as the preservation tax incentives do. Fifth, the investment tax credit as enacted is not available with regard to a property for which an election is made to take amortization deductions for the rehabilitation expenditures under section 191. Thus, taxpayers will be encouraged to use accelerated depreciation under the provisions of section 167(o) in conjunction with the tax credit. Sixth, this new tax credit will also discourage the revitalization of downtown residential property for continued residential use because it is not available for this purpose. Accordingly, landowners will be encouraged to convert downtown residential property to commercial use in order to obtain the substantial benefits of this tax credit.

In order to advise a client properly on the use of these various preservation and rehabilitation tax incentives, it is necessary to prepare an economic and tax analysis of the net return to the taxpayer in each of the following circumstances in which these tax incentives may be used for a property:

1. All rehabilitation expenditures are amortized pursuant to section 191 and all other property is depreciated on a straight-line basis;

2. All rehabilitation expenditures are amortized under section 191, all expenditures that would qualify are depreciated on an accelerated basis and any other expenditures are depreciated on a straight-line basis;

3. All rehabilitation expenditures are depreciated on an accelerated basis pursuant to section 167(o) and all qualified expenditures are taken as a tax credit under the investment tax credit;

4. All rehabilitation expenditures are depreciated on a straight-line basis, the section 167(o) and 191 incentives are not used and instead the investment tax credit alone is taken.

A cash-flow analysis for a 10-year period should be prepared in each of these cases. Further, the adviser should assume that the property is sold at the end of the tenth year for the original acquisition price plus rehabilitation costs. Then the adviser should prepare an investment analysis projecting the net return on the invested dollar for the client. The adviser will in most cases recommend that the client depreciate the rehabilitation under section 167(o) using an accelerated method of depreciation and take the investment tax credit if the property will constitute commercial, nonresidential property following the rehabilitation.

It should be noted that if the adviser can attach the gift of a facade easement to using accelerated depreciation under section 167(o) or amortization under section 191, it may be possible to structure a proposed rehabilitation project so that by using these tax incentives alone the investor may obtain a tax loss of approximately three dollars for each dollar of invested capital. For example, assume in one project the acquisition cost for a building is $250,000, the cost of facade rehabilitation is $150,000 and the remaining rehabilitation costs $400,000. The transaction could be structured so that the value of the gift of the facade and the restoration expenditures to the facade are deducted immediately as a charitable contribution, and the investor would be entitled to deduct $80,000 for each of five years as the amortizable rehabilitation cost. The total cost of the project would be $800,000, of which the investor's initial equity contribution hypothetically would be approximately $100,000. In this circumstance the investor would be entitled in the first year to a deduction of approximately $300,000 from these tax incentives alone, representing the $150,000 facade rehabilitation, approximately $70,000 for an assumed value for the gift of the facade and the $80,000 deducted pursuant to section 191.

One other example that might be helpful is that of a rental project requiring an equity investment of approximately $100,000. The projected net income for the project before tax and depreciation is approximately $7,600. Assuming a 50 percent tax bracket and traditional methods of depreciation, the net return on equity would be approximately 11 percent, not a satisfactory return for an investor in view of the substantial risk inherent in rehabilitating older properties. By taking full advantage of section 191, however, the first year return on equity may be increased to 25 percent, which makes the project much more palatable to the investor.

Conclusion

As can be seen, there are numerous incentives and disincentives that have been adopted by recent legislation in order to encourage the preservation of our historic properties. Congress has recognized that part of the heritage of our country is the architecture of its buildings and that this heritage should be sustained. In most of the instances I have discussed, however, Congress has imposed a specific deadline on when the incentive or the disincentive will lapse, the purpose of which is to give Congress an opportunity to study their effectiveness. Thus, I encourage people to pursue actively the use of these incentives and disincentives so that the Secretary of the Interior will be able to compile favorable statistics to present to Congress in order to obtain an extension of their applicable periods.

William Matuszeski

LESSONS IN PREPARING
FEDERAL TAX PROPOSALS

In 1970, the Council on Environmental Quality sought to establish a broad program on the environment for President Nixon. Discussions were held with persons interested in historic preservation and with the U.S. Department of the Treasury on a series of provisions to redress those features of the tax laws that hindered preservation and other environmental goals. One of the provisions was H.R. 5584, the proposed Environmental Protection Tax Act, most of whose tax incentives for the preservation and rehabilitation of historic structures were incorporated into section 2124 of the 1976 Tax Reform Act.

The experiences during that period of the Council on Environmental Quality, of which I was then a staff member, may give preservationists some insight into the way government tax officials think and may also provide a better understanding of the way those who run tax programs react to proposals. For example, with more knowledge of what kinds of information tax officials respond to most favorably, preservationists can better understand the arguments they will face in working on federal, state or local taxes.

The council identified certain critical issues that should be investigated to determine how the tax laws might more positively affect them. The issues identified were wetlands, designated historic structures and donations of open space. The council also identified the problem of old buildings that are suitable for rehabilitation and adaptive use, many of which are not listed in the National Register. These buildings are still worthy assets of cities and should be considered for preservation.

After preliminary discussion with the Treasury Department, the council decided to examine the effect on these critical areas of four basic tax tools: depreciation, recapture, business expense deductions and charitable donations.

Depreciation

Concerning depreciation tax deductions, it is important to realize that Treasury Department officials and tax officials in general consider the status quo as tax equity, and prefer straight-line depreciation over accelerated methods. Straight-line is the best depreciation method to them because it yields the smallest depreciation deductions for the taxpayer and so retains the most tax revenue in a current year. As a general rule, tax officials would much rather have money this year than the prospect of money three or four years later. Any tax proposal that requires or favors straight-line depreciation, therefore, is usually one that tax officials find attractive.

From the viewpoint of the taxpayer, the priorities naturally are somewhat different. The taxpayer likes accelerated depreciation and special write-off provisions—whether for three years, five years, eight years or however long the law allows.

Mr. Matuszeski is associate director for state programs, Office of Coastal Zone Management, U.S. Department of Commerce, Washington, D.C.

The then current law permitted accelerated depreciation deductions as follows: For new depreciable residential property (i.e., residential property held in whole or in part for rental purposes), in the first year the taxpayer could deduct double the normal straight-line depreciation and then each year thereafter a gradually smaller part of the undepreciated basis (cost) of the property. Because there is a doubling of the straight-line depreciation deduction in the first year, the method is called 200 percent "declining balance" depreciation. When people refer to 200, 150 or 125 percent depreciation, the declining balance method is what they are talking about. They are discussing how one measures that first year of accelerated depreciation. At that time 150 percent depreciation was allowed for new commercial structures other than rental housing, 125 percent for existing rental housing and 100 percent (or straight-line) for existing commercial structures. These provisions were not equitable, because they provided an incentive for new construction. More important, perhaps, is that Treasury officials are generally disposed to reducing all available depreciation deductions to straight-line for the reasons indicated earlier regarding the flow of tax dollars and because they believe accelerated depreciation serves essentially social, rather than revenue, purposes.

Recapture of Tax Deductions

The second tool the council focused on was the recapture upon resale of a structure of depreciation deductions previously taken. Owners typically have used accelerated depreciation and thereby reduced the basis or cost of their building for tax purposes, and then have sold it for more than this remaining basis. The question then arises of how the amount of money representing the difference between the depreciated value of the building and the sales price should be taxed. This amount has traditionally been treated for tax purposes as a capital gain, which is taxed at a lower rate than is ordinary income.

The Treasury Department dislikes the fact that in these cases owners benefit from the extra bonus of accelerated depreciation, sell the building for more than it is allegedly worth (the depreciated basis) and qualify for a capital gain rate of taxation on that bonus. The council found that the Treasury Department was ready to support a provision that would tax that entire amount of accelerated depreciation taken as ordinary income. This provision, in turn, serves as a disincentive to those who would hold a building long enough to take best advantage of accelerated depreciation and then sell it for demolition.

Business Expenses

The third tax tool the council focused on was in the area of business expense deductions. In particular, the council looked at the deduction available for demolition costs. Under applicable law, a property owner could utilize not only accelerated depreciation for a new building, but also could deduct as a business expense the cost of tearing down the structure that stood on its site. The owner might also deduct interest on loans and taxes during the construction period of the new building. And finally, the owner might deduct the undepreciated balance of the cost of the old building.

Of these three deductions, Treasury tax officials offered most support for removing the deduction for interest and taxes during construction. A building at that time is not generating revenue, so the owner is receiving the benefit of a current deduction for an economic activity producing no return. In contrast, the tax officials gave less support for disallowing the demolition and undepreciated basis deductions, because these tend to impinge more on routine business activities.

Charitable Donations

The fourth tool focused on by the council was the charitable donation of real property for historic and natural preservation purposes. Because of a series of confusing last-minute changes in the 1969 amendments to the Internal Revenue Code, charitable donations of partial property interests that are eligible for tax deductions were limited to life estates on farmhouses and private dwellings and to perpetual open space easements in gross. Because these terms can mean one thing in Maine and quite another in Alabama, there was a need to make the deductions apply more clearly and openly to remainder interests and donated easements related to environmental efforts and historic preservation. Treasury was generally reluctant to go along with these proposals for two reasons: They increased allowable deductions and they required the exercise of considerable judgment by the taxpayer in order to determine eligibility.

Tax Provisions

Tax relief proposals resulting from the council's efforts were submitted to Congress by the Nixon administration in 1971 and addressed a number of different conservation issues. Included were provisions affecting wetlands, such as depreciation tax deductions for structures built in wetlands, deductions for expenses incurred in draining and dredging wetlands and for interest and taxes during construction in those areas. Other proposals, in turn, called for preventing demolition expenses and the undepreciated costs of demolished historic structures from being deductible on an annual basis. For a developer wanting to take as many expenses as possible during the current year, these provisions would serve as disincentives to demolition. The proposals also called for limiting depreciation on new buildings erected on the sites of demolished historic structures to the straight-line method and for offering a five-year rapid tax write-off of rehabilitation expenses on historic structures.

Another set of proposals benefited all buildings undergoing substantial rehabilitation, regardless of historical significance. In cases where rehabilitation expenses exceeded the undepreciated cost of the building, the owner would be able to treat the rehabilitated structure as a new building for tax purposes, adding these expenses to the undepreciated cost and using accelerated depreciation for the entire amount. The council believed that this provision eliminated a crucial inequity in the law between new construction and rehabilitation.

The provisions also clarified the availability of deductions for the charitable donation of partial interests in land. The proposals specifically extended these deductions to include the charitable donations of leases, options to purchase and, most importantly, easements for both historic and natural preservation purposes.

Lessons

The success of the council's efforts and the soundness of its proposals for historic preservation are now evident from the enactment by Congress of most of the proposals in section 2124 of the Tax Reform Act of 1976. Of further interest were the lessons learned from the experiences of the Council on Environmental Quality in preparing these provisions. Four important lessons bear discussion:

1. *Choose one set of issues.* One of the problems with the proposed, but never enacted, Environmental Protection Tax Act of 1974 was that it offered too much—wetland provisions, open space provisions, a number of historic preservation provisions advocated by the council and general rehabilitation provisions. As a result, it was difficult to generate the necessary intensity of support. Environmental groups were not excited about the rehabilitation proposals, and historic preservation groups were not highly interested in wetlands preservation. A strong focus on the issues that the proposed legislation was trying to affect was lacking. In retrospect, the approach of the proposed Historic Structures Tax Act (now section 2124 of the Tax Reform Act of 1976) in addressing itself solely to tax relief for historic preservation was better.

2. *Keep it simple.* Make the proposed legislation understandable. Disallowing a tax deduction is easily understood if it provides, for example, that you cannot deduct the cost of tearing down a building. On the other hand, a set of detailed tax recapture provisions outlining the interplay of capital gains and ordinary income tax rates upon sale confuses people. The average taxpayer or even the average supporter of the legislation cannot be expected to understand the provisions.

3. *Focus on inequities in the current law.* Do not seek tax shelters or special privileges for preservation interests. Those whose work involves the preparation and enactment of tax laws will always think of preservationists as a special-interest group. To tax officials, people interested in historic preservation are grouped with those who are interested in a tax break for storing barber chairs and those who want a deduction for renting umbrellas. What preservationists must do, and were able to accomplish in the enactment of preservation incentives in the 1976 Tax Reform Act, is to make tax administrators understand that they are not proposing special privileges but instead want to remove from the law existing inequities and special privileges discouraging preservation. This approach opens many doors. Treating rehabilitation as equivalent to new construction for tax purposes, as the Tax Reform Act now provides, is a matter that can be presented as removing an inequity in the law. But asking for preferential treatment is a request for a privilege.

4. *Do not be intimidated.* Preservationists can easily become discouraged during the lengthy negotiations necessary with Treasury Department officials and tax administrators. For example, Treasury staff assume that all of the effects of a provision will create a revenue loss. They estimate the degree of revenue loss by deciding who will use the provision and how much it will be used. They seldom consider that the loss resulting from existing law offsets part of this proposed loss.

In the case of the proposals incorporated into the 1976 Tax Reform Act, Treasury asked how many people will benefit from the new tax deductions for rehabilitation expenditures. The more important question was not asked: How many of the people who use these rehabilitation tax deductions would otherwise have been tearing down buildings and getting deductions for the building's undepreciated cost plus all of the other business expenses associated with demolition and new construction? As a result of this narrow view of the impact of a tax provision on decision making, the Treasury Department is often able to find that the status quo is the least expensive alternative from a revenue perspective.

The Treasury Department is also an experienced user of the "revolving door trick." If Treasury tax analysts estimate that a provision will have a heavy impact and cause an undesirably large loss of revenue, they recommend its rejection. If preservationists redraft the proposal in response to this concern and soften its effect, the tax analysts then respond that the proposals do not create any revenue impact, therefore they must be ineffective, and so they block any change in the law. The preservationists are back on the streets shaking their heads. Quite often in this process, it is necessary to reassure oneself of the basic soundness of one's position in order to continue fighting for the needed changes.

It was this attitude of informed persistence that worked so well in the enactment of section 2124 of the Tax Reform Act. These lessons from our work in the early days at the Council on Environmental Quality should be helpful in obtaining from Congress an extension and perhaps improvement of the federal preservation tax incentives beyond their scheduled expiration in 1981, and in efforts to enact state and local tax relief for historic preservation.

2. State and Local Tax Law

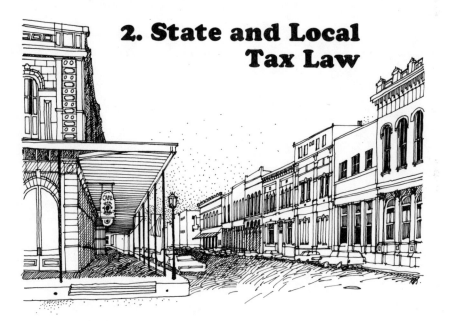

Robert E. Stipe

STATE AND LOCAL TAX INCENTIVES
FOR HISTORIC PRESERVATION

When Chief Justice Marshall stated the now familiar principle that "the power to tax is the power to destroy," the applicability of taxation to historic preservation was doubtless far from anything he then had in mind. Yet, he was perhaps a better prophet than he intended. In preservation terms, the question is whether the potentially destructive power of taxation of which Justice Marshall spoke can be reversed to become a positive power for the protection of historic buildings.

This discussion will not provide a detailed catalogue of statutes and practices in every state and territory, but instead will attempt to place the broad subject of state and local tax incentives in perspective.[1] It will describe some of the major successes and problems to date and speculate in a general way about some of the major problems that may be encountered as state and local governments continue to experiment with tax incentives as a financial incentive for historic preservation.

To outline the main points, one must oversimplify a bit and say that there are essentially two methods by which state and local governments provide aid for preservation through the use of their taxing and spending powers. The first is what might be termed the direct approach, dealing with the means by which state governments raise and spend dollars for preservation activities—whether in the form of direct expenditures for public projects or in the form of loans, grants or other subsidies to public, quasi-public or private agencies or individuals. Also included in any consideration of the direct approach would be the means by which local units of government, deriving their authority from the state, tax and spend specifically for these purposes.

The second method might be termed the indirect approach and would include all of the varied means by which the states, directly and through their local units of government, aid preservation efforts indirectly through authorized manipulations of the state and local taxing systems. These means include a variety of schemes for tax abatement or deferral through special classification of historic properties for tax purposes, the outright exemption or forgiveness of taxes, tax credits for restoration and maintenance expenditures by the property owner subject to limitations, freezing assessed valuations on historic properties before rehabilitation and so on. Obviously, the two basic approaches are not mutually exclusive.

At the state level, the principal revenue sources of interest are the income

Mr. Stipe is professor of design, School of Design, North Carolina State University, Raleigh, and visiting professor, Department of City and Regional Planning, UNC-Chapel Hill. He is currently co-chairman of the North Carolina Attorney General's Select Committee on Preservation Law Revisions and was for 17 years Professor of Public Law and Government at UNC's Institute of Government, Chapel Hill.

and inheritance taxes. At the local level, the major revenue source of interest, based on experience so far, is the property tax. While in every case the use of either the direct or the indirect approach may pose a variety of technical legal questions, the principal issue to bear in mind in discussing state and local tax incentives is that these incentives address themselves more to issues of policy, administration and politics than to questions of law.

Thus, it should help place the matter in perspective to summarize briefly the experiences of a sampling of those few states that are frequently or widely cited as active in this area, note some of the problems that have already arisen and attempt to draw some guidelines for the future. Throughout, however, it is important to keep three considerations in mind. First, most of the actual experience is of recent origin and any overall appraisal may be premature. Second, there is more than a little risk in drawing hard conclusions from a limited sampling of states. Third, it is important to note that in the realm of tax incentives, as in most other areas of government activity, the political, economic and administrative realities of the situation may have a more direct effect on the end result then the wording of the law itself.

State Revenue and Expenditure Considerations

It is common knowledge that since the passage of the National Historic Preservation Act of 1966, states have increasingly appropriated money from their general funds and occasionally other revenues for preservation purposes, supplementing federal funds distributed through the Heritage Conservation and Recreation Service (HCRS) under the 1966 act. Nevertheless, the major point to be made is that there is no state in which appropriations for historic preservation, from whatever source derived, even begin to approach one-half of one percent of the total state budget. These appropriations fund such typical preservation activities as research, survey and planning; preservation, restoration and maintenance of state-owned or state-subsidized historic sites; technical assistance and publications; grants or loans to local preservation groups; adequate staff for the state historic preservation offices created pursuant to the 1966 act; and all the other basic components of an effective state historic preservation program.

Qualitative Aspects of State Spending

92

Rather than dwell on the quantitative side of state preservation funding, it may be of more immediate interest to comment briefly on the qualitative aspects of state expenditures. In this connection, two speculations immediately come to mind.

First, one might reasonably expect some shift in the state preservation expenditure pattern over the next decade. For example, it is likely that there will be a shift away from direct appropriations supporting state-owned and maintained historic sites and a corresponding move toward greater support for private preservation endeavors. This shift will occur as a natural result of several factors, all tending to work in the same direction: (1) the effect of inflation, particularly with respect to restoration projects and their maintenance, which are both labor intensive and recurring; (2) a general recognition by the public, preservationists and politicians that public funds can support only a limited number of house museums and museum villages and an increasingly widespread feeling that already there may be too many of these; (3) pressures from the Heritage Conservation and Recreation Service to change the image of the national preservation program from that of a public works program with a heavy emphasis on full-scale period restoration to one emphasizing a more broad-based approach, as was originally intended by the framers of the 1966 act; and (4) a tendency to make greater use of fees and charges wherever possible to relieve the strain on other revenue sources. It is also quite possible that the recent emphasis on rehabilitation, architectural conversion, adaptive use and conservation generally (as opposed to restoration) will be sufficiently successful to diminish substantially the political will to support additional state-owned historic sites and programs.

Second, one may anticipate pressures on state legislatures, even in those states such as North Carolina that currently provide direct matching subsidies to local preservation projects, to contribute either alternatively or additionally (more likely the latter) to general state or local revolving funds, such as those that are a part of the growing number of state or local historic preservation trusts. The March 21, 1978, cooperative agreement under which the North Carolina state historic preservation office annually allocates part of its apportionment from HCRS to the statewide Historic Preservation Fund of North Carolina, Inc., represents the start of this statewide trend. State trusts or revolving funds also operate in New York, Maryland and Massachusetts, to cite a few examples, and one may confidently expect that they will multiply rapidly. Economically, such funds make sense, because they provide more possibilities for leveraging and fast action and are relatively free of political constraints. It is significant that the National Preservation Revolving Fund, administered by the National Trust for Historic Preservation, is already active in stimulating public and private revolving fund efforts through its loan program.

The shift in state funding from the public toward the private sector will not happen overnight. In fact, it will be rather slow in coming, largely as a result of political considerations. For several reasons, the shift will be especially slow in those states that currently provide matching grants for local projects. One reason is that legislators have an inherent distaste for giving up control over specific appropriations for individual projects and for, in effect, writing "blank checks" to nongovernmental groups, no matter how capable or well organized they are and no matter how worthy the cause. A second reason, representing a special problem in states with matching grant preservation programs, is that, even with logrolling or pork barrel elements under control, individual legislators like to "take home" a small appropriation for local preservation projects as demonstrable proof that they really are in favor of culture and that they do indeed have clout in the state capital. Locally, such grants tend to build support for the reelection of the individual legislator but, as some have remarked, the grants are insignificant.

A major problem in gaining state support for revolving fund appropriations (which sound like big-ticket items, although they may represent the wiser and more cost-effective public investment in the long run) is that money is in short supply in the states. The old axiom that "the federal government has the money, the states have the power and local governments have the problems" hardly bears repeating, but it is indicative of the situation in which the states (and the cities) find themselves.

93

State Sources of Revenue

The traditional source of state preservation appropriations has been the general fund, although there are notable exceptions. For example, if a prize were to be given for sheer ingenuity in finding new ways to support preservation projects, it should perhaps go to New Hampshire for a 1973 law that authorizes the state liquor commission to contract for the manufacture and purchase of commemorative liquor bottles of historical significance, adding the cost thereof to the price of the product within and segregating the profits in a special fund to be used for the exclusive support of a special historical fund.[2] Texas uses a portion of its cigarette tax for parks and preservation.[3] These approaches to financing preservation are interesting, but at the same time they are somewhat worrisome. Although from a purely pragmatic standpoint one preservation dollar spends as well as another regardless of the source, such approaches raise disturbing questions. Why, to take the two examples cited, should drinkers in New Hampshire and smokers in Texas bear a relatively heavier burden of taxation for financing preservation than the consumers of yogurt and milk? Philosophically, at least, the 1976 amendments to the Land and Water Conservation Fund Act, which created the National Historic Preservation Fund from the proceeds of off-shore oil leases, in effect shoring up one resource while depleting another, make more sense in terms of a rational preservation ethic. Nevertheless, it would appear that the question of "who should pay?" is one that current preservation philosophy has yet to address in a systematic, logical way.

Legal Implications

As for the legal implications of what may eventually be a major shift in the use of state funds for essentially private purposes, one should be mindful, if such a shift takes place, of the typical state constitutional admonitions that public funds from whatever source may be spent only for "public" purposes and the corresponding prohibitions in those same state constitutions against the granting of private emoluments or benefits except in consideration of public service. As was the case with urban redevelopment and renewal, there may be a problem of drawing lines. For example, the expenditure of public funds for the preservation of yet another of the many places visited or slept in by George Washington (by, for example, a private individual seeking to use HCRS or HUD Community Development Block Grant funds) would be, presumably, for a public educational purpose. Not to make light of the matter, a bed in which President Washington slept is demonstrably more important than one slept in by the author. But somewhere in between these two deliberately overdrawn extremes, there is a line that defines what is and what is not a "public purpose" in the constitutional sense. One may reasonably expect that the courts will have an interest in such matters as time goes on. There may be other legal problems that will be encountered with respect to both the direct and indirect approaches mentioned earlier, but this one example will suffice to illustrate the point.

It would appear, then, that the legal problems related to state tax and expenditure efforts, while not insignificant, are presently insubstantial. The real challenge for preservationists is to convince increasingly hard-pressed state governments that preservation is truly worthy of added financial support, to devise specific tax incentives to deal with specific preservation problems, and eventually to develop an economically and politically plausible rationale or ethical base for this additional support.

State and Local Tax Incentives Encouraging Preservation

Tax incentives are the indirect approach of providing preservation support. It is recognized that no preservation program can be totally dependent on public funding. The somewhat overworked name of today's game is economic viability—assuring that the bottom line of a preservation project balances out, providing a satisfactory return on the owner's or developer's investment. Experience shows that subsidies, whether direct or indirect, are often a key aspect of this balance, and it has recently become politically acceptable in a few states to provide a portion of this subsidy indirectly through various tax exemptions, reductions, deferrals and so on.

Although not claiming to have covered every jurisdiction, the author has found that only one state, Maryland, gives preservation projects a special state tax credit or deduction from state income or inheritance taxes.[4] Those other states that tax income tend to follow the general pattern of federal law with respect to exemptions and deductions. This would suggest that changes in state income tax practices to provide strong preservation incentives will follow the preservation tax incentives incorporated in the Internal Revenue Code by the Tax Reform Act of 1976 and the Revenue Act of 1978. But even with those new federal income tax incentives, state income tax laws have largely failed to fall into line.

The combinations and permutations of preservation tax incentives now authorized at state and local levels vary from state to state, so it may be helpful to summarize briefly some of the approaches that have been suggested, authorized or actually implemented in a few selected jurisdictions.

Deduction or Credit for Project Costs

One obvious approach would be to allow a deduction or credit (as in Maryland) for restoration or preservation project costs from state or municipal income taxes, with provisions for a carry-forward to certain expenses for a stated number of years to take account of major capital expenditures during the early years of a project. Such an approach was attempted in North Carolina in 1971. A draft bill authorized an annual deduction against adjusted gross income of up to 20 percent of restoration or preservation expenses incurred during that year, with a five-year carry-forward on properties listed in the National Register or designated by a local landmarks commission. The bill required that the expense provide a substantial educational benefit to the public, that the completed project measure up to accepted professional standards and that the whole arrangement be secured by recorded covenants. Before attempting to introduce the bill in the state general assembly, its sponsors did some checking and were discreetly informed that the state revenue department would be extremely reluctant to support any bill that would have the effect of "eroding the state tax base." Even a number of important preservationists would not support the measure, and the proposal has not been reintroduced since.

A variation on this proposal found support in the 1969 enactment of a New Mexico statute that allows the cost of restoring historic buildings listed in the state register and available for educational purposes (meaning, in practice, open to the public one day each month for eight, not necessarily consecutive, hours) as a credit against local real estate taxes.[5] After almost 10 years, only 12 properties have applied to take advantage of the law—principally, it is thought, because the property tax rate is low and historically accurate restorations are required.[6]

Maryland law provides that counties may elect to allow as a credit against local real estate taxes up to 10 percent of an owner's cost of maintaining or restoring a historic building in a historic district or up to 5 percent of the cost of constructing a new building in a historic district if the building is compatible with the character of the district.[7] This law has not been used for several reasons: People do not know about it, local officials believe that there are likely to be problems of administration and revenue loss, and some local officials believe that the wording of the statute is too vague to be workable.

Tax Relief from Increased Assessment

A second basic approach is one that protects the owner of historic property from higher property taxes that are the result of an increase in the assessment of the property after rehabilitation. Such an approach was attempted in Washington, D.C., based on a 1974 act of Congress that instructed the city council to adopt regulations providing tax relief for the rehabilitation of designated historic properties by ignoring the increased value of improvements for up to five years. The city never implemented this provision, largely because of the fear of further erosion of its already small property tax base. The law was repealed in 1978.[8]

Oregon has had much success with its 1975 law that provides a 15-year freeze in assessment at current true cash value for properties that are rehabilitated or preserved subject to conditions imposed by the state historic preservation officer (SHPO).[9] This law helps historic properties avoid the upward revaluation and increased taxes that would result from improvements. To qualify for the freeze, the property must be individually listed in the National Register or located within a National Register district and shown to be significant to the district, and it must be made available for public visitation at least one day a year. Generally, the owner must maintain the property and must agree to give the SHPO an opportunity to review any building permit applications that would change or diminish the character of the property. Because property taxes are fairly high in Oregon, the incentive that results is a strong one. It is also important to note that the decisions regarding which buildings qualify as significant are made with the advice of the SHPO and the local landmarks commission. There is a complicated formula for the recapture of back taxes and a very substantial penalty if the certification of the property for reduced valuation is removed. The Oregon act went into effect January 1, 1976, and was reenacted in mid-1979 to avoid its scheduled expiration at the end of the year. To date, about 130 property owners have applied for this tax relief.[10] The freeze approach in Oregon carries no relief provisions for owners of buildings that have already been restored and whose taxes are already based on the higher valuation resulting from earlier improvement or restoration.

Tax Abatement for Historic Properties

A variation on this approach is tax abatement resulting from assessments based on current use, such as is found in California. A 1977 law authorizes the owners of qualifying historic properties to enter into 20-year renewable contracts with a city or county, in which the owner agrees to maintain the property in good condition and to make it "visually accessible" to the public, and which may restrict the use of the property. In exchange for the agreement, the local government directs the assessor to value the property for tax purposes on its existing use, rather than its speculative "highest and best use" value.[11] The practical value of this law is questionable, because local tax assessors reacted to a similar 1970 law that was invalidated with a marked resistance to taking advantage of the authorization and a decided skittishness in considering any buildings other than residences for the program.

Tax relief in the District of Columbia is also tied to a 20-year covenant between the owner and the city, in which the owner agrees not to change the exterior (and in some cases the interior) without permission, to maintain the site in good condition, to permit inspections as necessary and so on. The quid pro quo for the covenant is reduced valuation of the site in cases where its value as a historic site is less than the full market value for purposes of computing the local property tax assessment.[12] That only two properties have applied for and received this tax relief may be attributable to several factors, among them the fact that a perhaps uniquely high percentage of the approximately 350 designated landmarks in the capital are already tax-exempt because they are governmental, religious or other property for which relief already is granted.[13] Questions have also been raised about the efficacy of the dual assessment provision. For example, in Georgetown a historic row house may already be valued (and taxed) at its highest and best use in its current form as a residence because it is located in a residential zone. However, a large mansion on Massachusetts Avenue, if located in an area zoned for business, will have substantial speculative value as commercial property and so may find the new law advantageous. The unique circumstances of the District may not indicate fairly the value of this form of tax relief.

Connecticut is another state frequently cited as having a model tax-abatement statute. This law authorizes municipalities to enact ordinances abating real property taxes on historically and architecturally significant buildings where "the current level of taxation is a material factor which threatens the continued existence of the structure, necessitating either its demolition or re-modeling in a manner that destroys the historical or architectural value."[14] The state legislature may, through the Connecticut Historical Commission, reimburse municipalities for tax revenues lost on account of this abatement. However, the Connecticut law has never been used, principally because the Connecticut Historical Commission has never received appropriations from the state with which to reimburse localities, notwithstanding several attempts in the legislature to obtain funding for the program.

A North Carolina law adopted in 1974, and differing substantially from the 1971 bill that found no support, has proved to be especially troublesome in operation. Rather than providing an across-the-board reduction in city and county property taxes levied each year on historic landmark properties, North Carolina law authorizes the deferral of 50 percent of annual property taxes indefinitely so long as the property continues to qualify as a historic property, which means that it must meet National Register standards as these are interpreted and applied by local landmarks commissions. No rehabilitation work is required to be done, no guarantees must be given that the property will be maintained, and there is no requirement of any public access to the property. Except for "acts of God," the deferral privilege may be lost by demolition, "over-restoration" and so on, but not by a change of use or ownership alone. The deferral privilege lasts as long as the property qualifies as a landmark. However, the state tax law to which the historic properties amendment was attached originally carried with it a five-year recapture provision (reduced in 1977 to three years) that, with interest on the unpaid amount increasing to 47 percent for the sixth fiscal year previous and decreasing by only 9 percent for more recent years, has proven to be a substantial deterrent to its use.[15]

This summary of recent legislation in Maryland, North Carolina, New Mexico, the District of Columbia, Oregon, California and Connecticut is necessarily superficial and is intended to be illustrative rather than comprehensive.[16] Other manipulations of state and state-authorized local systems of taxation designed to enhance the economic climate for preservation come readily to mind. A required reduction in property tax assessments to the extent that property values have been reduced through the imposition of recorded preservation restrictions is one possibility. Illinois, Virginia, Oregon, North Carolina, Tennessee and West Virginia are among those states having acts that in essence direct local tax assessors to consider preservation and open space restrictions when valuing property for tax purposes.[17] In light of the common requirement that property be valued for tax purposes at its highest and best use, one would think that such restrictions would be considered in any event. Nevertheless, such a specific directive may be helpful, especially in those states where assessors are elected rather than appointed on the basis of professional qualifications. The difficult problems relating to how an acceptable valuation of such interests may be accomplished is the subject of other papers.

General Problems Encountered with Tax Incentives

Notwithstanding the fairly recent origin of the programs outlined here, and at the risk of oversimplification, a few generalizations can be made about problems encountered with tax incentives based on experience to date. As a general caution, it should be stressed that one overriding problem of preservationists is letting enthusiasm for preservation or the desperate need for a bottom-line balance on preservation projects get out of hand. Preservationists must first acknowledge that serious problems can arise, especially in the local tax arena, depending on which approach is taken. Some of the more apparent problems can be summarized as follows.

Dollar Value Compared with Direct Aid

One thousand dollars in "saved" property or other taxes has the same dollar potential for preservation as a $1,000 grant of direct aid from federal, state, foundation, private or other sources. However, depending on the particular scheme selected, the $1,000 of tax advantage may or may not be put to work for a preservation purpose. For example, under the North Carolina act described earlier, one landmark owner could take the $1,000 and sail away on his yacht. Another individual owner may have genuine need to put the $1,000 to a preservation purpose and would so use it. In other words, the incentive value of the law depends heavily on the individual owner's personal financial circumstances. However, other state programs cited previously impose a positive duty on the landmark owner to put the tax incentive to work for preservation. This requirement is important because tax schemes that are not geared to need or that do not require an effort on the part of the owner are politically suspect, and perhaps rightfully so.

Perceived Inequity

Where landmark designation by a local landmarks commission not only triggers the traditional police power landmark protection regulations (a stay of demolition, for example) but also qualifies a property for tax exemption, abatement or deferral, the tax exemption alone may put an early end to both efforts because of the tax inequity perceived by the public. Landmark protection programs have failed dismally in several North Carolina cities and counties, not so much on the basis of the proposed landmark regulations as on the grounds of the concurrent tax break, widely considered locally to be inequitable and more often than not incorrectly described and misinterpreted by the local press. Any observer of local government knows instinctively that perceived fairness or equity vis-a-vis one's neighbors by all taxpayers in a jurisdiction is an essential foundation of the local property tax system. New tax preferences introduced into that system require thoughtful, deliberate and usually prolonged explanation to legislators, local officials and the public at large. This is one area of local government where the old saying that "haste makes waste" has special application and importance.

Whether or not it should be, the property tax has been, is and will continue for many years to be the principal source of revenue for cities and counties. Any scheme that gives even the appearance of diminishing that tax base reasonably may be expected to promote howls of objection not only from local officials but from their powerful state-level representatives as well (statewide, municipal and county leagues, etc.). A corollary is that attempts to provide indirect subsidies for preservation through deductions and exemptions from state income, inheritance or other taxes are apt to be viewed by state revenue departments and commissions with the same skepticism.

Public Opposition to "Loopholes"

The country is literally awash with talk of tax reform and the need for the elimination of tax "loopholes." As a number of legislators have been heard to observe, "Our job is to close loopholes, not open up more of them!" Perhaps one of the more subtle but nonetheless important tasks for preservationists is to help the public begin to understand that there is, in fact, no such thing as a tax loophole. Whether the talk is of income tax credits or deductions for education, medical expenses or mortgage interest, property tax abatement or credit for open space, estuarine areas, fallout shelters or pollution control facilities—all of these are nothing more nor less than deliberate, conscious statements of public policy, cast into law by democratically elected representatives, declaring that certain types of activity in the public sector are to be encouraged. One does not have to be for or against education, health care or historic preservation to accept the fact that there is no such thing as a loophole.

Nevertheless, the public sentiment is strong, suggesting that preservationists tread carefully in proposing modification of state and local tax systems to encompass preservation objectives. The sentiment is often confused with the notion of tax simplification, a strong advocate of which was former Secretary of the Treasury William Simon, who proposed doing away with all exemptions and deductions and taxing all income at a lower base rate. This aspect of the argument for tax reform may confront the preservationist with a dilemma. For example, the laws in New Mexico, Oregon, California and the District of Columbia discussed previously impress one not only as equitable but also as reasonably related to a preservation effort. However, when one examines the details of administration and procedure involved in the implementation of these programs, it becomes apparent that they are not self-executing, nor are they necessarily inexpensive. In fact, it has been argued that they add an element of audit to local and state property tax administration to the extent that preservation projects must be approved and inspected as they proceed, and periodically inspected and monitored for compliance on completion. These hidden costs may be said to strengthen the traditional argument that the purpose of taxation is to raise revenues for the running of the government and that public policy and democratic ideals are better served by approaching preservation (or any other) problem through the front door of loan and grant rather than through the back door of hidden tax preferences.

Erosion of the Tax Base

Wall and Hagman have observed that cities and counties in many states are directly dependent on the size of their tax base (i.e., total assessed valuation) in qualifying for federal and state grants as well as for maintaining their bonding capacity and that officials fear erosion of the tax base.[18] In those cities and towns where a substantial portion of the property tax base is already exempt (as in university towns, state capitals, counties with substantial federal lands and so on), there is an even stronger argument against removing additional property from the tax lists. In such situations, impact studies of the type conducted in Portland, Ore., prior to the enactment of that state's tax relief measures, which indicated that in the short run frozen assessments on historic properties would be only minimally harmful to the tax base and that in the long run they would be beneficial and take on a special significance. It seems obvious to recommend strongly that detailed cost-benefit studies should be undertaken to determine the actual impact of any proposed plan of tax incentives and that preservationists should welcome the opportunity to participate fully in such studies.

Minimal Financial Impact

Proposed tax incentive schemes at state or local government levels should be carefully analyzed to assure that the effect of the proposal will have a real dollar impact on preservation. For example, a plan to reduce property taxes on historic buildings by 50 percent annually may be sound in principle but only marginally effective in execution. In a city where the property tax rate is $3 per $100 of assessed valuation on the structure, and where there is a compelling need to replace a slate roof on a Victorian mansion valued at $30,000, an annual tax saving of $450 would not likely go far in replacing the roof.

Inherent Limitations on Taxation as a Planning Device

Not all writers are convinced that efforts to use the taxing system as a land use control device have met with unqualified success. Wall notes that "these programs have their roots in economic theory that suggests urban growth and development can be controlled through the manipulation of property and other tax policies."[19] The property tax in particular has generally been regarded by most writers as a relatively crude planning tool, and sufficient evidence is not yet at hand to demonstrate conclusively that more than ad hoc benefits

99

will result from extending its use into the preservation domain. In my opinion, it is an area to be approached with specificity and caution.

However, regardless of the tax under consideration, it appears that the most fruitful avenues for further experimentation are those that provide a tax subsidy only in exchange for preservation or restoration services rendered, plus repairs and maintenance, a reasonable amount of public access to the property benefited, agreements not to demolish the property either purposefully or by neglect, perhaps a preemptive option to purchase and so on. The direct and overhead costs of administering the plan should be noted as offsets with as much precision as possible, and policy decisions should be made with respect to the allocation of costs.

State and local tax advantage schemes on behalf of preservation—like zoning, landmark protection ordinances and other tools—are but one means of approaching the problem. Potentially, these tools perform at their best when the effort to subsidize preservation through tax incentives is a coordinated one that makes equally sensitive and sensible use of the other major governmental powers, such as the police power, eminent domain and, above all, the power to plan precisely and wisely. Taxation as a preservation incentive is new, tends to be highly site specific and has provided uncertain results. The proof is in the pudding, and preservationists have not yet had enough of the pudding to measure adequately either its taste or its quality.

It appears that the goal for preservationists is essentially the same as that faced by other special-interest pleaders of environmental causes: to convince the body politic that preservation purposes are indeed worthwhile and to assure that preservationists have their own values sorted out, especially for such critical and as yet unresolved issues as who should pay, for what and subject to what conditions. When preservationists have accomplished this much, the taxation techniques will fall into place.

NOTES

1. The generous assistance of certain persons in gathering information and discussing the tax assistance programs in the following jurisdictions is gratefully acknowledged. Oregon: Paul Hartwig, chief, Office of Archeology and Historic Preservation, state of Louisiana Department of Culture, Recreation and Tourism and former historical programs coordinator, State Parks Branch, Oregon Department of Transportation; District of Columbia: Ellen Kettler, former regional counsel, Midwest Regional Office, National Trust for Historic Preservation; New Mexico: Thomas W. Merlan, state historic preservation officer, New Mexico State Planning Office; New York: Frank Gilbert, chief counsel, Landmarks and Preservation Law, National Trust for Historic Preservation; Connecticut: John Shannahan, state historic preservation officer and director, Connecticut Historical Commission; California: John D. Henderson, AIA, San Diego, member, Board of Advisors, National Trust for Historic Preservation; Maryland: Henry Lord, Esq., Baltimore, former assistant attorney general, and St. Clair Wright, chairman, and Pringle Symonds, President, Historic Annapolis, Inc.

2. 1973 *N.H. Laws* ch. 376, § 66.

3. *Tex. Tax-Gen. Ann.* art. 7.06(3)(a) (Vernon 1969), which provides that 50 cents of the cigarette tax levied on each 1,000 cigarettes shall be credited to the Texas Parks Fund. This money is explicitly set aside for use by the State Parks and Wildlife Department for the acquisition, planning and development of state parks and historic sites.

4. *Md. Ann. Code*, art. 81, § 281A (Supp. 1977), *as amended* by 1978 Md. Laws, ch. 119.

5. *N.M. Stat. Ann.* § 18-6-13.

6. Levy, "The Manipulation of the Real Property Tax to Encourage the Preservation of Historic Structures," 26 (1978) (unpublished report in library of National Trust for Historic Preservation; hereafter cited as "The Manipulation of the Real Property Tax").

7. *Md. Ann. Code*, art. 81, § 12G (Supp. 1977). This tax credit may be spread over up to a five-year period.

8. District of Columbia Property Tax Revision Act of 1974, § 431 (current version at D.C. Code § 47-651).

9. *Ore. Rev. Stat.* §§ 358.475-358.545.

10. "The Manipulation of the Real Property Tax," note 6 above, at 9.

11. *Cal. Gov't. Code* §§ 50280-50289 (Deering); *Cal. Pub. Res. Code* §§ 5031-5033 (Deering); and *Cal. Rev. & Tax. Code* §§ 439-439.4 (Deering).

12. *D.C. Code* § 47-652 *et seq.*

13. "The Manipulation of the Real Property Tax," note 6 above, at 10.

14. *Conn. Gen. Stat. Ann.* § 12-127a.

15. *N.C. Gen. Stat.* 105-278. Informed opinion in the North Carolina preservation community acknowledges this to be a "bad" law. Notwithstanding the efforts of two successive study committees to rewrite it, it remains as originally written except for 1977 amendments reducing the recapture period from five to three years and providing for "acts of God." This demonstrates the truth of the adage that once a special tax benefit is enacted, it is almost impossible to eliminate.

16. The summary deliberately avoids any discussion of yet another approach, which is to exempt completely from local property taxation properties owned by historical societies, museums and similar nonprofit educational organizations. This practice is followed in approximately 15 states. Similarly omitted is any discussion of such provisions as found in *N.Y. Gen. Munic. Law* § 96-a, which in essence authorizes the partial remission or forgiveness of property taxes that threaten the continued existence of a historic structure faced with an antidemolition order from a local historic district or landmarks commission. Such provisions were designed to avoid the question of "taking" under police power regulations, and it is the author's understanding from Frank Gilbert, chief counsel, Landmarks and Preservation Law, National Trust for Historic Preservation, that this law has not been used to any extent. Discussion of the Puerto Rico law, which exempts from local taxes property located in the Old and Historic District of San Juan, is yet another purposeful omission. A detailed analysis of the Puerto Rico law is to be found in Louis Wall, "The Feasibility of Tax Credits as Incentives for Historic Preservation" (National Trust for Historic Preservation, 1971), available on loan from the National Trust library (hereafter cited as "Feasibility of Tax Credits"). Recent information concerning the impact of the Puerto Rico law is not available. Although the conclusions of the Wall study are perhaps a bit dated and also will not be enthusiastically received by preservationists, it is still one of the best studies of its kind available. Steven Levy, a graduate student at George Washington University, has written a fine study, "The Manipulation of the Real Property Tax," cited fully in note 6 above, that provides recent statistics on the comparative effectiveness of a number of the state and local statutes offering tax relief for historic preservation. This unpublished paper is also available at the National Trust library.

17. *Ill. Munic. Code* § 11-48.2-6; *Va. Code* §§ 10-139, 10-140, 10-142 and 10-155; *Ore. Rev. Stat.* §§ 271.710-271.750; *N.C. Gen. Stat.* 160A-399.5(6); *Tenn. Code Ann.* § 67-519; and *W. Va. Code* §§ 8-26A-4 and 8-26A-5.

18. "Feasibility of Tax Credits," note 16 above, at 23-24; Hagman, *Urban Planning and Land Development Control Law* 347 (St. Paul: West Publishing Co., 1971).

19. "Feasibility of Tax Credits," note 16 above, at 100.

101

Joseph H. McGee

STATE AND LOCAL TAXATION:
CURRENT PRACTICES, PROCEDURES AND EFFECTS

Although many state and local governments have contributed to conservation of the built environment through passage and administration of innovative laws, notably in the related areas of zoning and planning, most have ignored any suggestion that local tax relief be employed as an incentive for owners of historically or architecturally significant buildings to conserve and maintain their properties.

The suggestion that such properties should receive special tax treatment is apt to produce varied reactions depending on the point of view of the person to whom the proposal is made. First there is the state or local legislator, striving to meet the demands for more and more local services in times of increasing costs and still largely dependent on a single source, the property tax, with which to adjust local revenue. Then there is the tax assessor or administrator, charged with carrying out an already difficult tax procedure and reluctant to complicate this duty further. On the other hand, there are the property owners who would benefit from such tax relief. Some may be the owners of landmark buildings or estates saddled with burdensome property taxes on top of enormous costs to maintain their properties, not only for their own enjoyment but also for the preservation of what may be nationally important structures. Others may live in an old and historic district where they are probably subject to additional building and maintenance costs because of strict architectural controls established in an effort to conserve an ambience for all to enjoy. Finally, there is the great vox populi, expressing interest in preservation of its environment but above all sensitive to the tax bite on its own pocket and deeply suspicious of any system that allows a neighbor a different, and perhaps more favorable, standard of taxation.

The tax policy of most United States cities and other local governmental entities is centered on the ad valorem taxation of private property, which includes some personal property but is primarily real property. This property tax is one of the oldest forms of taxation known, and yet it is also one of the most hated government revenues. It has been criticized by those who must administer it as well as those who pay it; it has been faulted for having no direct relation to the ability to pay or to services rendered; and it is called regressive, inequitable, difficult and costly to administer and susceptible to fraud. Nevertheless, the property tax remains the chief source of revenue for the almost 100,000 units of local government in this country. The federal government, of course, derives the bulk of its income from individual and corporate income taxes. The states rely primarily on the sales tax and to an increasing degree on

Mr. McGee is attorney and partner, Buist, Moore, Smythe and McGee, Charleston, S.C., a past president of Historic Charleston Foundation and a former trustee of the National Trust.

their own income tax and, while a few cities tax income and sales, the overwhelming majority of local governments are left almost solely dependent on the property tax. In addition, the property tax is for most cities and counties the only revenue source that can be adjusted to produce more or less revenue as needed to balance a budget.

In the 1976 budget of Charleston, S.C., the property tax produced only about half of all income but, after deducting receipts from various city opertions such as utilities and franchises and all forms of indirect state and federal aid, there remained only two direct taxes producing income, the other being the business license tax, which is fixed and difficult to change and produces less than 5 percent of the total revenue.

For these reasons, it appears that the only significant effect local tax policy can have on conservation of the environment is through the administration of the real property tax. In considering local administration of this tax, it is important to remember that all local governments lack an inherent power to tax. They derive their taxing authority from state constitutions, from state statutes and from charters of incorporation granted by the state. While there seems to be an increasing interest in true home rule (in which a state, presumably by or pursuant to an amendment to the state constitution, gives to a local unit full autonomy), this is not the usual situation today. By and large, state laws, and in many instances state constitutions, prescribe what kinds of property shall be taxed, how they shall be appraised and how their assessments are to be determined and then, finally, allow the local government to determine the millage to be applied. Without the necessary enabling laws, most local governments are without authority to grant the owner of historically or architecturally significant buildings any relief from the property tax.

Administration of the tax, however, is invariably a function of local government. The local assessor is usually a city or county employee—elected in 23 states, politically appointed in 15 states and selected on the basis of professional competence in only 12 states. The tax bill that the property owner receives is the product of several different factors. First, the property is appraised. Then the appraised value is multiplied by the assessment ratio to produce the assessed value. Finally, the millage, which is set by the local governmental tax unit, or units, is multiplied by assessed value to give the actual tax due.

The first concern is with appraisal. The majority of laws direct the tax assessor to appraise real property at its fair market value, and this in turn is interpreted to mean at its "highest and best use," a rule that probably causes most of the resentment against tax appraisals. To understand its effects, consider the case of the owner of a large tract of land. Formerly a country estate, it is now surrounded by urban sprawl. Although the owner may fervently wish to retain the property for continued personal enjoyment, its location now makes subdivision a possibility and ultimately perhaps an economic necessity, for the tax assessor must appraise the estate at what it would bring if offered for immediate sale to the highest bidder without restriction on use. This is the highest and best use doctrine. It is understandable that the loudest cry against this method of appraisal should come from agricultural interests, but the same argument is now heard from many who own historic properties, both in and outside the inner city. The fact that an early 19th-century residence is an excellent example of an architectural style or that the building may be associated with an event of historical significance is not likely to influence its resale value so much as is its location in a strategic point within a proposed highrise development.

Classification by Use

A solution to this complaint may be the enactment of a "classification by use" system of appraisal. Generally, classification systems provide that assessments shall be based on current use, rather than on fair market value and distinguish the following uses of property: utility, agricultural land, commercial and industrial, residential, livestock, railroads, mining, gas and oil properties and merchandise inventories. Such a system requires a change in law at the state level and, in many instances, amendment of the state constitution. Of the 49 states and the District of Columbia that responded to a 1972 questionnaire from the U.S. Senate Subcommittee on Intergovernmental Relations, 25 states and the District did not have a classification system of any kind and 15 had only partial systems.[1] Included in this latter category were provisions for special farmland assessments that in six states represented the only special property classification. The provisions of the classification systems in eight states that do have them vary considerably.

California has a classification by use law of special interest to historic preservationists.[2] Qualifying property owners may have their assessments based on the property's actual use rather than potential highest and best use—if the property is a landmark listed in the National Register of Historic Places, the state properties register or a city or county register, and if the owner has signed a 20-year contract to preserve and maintain the property, restrict its use and allow reasonable public visitation.

In the District of Columbia, properties designated as historic may be assessed on two bases for real estate taxation: the traditional basis of highest and best use and also the basis of actual current use. If the actual use assessment of a site with a historic building is less than its highest and best use assessment, the property will be taxed on the basis of the lower assessment if the property owner agrees, under a minimum 20-year contract with the District, to preserve and maintain the building.[3]

Any such classification system is likely to beget as many problems as it solves, and the opponents of such programs are convinced that their inequities are as great as the system they replace. But, from the point of view of the owner of a historic property, a use classification is likely to produce a lower tax if the property is susceptible to resale for a different purpose.

Differing Ratios

The effect of a high appraisal may also be reduced by the use of different ratios to determine tax assessments. In some states all real property is assessed at the same rate, but in many the applicable rate is determined by the property's use. This, too, is a form of classification. When a state changes from a single appraisal method and a uniform assessment ratio to appraisal by use and a varying assessment ratio dependent on use, the total effect can be to reduce drastically the assessed value of certain properties. This is what happened in South Carolina as the result of an act passed by the state legislature in 1975.[4] Owner-occupied residences and certain agricultural lands are now assessed at 4 percent of appraised value. Some industrial uses are assessed at a ratio of 10 percent, but all other properties are assessed at 6 percent of appraised value. There is no provision for special treatment of historic buildings or areas, despite the efforts of one Charleston senator to incorporate such a provision.

In 1977 Arizona enacted a law authorizing separate assessment ratios for various classes of property. The Arizona law provides that historic property may be assessed at 8 percent of its actual cash value for 15-year renewable terms. Properties qualifying for this special rate must be listed in the National Register of Historic Places, be open to the public at least 12 days a year and be maintained in accordance with special state standards. Property owners must also agree not to use the property for profit-making purposes or to charge an admission fee greater than is necessary to recover maintenance or restoration costs.[5]

Although state laws usually define both the appraisal technique and the application of ratios, practices and procedures can vary from county to county in a given state. Local attitudes invariably influence the appraisal technique and unless there is specific control and supervision of a continuing reassessment program from the state capital, there is likely to be wide variation in local practices and procedures.

Easements

The effect of historic preservation easements and restrictive covenants on the appraised value of taxable property is omitted from this discussion except for one comment. It is frequently suggested that a property owner who grants a scenic or facade easement, or who voluntarily subjects property to restrictive covenants limiting its future development, has substantially reduced the resale value of the holdings and that the assessed value should be reduced accordingly. While true in theory, and perhaps often true in reality as well, the promoters of such easements and restrictions have been heard to recite, in almost the same breath with which they claim lower taxes, that if all property owners in the same neighborhood agreed to the same restrictions the integrity of the neighborhood would be preserved and land values would go up—an anomaly indeed.

Exemption

Tax relief for historic properties may also take the form of direct exemption or abatement from property tax liability. Probably the most common property tax relief granted to historic buildings is outright exemption. Most state constitutions provide for exemption of certain classes of property, such as those owned by organizations having charitable, educational, governmental, religious or other nonprofit purposes. While these exemptions are sometimes spelled out in detail, the constitution may instead contain only a broad authorization for this purpose. The state legislature must then enact a bill exempting specific property.

While such exemptions directly affect many historically and architecturally significant buildings, there are two important observations to be made. First, the exemption is generally granted to the owner of the property because the owner is a nonprofit association maintained purely for the public good. Second, this exemption typically is granted without reference to the significance of the building itself. There are exceptions to this last generalization. New Jersey, for instance, provides that historic buildings listed in the state register and owned by nonprofit corporations are exempt from the property tax.[6]

In Charleston, S.C., general tax relief is not granted to the nonprofit Historic Charleston Foundation. Its Russell House, however, has been granted tax immunity by the local Tax Exempt Board, which ruled that this house museum serves an "educational purpose" as contemplated by the state constitution.

While property tax exemption has been a legitimate form of relief for bona fide nonprofit activities, generally it does not benefit most privately owned property. In an urban area, the concentration of government buildings, schools, churches, hospitals and other exempt properties continues to erode the all-important property tax base by the enlargement of these tax-exempt activities. Since property tax exemptions impair the ability of cities to generate tax revenues, they thus cause ever higher tax rates for nonexempt properties. Local resistance to the extension of exemption policies to include privately owned historic properties is, therefore, justified in most instances, unless the extension is part of a comprehensive tax reform program.

Tax Credits or Abatement

Perhaps the most practical form of tax relief for privately owned properties worthy of historic preservation is some form of tax credit or temporary abatement or exemption for preservation or restoration expenses. Preservation forces have clamored for such relief for years, and several states have passed enabling acts, but few local governments have implemented this tax relief.

However, similar tax breaks to encourage economic development have enjoyed widespread use and success. The basis for such a program must, of course, originate with an authorization under the state constitution. It is not unusual for cities and towns to be allowed to exempt new industry from taxation by general or special ordinance for a limited period of time. In South Carolina, for instance, the state constitution permits the legislature to provide for industrial abatements, which have been used to some extent in all counties.[7] Tax abatement for new industry is acceptable to the public because it does not reduce the existing tax base and consequently shift the tax burden to them. By holding taxes on new industry at a constant rate for a limited period of years, the community is able to subsidize industrial development in a uniform manner to obtain desirable growth. This approach has also been used in Missouri, where property owned by urban redevelopment corporations is authorized by state law to be exempt from property taxes for 25 years.[8] While the law does not apply solely to historic properties, it has provided a measure of tax relief that has encouraged preservation of historic sites in certain urban renewal areas.

Another tax incentive plan not necessarily designed to preserve historic structures but applicable in most instances would grant partial exemptions in return for maintenance and repair. Providence, R.I., in accord with a State Neighboring Act, has such a program administered by the city assessor.[9] For five years, the tax assessment of dwellings used exclusively for residential purposes will not be raised to reflect the cost of specified alterations and improvements. It should be underlined that this program is not limited to historic districts. A significant effort in the direction of exemptions based on maintenance has occurred in Maryland.[10] Each county or municipality may elect to allow as a credit against local real property tax up to 10 percent of an owner's cost of restoring or preserving a historic building individually designated or in a locally designated historic district, or up to 5 percent of the cost of constructing a new building that is architecturally compatible with the surrounding historic district. Unfortunately, the act, which is highly acclaimed by preservationists, has not yet been implemented by any jurisdiction. Some use has been made of another Maryland law authorizing certain counties to exempt, for up to five years, properties in local historic districts from increases in their assessments caused by structural improvements.[11]

The New Mexico Cultural Properties Act of 1969 exempts privately owned property that is in the state register of historic places and available for educational purposes from local property taxes in the amount of approved restoration, preservation and maintenance expenses. The act also provides that qualifying amounts expended in a given year may be carried forward for credit against property taxes for up to 10 subsequent years.[12]

Conclusion

Among the greatest problems facing any effort to provide tax incentives for historic preservation is the task of defining a historic building or district. If tax relief is limited to those structures that have some particular association with events or lives of historical significance, or if the building must be of landmark architectural significance, then the relief is so limited as to be of questionable worth. Most truly historic buildings are already tax exempt and the number of landmark buildings in private ownership is not large. If tax incentives are to become a true encouragement to preservation of the built environment, then a larger definition must be found, one that recognizes the concept of an architecturally significant district and the importance of every building within it as a part of the whole.

Although this discussion has underlined the complications that beset any form of tax relief at the local level, some progress has been made and there is reason for preservationists to continue their efforts to find a worthwhile workable program.

NOTES

1. U.S. Senate, Subcommittee on Intergovernmental Relations, 93rd Cong., 1st Sess., *Status of Property Tax Administration in the States,* 1973.

2. *Cal. Gov't. Code* §§ 50280-50289 (Deering); *Cal. Pub. Res. Code* §§ 5031-5033 (Deering); and *Cal. Rev. & Tax. Code* § 439-439.4 (Deering).

3. *D.C. Code Encycl.* § 47-652 *et seq.* (West).

4. *S.C. Code* § 12-43-220.

5. *Ariz. Rev. Stat.* § 42-139.

6. *N.J. Stat. Ann.* §§ 54:4-3.52 to 54:4-3.54.

7. *S.C. Const.* art. X, § 3(g).

8. *Mo. Ann. Stat.* §§ 353.110 (Vernon).

9. 1966 Rhode Island Public Laws, chapter 15. This statute, which as enacted applied to alterations and improvements commenced between June 1, 1966, and June 1, 1968, has been extended several times and is still in effect, according to the Rhode Island Historical Preservation Commission.

10. *Md. Ann. Code,* art. 81, § 12G. These credits may be spread over a five-year period. The law grants jurisdictions the right to condition tax relief on agreements by owners to exhibit their properties periodically for educational purposes.

11. *Md. Ann. Code,* art. 81, §§ 9C(b)(4)(Allegheny County); 9C(j)(3)(Frederick County) and 9C(0-1)(3)(Washington County).

12. *N.M. Stat. Ann.* § 18-6-13.

Lonnie A. Powers

STATE HISTORIC PRESERVATION TAX STATUTES: THREE CASE STUDIES

A large and growing number of state and local governments have enacted measures designed to give tax relief to owners of historic properties. Such measures range from the fairly traditional property tax exemption given historic properties owned by nonprofit historic preservation organizations to the credit given against state income tax in Maryland for a portion of the amount spent on proper rehabilitation of privately owned historic structures not otherwise tax exempt.

To provide a basis for comparing state historic preservation tax statutes and for illustrating their various advantages and problems, the laws of Oregon, Maryland and the District of Columbia are examined here in some detail. This is not intended to be a definitive analysis of these statutes; rather, it is intended to stimulate discussion and comparison of them.

In brief, Oregon's law offers owners of property currently listed in the National Register of Historic Places a freeze in the real property tax assessment of their property for a period of 15 years in return for an agreement to maintain the property and to open it to public visitation at least one day each year. The freeze allows renovation of the property without fear of an increase in assessment during the 15-year period. Maryland, in contrast, has a statute quite similar to the federal income tax incentives for historic preservation found in the 1976 Tax Reform Act except that the Maryland law applies only to non-depreciable, owner-occupied property. Over a five-year period, an owner of a qualified structure can deduct from state income taxes money spent for "certified rehabilitation." Unlike Oregon or Maryland, the District of Columbia offers a reduction in property tax assessment by providing for assessment at current use rather than "highest and best use" (most economically advantageous) of the property.

Oregon

The Oregon statute providing for frozen assessments on historic property[1] has been very successful. The law has been in effect only a little less than four years and 192 of an estimated 500 eligible properties have been certified under it.[2]

The statute declares that it is in the "best interest of the state to maintain and preserve properties of historical significance," and defines historic property qualifying for tax relief as real property currently in the National Register, open

---

Mr. Powers is a lawyer in Little Rock, Ark., a former board member of the Quapaw Quarter Association of Little Rock and is currently completing requirements for an LLM degree from the George Washignton University School of Law specializing in land use management law.

to the public at least one day a year and maintained according to minimum standards established by the state historic preservation officer. Purchasers under recorded instruments of sale fall within the definition of owner.[3]

Application for classification and special assessment as historic property is made to the assessor of the county in which the property is located. An applicant must "consent in writing to the viewing of the property (inspection) by the state historic preservation officer and any state advisory committee on historic preservation."[4] Under the statute, applications must be made by December 31 of any year for the freeze in assessment to begin on January 1 of the following year (i.e., December 31, 1979, for assessment as of January 1, 1980).[5]

The county assessor has 10 days to forward the application to the state historic preservation officer, who "shall review the application and may view the premises" and who may approve, disapprove or partially approve the application by April 1 of the year following the year of the receipt of the application; the application is "deemed approved" if no action is taken by April 1. Property owners whose applications are rejected or partially denied may appeal to court. Approved applications are certified in writing to the county assessor and the certificate must state the facts on which approval is based.[6]

For the 15 years following certification, the property's assessment is frozen at its true cash value "at the time application was made" unless it becomes disqualified. Disqualification can result from voluntary termination by the owner, sale of the property to a tax-exempt owner or discovery by the assessor that the property no longer qualifies (examples are failure of the owner properly to maintain the property or improper changes to the property). A penalty equal to the amount by which the tax would have been increased, but for the frozen assessment, during the assessment year in which the property lost its certification times the number of years it was certified attaches to disqualified property unless the reason is transfer to a tax-exempt owner or destruction by "fire or act of God."[7]

Under the statute and its subsequently adopted administrative rule[8] (see page 117), a property owner is obligated only to open the certified property to public viewing one day each year,[9] to preserve it in its condition as of the date the assessment was frozen and to allow periodic inspection by the state historic preservation officer. Any repairs, alterations or improvements to the property must be approved in advance through review of building permit applications by the state historic preservation officer.[10]

By a resolution dated December 30, 1975, the state historic preservation officer adopted rules, as authorized by the statute, providing for "allowance and substantiation" of public viewing and for minimum maintenance standards. Owners of certified properties are required to file a statement during the first month of each assessment year setting out the specific day or days and hours during which the building is open to the public. Also, application for a building permit for work on a certified structure must be approved by the state historic preservation officer and the owner must "covenant that any such alterations, improvements or repairs shall be made in a workmanlike manner using sound historic preservation techniques" before beginning any work covered by a building permit.[11] The state historic preservation officer also has the authority to demand reports from owners of benefited historic property as to the property's continued qualification for frozen assessment, and may decertify the property if such reports are not received within 90 days after a request has been mailed.[12] No rules have been adopted implementing this particular power, however.

High property taxes and the straightforward nature of the Oregon law enabling a property owner to know what the property tax will be are the two main reasons why the law has been used so often.[13] Other reasons that contribute to its popularity are its relatively minor burdens on the property owners and the slight effect it has on property tax revenues.

Since the Oregon law was passed, two studies have been made of the effect on general property tax rates of freezing assessments on historic properties. The first, by the Oregon Legislative Revenue Office, concerned only the effect of freezing historic property assessments in Jacksonville, a community of 2,116 persons.[14] The second study, by the Bureau of Management and Budget, examined Portland, population 375,752, and assessed the impact of several state statutes, including the historic property frozen assessment statute, on property tax rates in that city.[15]

The Jacksonville study identified more than $2.1 million (fair market value) of historic property in that town that potentially could qualify for the assessment freeze. The study assumed that all of the property would qualify at various times over the original five-year life of the statute. Properties having an aggregate value of $436,190 actually had been frozen by June 16, 1976, leaving properties with a value of $1,396,120 that could be frozen between 1977 and December 31, 1980, the original expiration date of the statute. This law was extended in 1979 and will now expire on December 31, 1985 (see note 5). The study also assumed that with only routine maintenance, inflation would cause the fair market value of the historic property to increase at an average rate of 9 percent each year, the same average rate as for nonhistoric property. Based on those assumptions, the report concluded with two findings. First, in order to sustain a 6 percent per year increase in overall property tax revenue for each of the 10 years, 1975-1985, Jacksonville would have to increase its tax rates by less than one cent each year to compensate for tax revenues lost by freezing assessments. In order to achieve a 9 percent growth in revenues, despite the frozen assessments, the city would actually have to increase the tax levy by an average of only one cent a year during the same period. The maximum amount of property taxes shifted to owners of nonhistoric property in any one year would be $4,787 in the tenth year under the 9 percent scenario.[16]

The Portland study assumed that owners of all of the 128 properties in Portland identified by the city's Bureau of Planning and Development as being potentially eligible for tax relief would apply for it and have their assessments frozen. The true cash value of the 128 properties was calculated at just over $24.3 million in 1975 and was expected to rise to $38.8 million by 1983. (The study did not give figures for the value of the total tax base.) Therefore, by 1983 the city would be losing tax revenues on, approximately, an additional $14.5 million worth of real property. However, the anticipated increase in the tax rate by 1983 to compensate for the effect of this exemption would be only four cents above the 1975 tax rate of $28.01 per $1,000 of assessed value.[17] The study found that if the average price of a house in Portland was assumed to be $25,000 in 1975, the impact on the average homeowner would be a 75-cent increase in property taxes.[18]

Despite this evidence of only a small increase in taxes resulting from the operation of Oregon's law, the statute has generated some resistance to the creation of new National Register historic districts. According to the statute, all properties in National Register historic districts are eligible to have their assessments frozen for the 15-year period stipulated.[19] The fear, apparently unjustified, is that additional Register districts could seriously erode the tax base of small communities.[20] This fear is present in towns like Jacksonville, where almost the entire town is or is proposed to be included in a National Register historic district.[21]

To meet this resistance, an amendment to Oregon's statute was offered in the 1979 legislature to provide that the periodic "trending," or readjusting, of all property assessments to reflect inflation would hereafter apply to historic properties whose assessments had been frozen.[22] Oregon conducts a general on-site reassessment of all real property each sixth year, but in the interim it trends all assessments, except those frozen, in order to reflect inflation. The assessors determine the average percentage increase in fair market value by checking sales of property within their communities and then increase the assessed values of all property by that percentage. Despite the assessment freeze, then, historic property assessments would have been increased to reflect inflation. The assessment freeze, however, would still have protected them from any upward reassessment on account of improvements made during the 15-year freeze. The trending amendment would have removed the tax relief under the original law for historic properties that are not improved or rehabilitated following their freeze in assessments. Most preservationists opposed the amendment, therefore, and it was not enacted.

That the Oregon statute is encouraging restoration and rehabilitation is evident from discussions with Oregon preservationists. Leonard Gionet, one of three partners who converted an 1890s Portland building into a restaurant and apartments, gives the Oregon law credit for making the $250,000 project possible. The building's assessment was frozen at its pre-improvement level of $30,000, for a tax burden of about $850 per year. Gionet estimates that the net positive cash flow from the completed project, financed with bank loans, personal funds and public grants, will be approximately $150 to $200 a month. Were the improvements to be taxed, even this minimal cash flow would disappear and no bank loans would have been available.[23]

George McMath, a Portland architect active in preservation and the architect on several properties having frozen assessments, indicates that in several cases the freeze has tipped the balance in favor of restoration. The positive effects of the statute are seen in the increasing numbers of applications for frozen assessments. McMath thinks that the Oregon law has been much more effective than the 1976 Tax Reform Act in stimulating restoration. The primary beneficiaries of the federal act are, he observes, owners who have large enough incomes to make the resulting income tax deductions beneficial, while the Oregon law directly benefits all owners of historic property regardless of income.[24]

David W. Powers III, manager of the state historic preservation office, is most enthusiastic about the benefits of the Oregon law. In his opinion, it has been critical in several preservation efforts.[25]

111

It appears that Oregon has enacted a tax incentive substantial enough to encourage historic preservation but having such a slight impact on overall property tax revenues that it does not arouse serious opposition. Furthermore, the well-drafted Oregon law is accomplishing its purpose through efficient administration and widespread use by enthusiastic preservationists.

Maryland

Maryland has enacted two tax statutes designed to aid historic preservation; only one is being used, and it provides for deductions from the state income tax.[26] The other statute[27] provides for real property tax relief for historic property and is enabling legislation that allows individual counties to enact ordinances authorizing credits against local property taxes as incentives for private restoration. Thus far not one county has enacted tax relief of this sort, probably for fear of reducing their local tax base.[28]

Potentially this second statute is very useful because it would allow a credit against property taxes of up to 10 percent of an owner's expenditures for restoration and preservation of historic property or up to 5 percent of the cost of constructing a new building that is compatible with its surrounding historic district. The statute has a five-year carry-forward provision, which allows a taxpayer who cannot use up the credit entirely in one year to apply it against state taxes for up to five more years. Officials of the Maryland Historical Trust are unaware of any concerted effort by preservationists or others to persuade counties to use this statute; perhaps the counties will not act to implement it unless pressured to do so.[29]

Maryland's income tax statute was passed in 1975, and was adapted from early versions of federal legislation that became section 2124 of the Tax Reform Act of 1976.[30] The state act was amended slightly in 1976 and extensively in 1978.

In contrast to the detail of Oregon's statute, the Maryland law is quite brief, particularly after the 1978 amendments. An owner or life tenant of a "certified non-depreciable historic structure"[31] is allowed to deduct from state income taxes over a 60-month (5-year) period amounts expended for a "certified rehabilitation." Qualifying properties must be non-depreciable, i.e., not used in a trade or business or for any income-producing purpose and, therefore, typically would be owner-occupied residential structures. In addition, the property must be certified historic by being either individually listed in the National Register of Historic Places or located in a National Register, state or locally designated historic district and shown to be contributing to the significance of the district. To be certified, the rehabilitation work must be consistent with the historic character of the property and must have been done in accordance with regulations promulgated by the state comptroller, who administers all state income tax laws.[32]

The basic difference between the Maryland law and the federal Tax Reform Act of 1976 is that the Maryland law allows deductions only for expenditures on non-depreciable property, while the federal law applies only to depreciable property. As originally enacted, Maryland's law applied both to depreciable and non-depreciable property. Its limitation to non-depreciable property by a 1978 amendment was part of an effort to make its provisions complement the federal act and not allow any taxpayers a double deduction for the same expenditures.

Maryland's income tax statute is not being widely used. According to an official in the office of the comptroller, only one partial deduction and three full deductions were allowed from the nine applications filed for the 1976 tax year, while four deductions resulted from five applications filed for the 1977 tax year.[33] A number of administrative and staffing problems are responsible. A professional staff of architects and historians ideally is needed to prepare and administer the standards required for certifying the significance of structures and appropriateness of rehabilitation work. Since the Maryland Income Tax Division lacks the staff necessary to carry out the administrative duties delegated to it under the act, it has informally turned the certification process over to the Maryland Historical Trust. Despite its staff of design and preservation professionals needed to implement the act, the Maryland Trust is fully occupied administering its own programs and consequently lacks the resources to handle the tax laws.[34] The result is that the state income tax relief program is administered jointly by and not well coordinated between the Income Tax Division and the Trust.[35]

The underutilization of this statute takes nothing away from its inherent value. It offers an important tax incentive for private rehabilitation of residences and other non-income-producing property, an incentive not available under the federal act. Even before the 1978 amendment restricting the benefits of the law to non-depreciable property and changing the deduction amortization period for the deduction from 120 months to 60 months, the statute had benefited mostly residential structures—the 60-month amortization period of the federal law being more attractive for owners of depreciable properties than the pre-1978 120-month period of the Maryland law.[36]

Because so few persons have taken advantage of the law and because it benefits mostly residential structures, the total tax loss to Maryland has been less than $10,000 each year, with benefits to individual property owners averaging $1,500 to $2,000.[37] Maryland privacy legislation prevents the division from giving out the names of persons who have received credit under the statute, thereby making it impossible to discuss with property owners who have used the tax incentive their assessment of its value.

Both the division and the Maryland Trust think that the law is having a positive effect, but that lack of funds and staffing prevent them from properly implementing the statute. Ideally, Maryland should consolidate the administration of the statute in one agency having adequate funding and staff to assure its most widespread understanding and use. The Maryland statue could then provide an adequate complement to the federal act's benefits for owners of income-producing properties.

District of Columbia

The ineffectiveness in the District of Columbia of a statute providing for assessment of historic property on the basis of actual use, rather than the most economically advantageous "highest and best use,"[38] demonstrates the limited utility that an otherwise useful technique may have in the special circumstances of a city like Washington.

The statute offers real property tax relief only to buildings individually designated as historic by the mayor and the Joint Committee on Landmarks of the National Capital. Owners of eligible property can apply to the District government for assessments of their property based on its actual use and also on its highest and best use. If the actual use assessment is lower and would reduce taxes, the owner may opt for that assessment, but in exchange must enter into a historic preservation covenant agreement (see page 122) with the District for a period of not less than 20 years. Under the agreement, the owner gives reasonable assurances that the property will be properly used and maintained, and states that if the agreement is violated the taxes that otherwise would have been due will be recovered with interest.

According to District of Columbia officials, only two out of approximately 350 potentially eligible structures have taken advantage of the tax relief offered by the statute.[39] The failure to use the statute is due to three factors: (1) the statute applies only to individually designated historic properties, many of which are already tax exempt; (2) because many eligible properties are now being used for their maximum economic benefit available under applicable zoning, an actual use assessment would be no lower than one based on highest and best use; and (3) objections to the restrictions and 20-year life of the historic preservation covenant.

Of the approximately 350 structures eligible for relief, an estimated 200 are tax exempt because they belong to foreign governments, educational or charitable organizations or the federal government. About 70 eligible structures, mostly residences in Georgetown, are now being used for their most economically beneficial use. Existing zoning prevents these structures from being commercially used. Some 50 additional structures are being put to uses that are so close in value to their highest and best uses that they would not receive any substantial tax relief under the statute. Therefore, most eligible properties cannot, for one reason or another, actually benefit from this tax relief, offering nothing in exchange for encumbrances lasting the required 20 years. This leaves only 25 to 30 properties for which significant tax relief is possible under the statute.[40]

The District of Columbia government has sought to publicize the statute by including information on it when annual property tax assessments are mailed out. While some 20 to 25 inquiries are received each year as a result, the only structures that benefit from the statute[41] are a private residence at 1801 F Street, N.W., and the Potomac Boat Club. A review of the relief obtained by the owners of these properties demonstrates the potential utility of the law.

In computing the tax relief, the F Street residence was assessed on an actual use basis at $135,180 for the land and $212,500 for improvements, compared to $1,230,138 for the land and $362 for the improvements if put to their highest and best use. The low improvement figure results from the fact that the existing house would have to be torn down to make way for a highrise office building were the property to be used to its maximum zoned capacity; i.e., the $362 represents net salvage value. The owner, therefore, now is being taxed on almost $1 million less than would otherwise be the case.[42]

The Potomac Boat Club figures show a smaller but still significant drop in assessed value. The assessment for actual use is $99,180 and improvements $67,000, while highest and best use results in an assessment of the land at $192,822 and the improvements at $8,311. The decrease in assessment is almost $35,000.[43]

Prospects for expanded use of the District's law appear slight. The District government, under home rule, has been reluctant to provide tax relief for historic preservation.[44] The District's tax base is small, including only one-third of the real property in the District, because so much of it belongs to the federal government or is otherwise tax exempt. Also, the increasingly serious problem of displacement within the District, particularly in such historically significant areas as Capitol Hill, has made the government resistant to an action that would both shrink the tax base and, in the opinion of some, contribute further to displacement.

Conclusion

These three case studies demonstrate that state tax statutes can be effective tools for encouraging historic preservation. Their effectiveness will depend on, among other factors, simplicity and direct benefits to and lack of burdensome requirements imposed on the owners of historic properties. In order to insure their acceptance by tax authorities and the public, the incentives must fit effectively into the particular state's tax structure, must clearly aid only those owners who actively preserve their property and must not impose too great a burden on other taxpayers.

Oregon is an encouraging example of a state whose statute meets these criteria. Other states, too, can draft a simple statute keyed to their specific tax structures.

114

NOTES

1. *Ore. Rev. Stat.* §§ 358.475-.565 (Supp. 1977).

2. Telephone interview with David W. Powers, manager, Oregon State Historic Preservation Office (May 10, 1979) and Powers' testimony before the Senate Revenue and School Finance Committee, State of Oregon (Jan. 17, 1979) regarding Senate Bill 265, enacted in 1979 Ore. Laws, chap. 346.

3. *Ore. Rev. Stat.* §§ 358.475-.480.

4. *Ore. Rev. Stat.* §§ 358.485.

5. Under the original law, no applications could be made after December 31, 1979, *Ore. Rev. Stat.* § 358.485. However, a bill that was enacted by the 1979 Oregon legislature extends the time limit to December 31, 1985 (1979 Ore. Laws, chap. 346).

6. *Ore. Rev. Stat.* §§ 358.490-.495.

7. *Ore. Rev. Stat.* §§ 358.505-.525. See text at note 22 regarding trending values.

8. See note 1 and Resolution adopted pursuant to *Ore. Rev. Stat.* § 358.545 (hereafter cited as "Resolution").

9. The public viewing provision has caused some problems for owners of private residences. David Powers thinks that it may discriminate against them since owners of commercial or public

buildings are able to satisfy this requirement without any special effort. Also, at least two private homes were robbed shortly after being opened to the public, apparently by professionals who planned the crimes during the public visitation hours (telephone interview with David Powers, June 20, 1978).

10. Resolution, note 8 above, § E.

11. See note 8 above.

12. *Ore. Rev. Stat.* § 358.535.

13. Letter from David Powers to Carol Shull, Office of Archeology and Historic Preservation, Heritage Conservation and Recreation Service, U.S. Department of the Interior (March 15, 1978).

14. "Impact of Freezing Jacksonville Historic Property Value," memorandum to State Rep. Brad Morris from Stephen C. Meyer, economist, Oregon Legislative Revenue Office (June 16, 1976)(hereafter cited as "Impact of Freezing").

15. "Impact of Property Tax Exemptions on the Average Homeowner," memorandum submitted to the mayor and commissioners of Portland, Ore., by the Budget Division, Bureau of Management and Budget, Portland, Ore. (Dec. 31, 1975) (hereafter cited as "Impact of Property Tax Exemptions").

16. Since a 6 percent gain in tax revenues is less than the 9 percent rate of inflation anticipated by this study, the tax rate in the 6 percent hypothetical would actually drop over the 10-year period. If no historic property had its assessment frozen it would not be necessary to change the tax rate in order to achieve a 9 percent increase in revenue but the maximum estimated effect of freezing assessments would be a 10-cent increase in the tax rate in 1985. "Impact of Freezing," note 14 above, Tables I and II.

17. "Impact of Property Tax Exemptions," note 15 above, Table V.

18. *Id.,* at 16.

19. *Ore. Rev. Stat.* § 358.480(1).

20. The two studies cited above in notes 14 and 15 demonstrate that freezing property taxes will not cause a significant tax increase.

21. Telephone interview with George McMath, Portland architect active in historic preservation (June 22, 1978). Jacksonville now has a new city administration that is much more receptive to historic preservation and frozen assessments (Powers interview, note 2 above).

22. Senate Bill 265, 1979 Oregon Legislative Assembly.

23. Telephone interview with Leonard Gionet (June 21, 1978).

24. Telephone interview with George McMath (June 23, 1978).

25. Powers interview, note 2 above.

26. *Md. Ann. Code,* art. 81, § 281A (Supp. 1977), *as amended,* 1978 Md. Laws, ch. 119.

27. *Md. Ann. Code,* art. 81, § 12G (Supp. 1977).

28. Telephone interview with Louise L. Hayman, public relations coordinator, Maryland Historical Trust, by Jeff Tarplin, National Trust for Historic Preservation (June 27, 1977). (Memorandum concerning the interview is in the files of the National Trust.)

29. Telephone interview with Louise L. Hayman and Jack Finglass, Maryland Historical Trust (June 21 and June 24, 1978).

30. 90 Stat. 1916, § 2124. Opinion of the Attorney General of Maryland to Delegate Tyras S. Athey (March 23, 1977) (copy in files of the National Trust).

31. *Md. Ann. Code,* art. 81, § 281A(c), *as amended,* 1978 Md. Laws, ch. 119, § 1(b).

32. Finglass interview, note 29 above. Because the comptroller, through the Income Tax Division, relies on the Maryland Historical Trust to inspect and certify all rehabilitation work and since the Maryland Trust also administers in Maryland the federal 1976 Tax Reform Act, the standards used for certifying rehabilitation work under § 281A are those issued by the U.S. Secretary of the Interior for the Tax Reform Act of 1976.

33. Letter of James T. Swisher, assistant chief, Income Tax Division, Comptroller of the Treasury, to Jeff Tarplin (September 1977) (copy in files of the National Trust); telephone interview of author with Swisher (June 20, 1978).

34. Finglass interview, note 29 above.

35. The staffs of the division and the Maryland Trust have not coordinated effectively their information on the tax program, their status reports on the usage of and applications for the program or the process for applying for the tax relief. While the Maryland Trust does mail out applications for deductions (Maryland Tax Form 502H), the forms are returned to the division, which, after an unspecified time, sends them over for the Maryland Trust's evaluation of the structures and the rehabilitation work. Lack of staff prevents the Maryland Trust from inspecting each structure whose owner or life tenant applies for relief under § 281A; instead they rely on photographs and specifications submitted with Form 502H. It is conceded by Maryland officials that the questions included in Form 502H regarding the nature of the

rehabilitation work need improvement. Finglass and Swisher interviews, notes 29 and 33 above.

36. Prior to the 1978 amendment, Maryland used a 120-month amortization period, compared to the 60-month period in the federal law and the current Maryland statute.

37. Swisher interview, note 33 above; telephone interview with Jack Kates, attorney, Maryland Income Tax Division (June 23, 1978).

38. *D.C. Code Encycl.* § 47-652 to 47-654 (West Supp. 1977). These sections were enacted by Congress prior to its grant of home rule to the District. Before its subsequent revocation, section 47-651 provided that the District of Columbia City Council could by regulation impose different tax rates on land and improvements of designated historic property and may ignore increased valuation for improvements resulting from rehabilitation or new construction for up to five years. No regulations were ever adopted implementing this section. Concern over speculation and displacement prevented any use of the five-year deferment law and played a part in discouraging use of the actual use assessment law.

39. Telephone interview with Nancy Taylor, Department of Housing and Community Development, District of Columbia (June 20, 1978).

40. *Id.*

41. *Id.*

42. *Id.*

43. *Id.*

44. A District of Columbia City Council aide was quoted in 1976 as saying that it might be cheaper to give outright preservation grants than to lose tax revenues. E. Meyer, "Restore or Demolish," *Washington Post,* October 10, 1976. See note 38 above on the effects of displacement on the attitudes of the District of Columbia government.

116

RESOLUTION

WHEREAS, Oregon Laws 1975, ch. 514, provides for implementation of a special tax assessment applicable to historic properties which are currently listed in the National Register of
Historic Places; and

WHEREAS, Section 11 of Oregon Laws 1975, ch. 514 provides
that the State Historic Preservation Officer shall adopt rules
which:

(1) Encompass requirements for allowance and substantiation of public sightseeing of historic properties classified
under Section 1 to 11 of this Act;

(2) Provide minimum maintenance standards for the properties;
and

(3) Delineate any other matters necessary to carry out
the purposes of Section 1 to 11 of this Act.

NOW, THEREFORE, the following rules are adopted:

A. Definitions.

(1) "Open to the public" means that a reasonable portion
of the historic property, including exteriors and interiors of
structures and buildings, shall be accessible by the public for
visitation in accordance with these rules.

(2) "Reasonable portion of the historic property" is a
portion of the property substantial enough to provide a significant
benefit to members of the public who view the property.

(3) "Alteration" means a change, removal, or substitution of
a particular of one part of a building or structure which changes
the form or nature of the historic property without destroying the
identity of the historic property. Within the context of these rules,
"alteration" includes any willful change to the present state of the
historic property, including renovation or restoration, when any
apparent or detectable change in existing configuration, material,
architectural detail, or workmanship occurs.

(4) "Improvement" means everything that amounts to more
than repair that tends to add to the value or convenience of the
historic property.

(5) "Repair" means to mend, remedy, restore, or renovate to

a sound or good state after decay, injury, dilapidation, or partial destruction. Within the context of these rules, "repair" is construed as "alteration" or "improvement" if any apparent or detectable change in existing configuration, material, finish, color, architectural detail, or workmanship occurs.

(6) "Maintenance" means to preserve, to keep in a historic state or condition, to keep in good order, and relates to acts which prevent a decline, lapse, or cessation from that state or condition. Within the context of these rules, "maintenance" includes activities such as mowing lawns, cleaning, trash removal, and other such activities which are undertaken in the normal course of day-to-day living. Painting, gutter repair and other structural and electrical work will be construed as "repair", "improvement", or "alteration", if any apparent or detectable change in existing configuration, material, finish, color, architectural detail, or workmanship occurs.

B. Eligibility for Classification

(1) As noted in Oregon Laws 1975, ch. 514, property currently listed in the National Register of Historic Places is eligible for special assessment. National Register criteria refer to the characteristics of integrity of location, design, setting, materials, feeling and association in properties which are associated with significant historic events or persons; or that embody distinctive characteristics of a type, period or method of construction; or that represent a work of a master; or that possess high artistic value; or that are valuable sources of historic or prehistoric information.

(2) In the event that property eligible for the special assessment is located within the bounds of a National Register Historic District, the State Historic Preservation Officer will review recommendations from the appropriate local landmarks commission as to which buildings should be considered for the benefit of the special assessment.

(a) The local landmarks commission must be duly recognized by appropriate state, county, or municipal statute, and must have jurisdiction over the historic district in question.

(b) In compliance with Oregon Laws 1975, ch. 514, ultimate determination will be made by the State Historic Preservation Officer.

(3) The State Historic Preservation Officer may approve the application with respect to only part of the property which is the

subject of the application. However, if any part of the application
is denied, the applicant may withdraw his application.

C.   Inventory of Property

The State Historic Preservation Officer may take an inventory
of the property at the time he reviews the application for the
special tax assessment. The purpose of the inventory is to
establish the existing state or condition of the property. The
inventory will serve as a basis to determine owner's rights and
duties relating to proper maintenance of the property as detailed
in Section G.

D.   Public Viewing

(1)   The owner of the historic property will open to the
public a reasonable portion of the historic property qualifying
for the special assessment for at least one day in each year.

(2)   During the first month of the current assessment year
and each year thereafter, owner shall submit to the State Historic
Preservation Officer the specified dates and hours for the opening
of his property. At this time owner shall submit a description of
those portions of the historic property which he plans to open to
the public.

(3)   If there is any portion of this property that the owner
does not plan to open to the public, the owner must submit to the
State Historic Preservation Officer a detailed description of
the portion he does not wish to open and a statement explaining
why portions of the historic property should not be open.

(4)   If, the State Historic Preservation Officer determines
that extraordinary circumstances exist to justify not opening
certain portions of the historic property, and that even if the
described portion of the property is not open, a sufficient portion
of the property is open so as to allow members of the public a
significant benefit from viewing the property, then the Historic
Preservation Officer may allow the owner not to open the designated
portions of the property. Examples of such circumstances are where
an opening of certain portions of the historic property could
reasonably result in loss or destruction of property or appurten-
ances, thereto (e.g. where priceless antiques are too numerous to
guard) or where situations exist in which open house would place
an undue burden on the owner (e.g. where age or health of owner
severely impairs his ability to control activities).

119

·(5) If the Historic Preservation Officer determines that to
exclude the requested portion of the property is not reasonable,
then he shall notify the owner and state the reasons for the denial.

(6) A list of public viewing dates will be maintained by
the State Historic Preservation Officer.

E. Application for Alterations, Improvements and Repairs

(1) Before undertaking any improvements, alterations,
or repairs, as defined in these rules, owner shall submit an
application for a building permit in compliance with the Oregon
Structural and Fire and Life Safety Code to:

(a) The appropriate Building Official, and

(b) All other government authorities in compliance with
all applicable federal, state and municipal laws.

(2) The Building Official shall refer each application
to the State Historic Preservation Officer. The State Historic
Preservation Officer shall review the application for alteration
improvement or repair and will notify the Building Official and
applicant within 60 days of how the proposed work will affect
certification of such building for special tax consideration under
Oregon Laws 1975, ch. 514.

(3) If, in the judgment of the State Historic Preservation
Officer, further elaboration on the nature of the alteration,
improvement, or repair is needed, the State Historic Preservation
Officer may request further information from the owner prior to
certification.

F. Nature of Alteration, Improvements or Repairs

Owner shall covenant that any such alterations, improvements
or repairs shall be made in a workmanlike manner using sound
historic preservation techniques. The alterations, improvements
or repairs shall be done in a way so as not to destroy, alter or
modify the redeeming characteristics of the building to wit,
the characteristics that qualified the historical property for
the special assessment. If questions arise as to preservation
techniques, owner is encouraged to contact the State Historic
Preservation Officer for clarification.

G. Maintenance

Owner shall covenant that the historic property will be
maintained in such a way so as to prevent a lapse, decline or
cessation from the state of condition existing at the time the

120

application for the special assessment was granted. Maintenance
will be performed so as to reflect a spirit of historic authenticity.

H. Fire Insurance

While not required, it is highly recommended that the owner
purchase and maintain in effect during the term of the special
tax assessment period, policies of insurance written by a company
or companies qualified to do business in the State of Oregon,
providing insurance coverage against fire that may occur to the
existing structures, buildings, alterations, modifications, improvements, and repairs.

I. Owner's Acknowledgment of Rights and Duties

(1) The County Assessor shall furnish to the owner at the
time application for the special assessment is made an unabridged
copy of these rules, together with a copy of Oregon Laws 1975,
Chapter 514. The owner shall sign a statement that states that
he has read and understood Oregon Laws 1975, Chapter 514 and
applicable rules and agrees to comply with the law and rules
adopted pursuant to the law, and that he covenants to alter,
improve, repair and maintain his property in accordance with
Sections F and G of these Rules.

APPROVED:

State Historic Preservation
Officer   Dec. 30, 1975
                                        Date

121

HISTORIC PRESERVATION COVENANT

THIS HISTORIC PRESERVATION COVENANT made this _____ day
of _____, _____, by and between _____
_____,
(hereinafter called "Owner"), and the District of Columbia, a municipal
corporation (hereinafter called "District").

W I T N E S S E T H:

WHEREAS, Owner is the record owner in fee simple of certain real
property in the District of Columbia known as _____
Street, N.W. _____,
located on Lot _____, Square _____, including the
grounds and improvements located thereon as of the date hereon as is
more particularly described in Exhibit A, attached hereto and
incorporated herein, (all of which real property is hereafter referred
to as the "Site"); and

WHEREAS, the aforesaid Lot _____, Square _____ is
encumbered, as evidenced by Exhibit B, attached hereto and incorporated
herein; and

WHEREAS, the Site has been designated an historic landmark by the
Joint Committee on Landmarks of the National Capital, as evidenced by
Exhibit C, attached hereto and incorporated herein; and

WHEREAS, Owner and District desire to preserve and maintain the
present historical, aesthetic and cultural character and conditions
of the Site for a period of twenty years;

NOW, THEREFORE, in consideration of a real property tax reduction
for fiscal year _____ through and including fiscal year _____,
Owner and District covenant and agree for themselves, their successors
and assigns that the Site for the fiscal year _____ to and including
fiscal year _____ shall be subject to the following conditions,
limitations, restrictions and requirements:

Section 1. (a). If any permit or license is required by law for
any construction, demolition, alteration, or modification of the
exterior of the Site, or of its interior which would affect in any
way its exterior structure or appearance, Owner shall not apply to
the Office of Licenses and Permits, Department of Economic Development,
for such permit or license without the prior written approval of the
Director of the Department of Housing and Community Development, his

successor or designee (hereinafter the Director). If no such permit
or license is required by law, Owner will not, without prior written
approval of the Director, undertake or permit any construction, alteration, or remodeling to change the exterior of the Site, or its
interior which would affect in any way its exterior structure or
appearance, or the grounds, or improvements included in the Site as
depicted in Exhibit A. The Director shall approve or disapprove
Owner's written request within thirty (30) calendar days after actual
receipt thereof by the Director.

(b). Owner agrees at all times to maintain the Site in a good
and sound state of repair so that no deterioration shall take place
in its exterior appearance or in its interior which would in any way
affect its exterior structure or appearance, as depicted in said
Exhibit A.

(c). In the event Owner violates either covenant (a) or covenant
(b) of this Section, or both such covenants, the District shall assess
the Site, or part thereof, on the basis of full market value for such
fiscal year, or part thereof, in which the violation took place and
in which a real property tax reduction was granted pursuant to this
agreement. Any back taxes, plus interest at the prevailing U.S. Treasury
rate of interest for such fiscal year or part thereof involved in this
agreement, shall be due and owing the District and payable within
sixty (60) days after the date of mailing by the District of a notice
to the Owner of the amount of back taxes and interest due.

Section 2. <u>Inspection of the Site</u>. Owner hereby agrees that
representatives of the District shall be permitted at all times to
inspect the property. Inspections will normally take place from the
street; however, Owner agrees that the representatives of the District
shall be permitted to enter and inspect (a) the interior of the Site
to insure maintenance of structural soundness, or (b) the grounds, or
(c) improvements thereon. Inspections will not, in the absence of
evidence of deterioration, take place more often than annually.
Inspections will be made at a time mutually agreed upon by Owner
and District, and Owner covenants not to withhold unreasonably his
(their) consent in determining a date and time for inspection.

Section 3. _____. The covenants expressed herein
shall apply to and run with the Site for the benefit of the District
and its successors for twenty years commencing with fiscal year
_____ and ending on and including fiscal year _____.

Section 4. _____. The real property tax

reduction for fiscal years _____ through and including

_____ shall be based upon the difference for each fiscal

year between the full estimated market value of the Site determined

without regard to its historic nature and its value based on current

use and conditions as an historic site. If the value as an historic

site is less than the full market value determined without regard

to the historic nature of the site, the value as an historic site

shall be the basis of tax liability to the District. In case of any

dispute as to the valuation assigned to the Site by District or its

designated agent, Owner shall retain any right of appeal which Owner

may have as a taxpayer aggrieved by any assessment or valuation of

real property.

    Section 5. <u>Amendments</u>. The covenants expressed herein may be

amended during the time this agreement remains in force, upon the

consent of both Owner and District.

    IN WITNESS WHEREOF, the undersigned have executed this Covenant

this _____ day of _____, 19_____.

_____
                      (Owner)

_____
         (District's Representative)

124

Richard R. Almy

CONSIDERATIONS IN CREATING PROPERTY TAX RELIEF FOR HISTORIC PRESERVATION

The U.S. property tax, bulwark of local government finance, alternately is enlisted as an ally in the cause of land-use policies or is castigated for having caused their failure. It is natural then that as sentiment for the preservation of cultural artifacts builds, interest in the effects of the property tax on historic preservation also grows. Unfortunately, the effects of the property tax on investment decisions generally are complex, subtle and imperfectly understood.[1] The situation with respect to preservation activities is certainly not clearer.[2]

Ignoring for the moment such questions as who ultimately bears the burden of property taxes, some of its effects can be described. Property taxes are an expense of owning or using a property. Unless the nominal taxpayer can shift this expense to others by an increment in the price of products or services (an impossibility for idle or owner-occupied single-family residential property), the real or imputed income that can be received is reduced. If the reduction in income or the increase in operating expenses (of nonrevenue-producing properties particularly) caused by property taxes is greater than the owner or user can or is willing to tolerate, two basic strategies are available: An attempt can be made to reduce expenses or to increase income. Expenses can be reduced by deferring maintenance, ultimately leading to the deterioration and eventual abandonment of a property. Income can be increased by converting a property to a more profitable use.

Architecturally and historically significant properties represent intangible and unique resources that cannot be recovered once they have been demolished or too far altered, and both the deferred maintenance and conversion strategies pose a clear threat to their preservation. If property tax programs for historic preservation are to have even limited effectiveness, they must be designed to counter one or both of these strategies.

Current Practices

Preservationists in 36 states, the District of Columbia and Puerto Rico have been successful in persuading legislatures to enact measures that have the effect of providing a property tax incentive for historic preservation or providing property tax relief for historic properties. Although there is more diversity in the forms that "property tax incentives" for historic preservation have taken in comparison to the forms of other single-purpose incentives (e.g., for the preservation of farmland and open space), they may be classified according to their objective(s), operation and comparative strengths.

Mr. Almy is director, Research and Technical Services, International Association of Assessing Officers, Chicago. The views expressed in this paper are those of the author and not necessarily those of IAAO.

The classes into which these laws fall generally are: dual-purpose (restoration and preservation) incentives; restoration incentives; preservation incentives (encouraging maintenance of properties in their current uses); and exemption of historic properties, either individually or as a class, such as those owned by nonprofit preservation organizations. Property tax exemptions are comparatively weak preservation tools because to be eligible for exemption, explicit actions by owners to help preserve their historic property are generally not required. Measures containing an incentive to engage in a preservation activity, therefore, are preferred to those that merely provide property tax relief.

The effect of property tax exemptions as an incentive for historic preservation is still largely unknown.[3] Legislatures, however, are under pressure to do something, and the granting of an exemption is a time-honored response. Critics of the proliferation of exemptions notwithstanding,[4] property tax exemptions for historic preservation are comparatively innocuous. If the approximately 18,000 properties listed in the National Register of Historic Places could be taken to represent the maximum number potentially eligible for exemption, then the actual number of potentially eligible properties (i.e., properties now taxed) will be considerably less, since many are eligible for exemption on other grounds (e.g., publicly owned property and the holdings of religious, educational and charitable institutions). Thus, the group of potential beneficiaries is small in relation to the number of taxpayers generally, making additional exemption or "tax expenditure" a politically expedient course of action.[5]

A Structured Approach to Using Property Taxation

While it may not be possible to formulate a model preservation tax abatement program as Wall hoped to do,[6] it does seem possible to devise ways to utilize effectively property tax incentives in historic preservation. The evaluation of existing property tax incentives for historic preservation is complicated by the current conditions of property tax administration, land-use planning and controls and preservation practice. With respect to property tax administration, several considerations deserve simultaneous, explicit attention if effective historic preservation tax programs are to be designed.

First, a distinction should be drawn between property tax incentives for historic preservation and property tax relief for historic properties. Although it is difficult to make a clear distinction between the two, a property tax incentive implies that there is an explicit return (e.g., an agreement to restore, maintain or preserve a historic property) for the favorable property tax treatment. A secondary element of a property tax incentive program is a deferred or rollback tax provision, which is designed to recoup for the public all or a portion of the taxes foregone should the agreement be broken. Agreement requirements and deferred tax provisions create something of a dilemma. Although they are necessary to assure that the public interest is being served, they inhibit participation in incentive programs. Property tax relief measures, on the other hand, require nothing except that either the property be historic or the owner meet certain qualifications or both. No other preservation activity or commitment is required. Other things being equal, an incentive is preferable to tax relief alone.

Second, attention should be focused on the characteristics of architecturally and historically significant properties. For the purpose of designing property tax incentives, such physical characteristics as designed use, functional utility with respect to designed use and to compatible alternative uses, state of repair and location are of greater importance than other characteristics (e.g., style, architect and aesthetic qualities) that make a property architecturally or historically significant. Although the latter characteristics are more important in determining local, state or national historical significance, which in turn may influence incentive strategies, the former are more critical to private preservation. To state the obvious, unless a property has contemporary utility in its originally designed use, in a compatible alternative use or in tourist appeal, its private preservation will be difficult to assure. Unless zoning and other land-use controls prohibit more intensive land uses, property tax incentives should be keyed to narrowing or even closing the gap between assessments based on the market value and current use value of historic structures.

Finally, characteristics of state and local property tax systems must be taken into account. Property taxation in the United States is characterized by extreme diversity, but a given local property tax system may be examined from two broad aspects: its role in raising local government revenues and assessment practices, with the former perhaps the more important aspect. The potential strength of a property tax incentive is chiefly a function of the role of the property tax in the revenue system. This role is governed mostly by legislation (e.g., determining which property is to be taxed, at what rate, by whom and for what purpose), the pattern of political subdivisions and the pattern of urban development. If the property tax is a relatively important source of revenue (as it is for many local governments) and effective property tax rates are high, a property tax incentive program may prove effectual.[7] If the opposite is true, as Wall has shown to be the case in Puerto Rico, a property tax incentive is apt to be ineffectual.[8] The fiscal circumstances (e.g., high effective property tax rates, stagnant property tax bases, extensive amounts of tax-exempt property, etc.) that would tend to make a property tax incentive more effectual also are apt to diminish the chances of such an incentive being enacted. Jurisdictions in which there is a "revenue squeeze," such as a central city with a declining tax base and increasing service demands, are less apt to take actions that will further aggravate their fiscal problems. Similar resistance may be felt in capital cities and in other jurisdictions where there is already a concentration of exempt properties.

The potential impact of assessment practices on historic preservation activities is equally complex. In the United States today many real property assessment systems are based on the so-called cost approach to value in which land and buildings are appraised separately.[9] The approach derives its name from the fact that an estimate of the current cost of reproducing or replacing a building is made, from which an estimate of accumulated depreciation is deducted and to which an estimate of land value is added. The land value estimate is based on the estimated market value of the site as if it were available to be used in the most profitable way (the so-called "highest and best use"). The cost approach can be criticized because participants in real estate markets usually buy whole properties, not artificially separated land and building components. Nevertheless, it remains a useful technique for the mass appraisal of properties because information on the physical characteristics of properties is easier to obtain than market data (e.g., sales, rents and operating expenses).

127

Many assessing officers fully avail themselves of market information and also base assessments on "market approach" and "income approach" estimates of value and use available sales data in assessment ratio studies to improve the accuracy of their cost approach estimates.[10] Nonetheless, maladministration and errors in real property assessment are not uncommon, and although maladministration is not necessarily detrimental to historic preservation, a number of problem areas warrant attention by preservationists.

With respect to the estimation of land values, the greatest potential problem is ascribing a higher and better use to a site than is appropriate under the circumstances. Although most properties are appraised on the basis of current use, those properties that are located in transitional areas may be appraised on the basis of the most intensive permitted (zoned) use, even though the market demand for that use is uncertain and the current use value is much lower.

Assessing officers also may be unaware of restrictions and easements limiting the use of historic properties.

Numerous difficulties can also arise in the estimation of the value of historic buildings. Cost estimates of conventional buildings are usually based on published cost schedules.[11] These schedules are usually designed to produce an estimate of the cost of replacing a building with one of equal utility but constructed in a contemporary manner (the replacement cost), rather than an estimate of the cost of producing an exact replica of the building (the reproduction cost). In the case of older buildings that were constructed of expensive materials and in labor-intensive ways, replacement costs are normally lower than reproduction costs. Hence, the bias in cost schedules works to the advantage of older buildings. Architecturally unusual buildings, however, may not fit within the specifications of cost schedules, and appraisers may be forced to use more detailed cost estimating techniques. These techniques will usually produce a cost estimate that is based at least in part on the reproduction cost concept. The current cost estimating process is consequently a potential source of assessment bias.

Another aspect of the cost approach is the estimation of depreciation. Appraisal theory holds that depreciation is made up of three components: physical deterioration, functional obsolescence and economic obsolescence. Physical deterioration is simply the loss in value due to wear and tear. Functional obsolescence pertains to design features of a building that make it obsolete for its originally intended purpose. Economic obsolescence is caused by external factors that result in a lack of demand for a particular type of property (e.g., waterpowered gristmills), all properties in a particular area (e.g., a slum) or a combination of both (e.g., a mill town). Some forms of depreciation are held to be curable, while others are not, so methods for estimating depreciation vary. Owners and preservationists seeking property tax relief for historic buildings would be advised to examine closely depreciation estimating practices in their communities. Economic and functional obsolescences in particular are apt to apply to historic properties, and standard depreciation tables rarely incorporate these forms of depreciation.

A misconception related to depreciation concerns the effect of restoration and preservation expenditures on assessed values. Many persons believe expenditures to cure depreciation will necessarily result in an increase in assessed value. This misconception apparently stems from the fact that curable depreciation is measured by the cost of the cure.

It has been shown that the fear of reassessment is greatly exaggerated.[12] Reassessments may not be undertaken because (1) communities have policies encouraging maintenance activities by not assessing certain types of expenditures, (2) the depreciation cured by improvements was not previously recognized and (3) there is an element of inertia in reassessment systems.

A final consideration is the possibility that some historic properties may be more highly valued than other properties of similar utility.[13] Such properties should hardly be in need of, or eligible for, property tax relief or a property tax incentive for historic preservation, as the economics of the situation should be incentive enough.

Conclusion

There are two points in an assessment system at which property tax burdens can be reduced in the cause of historic preservation. First, legislation designed to provide a property tax incentive for historic preservation or property tax relief for historic properties can be enacted. Second, taxable historic properties can receive special attention in the valuation process. The first alternative can provide property tax relief but is of dubious effectiveness as a preservation incentive. Nevertheless, legislative placebos for historic preservation have been enacted in most states, and additional legislation may be expected in the future. More intelligent and effective assessments of historic properties can also provide relief, and a better understanding of assessment processes may lessen the need for property tax incentives for historic preservation. Both alternatives, if they are to be fair and effective, require a closer liaison between preservationists and assessing officers.

NOTES

1. The evidence of the land-use effects of property taxation is summarized in Denne, "Explicit Property Tax Policies and the Promotion of Specific Land Use and Economic Development Objectives: A Review," II *Assessors Journal* 13-46 (March 1976), a paper prepared by the International Association of Assessing Officers under contract to the U.S. Department of Housing and Urban Development.

2. Wall, "The Feasibility of Tax Credits as Incentives for Historic Preservation" 100-105 (Washington, D.C.: National Trust for Historic Preservation, 1971; unpublished research report in National Trust library) (hereafter cited as "Feasibility of Tax Credits").

3. "Feasibility of Tax Credits," note 2 above, at 58.

4. See, for example, Balk, *The Free List: Property Without Taxes* (New York: Russell Sage Foundation, 1971) and International Association of Assessing Officers, Policy Statement No. 2: Property Tax Exemptions (Sept. 22, 1971).

5. For a discussion of the impacts of property tax expenditures and methods for their measurement, see Kenne, "The Impact of Differential Assessment Programs on the Tax Base"; Harriss, "Discussion"; and Gloudemans, "Discussion," all in *Property Tax Incentives for Preservation: Use-Value Assessment and the Preservation of Farmland, Open Space, and Historic Sites* (Chicago: International Association of Assessing Officers, Research and Technical Services Department, 1975).

6. "Feasibility of Tax Credits," note 2 above, at 10.

7. The effective property tax rate of a property is the tax assessed against the property divided by the market value of the property. Effective tax rates are used to compare levels of taxation among localities that have different assessment levels, which make comparisons of nominal tax rates meaningless. In 1976, effective property tax rates for single-family residences were estimated to range between 0.13 and 6.77 percent of sales price among 353 cities having 1973 populations of 50,000 or more. See U.S. Bureau of the Census, Census of Governments, 1977 Vol. 2 *Taxable Property Values and Assessment-Sales Price Ratios* 25 (Washington, D.C.: U.S. Government Printing Office, 1978).

8. "Feasibility of Tax Credits," note 2 above, at 73-77.

9. See International Association of Assessing Officers, *Improving Real Property Assessment: A Reference Manual* 163-67 (Chicago: 1978) (hereafter cited as *Improving Real Property Assessment*).

10. In real property assessments the most interesting market approach application is the use of a statistical technique, multiple regression analysis (MRA), to estimate probable sales prices. For a comparatively nontechnical discussion of the use of MRA in assessing practice, see *Improving Real Property Assessment*, note 9 above, at 216-20. Assessment ratio studies are used either to derive adjustment factors for cost approach based appraisals or to identify areas or classes of property in need of reappraisal. For a discussion of the use of assessment ratio studies in assessment administration, see *Id.* at 135-37 and 210-16.

11. Examples of nationally published schedules include American Appraisal Associates, Inc. *Boeckh Building Valuation Manual* (Milwaukee: 2d ed., 1979) and Marshall and Swift Publication Company, *Marshall Valuation Service* (Los Angeles: 1975).

12. U.S. Department of Housing and Urban Development, *A Study of Property Taxes and Urban Blight* 3 (prepared by Arthur D. Little, Inc.) (Washington, D.C.: U.S. Government Printing Office, 1973).

13. For a discussion of the value of historical significance, see Buchanan, "Is There a Special Value for Antique Buildings?," 12 *Appraisal Institute Magazine* 37-42 (Fall 1968); and Reynolds and Waldron, "Historical Significance . . . How Much Is It Worth?," 37 *The Appraisal Journal* 401-10 (July 1969).

R. Lisle Baker

STATE TAX INNOVATIONS
IN THE CONSERVATION FIELD

Taxation can provide a useful complement to regulation and eminent domain as a means of land-use control.[1] Indeed, "green space" conservationists are beginning to understand the importance of center-city preservation—all too frequently the handsome old building that disappears downtown is replaced by a newer (and often uglier) version on prime agricultural land in the countryside. State tax innovations for open space preservation discourage undesirable changes in use and consequently may provide models for similar tax relief for historic preservation.

Unlike some forms of wealth, ownership of real property costs something extra: annual taxes based on the property value.[2] Questions of state and local taxation, therefore, are of immediate concern for property owners who do not have enough income to use federal tax shelters—the people for whom a distress sale is a real possibility. In short, if the federal taxation discussion might be entitled "Gimme Shelter," the state and local taxation might be called "Gimme Income," or at least "Gimme Relief."

Property value for tax assessment purposes is usually defined as the price that a willing buyer would pay a willing seller when both know the relevant facts. Because most owners are reluctant to time their property sales to provide local tax assessors with a ready-made valuation, real property is usually valued by one of three methods that theoretically produce the same results: (1) replacement cost less depreciation and obsolescence (useful for churches or other properties for which there is a small market); (2) comparable sales (the way most of us decided we paid too much for our last house) and (3) capitalized earning power (the value of an asset that would produce the actual or potential net income of the property).

Tax Relief

The need for tax relief arises when property taxes contribute to a distress sale. For example, if an existing land use is desirable but the return on the land cannot support the carrying cost (including the property tax), and the owner lacks either the will or the capacity to divert other sources of revenue to make up the difference, the property will be offered for sale. Often the sale will mean transfer to a purchaser who alters the use of the property to increase its value. A subdivision of farmland into small residential lots is a common example. When property taxes contribute to this process, pressure for relief arises.

Landowners who seek tax relief rarely argue that the goal is to dodge taxes. Instead, they lump themselves in a class with large numbers of other landowners and argue their cases on a higher plane. The most familiar of these

---

Mr. Baker is professor of law at Suffolk University Law School, Boston, Mass.

arguments are as follows: *Compensation:* The land has unfairly borne a tax burden that does not reflect a compensatory return in public services. For example, farmland grows no school children.[3] *Beneficial preservation:* The existing use constitutes an affirmative benefit to the public for which the property owner should be rewarded. For example, a forest protects watershed ecosystems, provides a renewable wood supply and offers visual amenity. *Personal hardship:* The landowner's property is poor and so is he.

These arguments often have some merit and occasionally find a receptive ear in a state legislature. Nonetheless, they bring to mind humorist Abe Martin's statement that "when someone says it is not the money but the principle— it's the money."

Property Tax Jurisdictions

Property tax jurisdictions fall into two classes: hydraulic and amputation. In a hydraulic jurisdiction, a reduction in the burden of one taxpayer means an increase in that of another. For example, in Massachusetts a locality determines the budget to be raised from property taxes and apportions it to cover the total nonexempt assessed valuation of properties in the municipality. (Here, income rises to meet expenditure, despite Parkinson's Second Law.[4])

In an amputation jurisdiction, a reduction in one taxpayer's burden means a decline in public revenues (and usually services). Unlike the rate in the hydraulic jurisdiction, the tax rate in an amputation jurisdiction is fixed and can often be increased only through voter referendum. (Kentucky was such a jurisdiction for a short period.) The federal income tax system is also an example of an amputation system at work. However, an amputation jurisdiction may perform like a hydraulic jurisdiction in that attempts at tax relief for certain classes of taxpayers are often accompanied by questions regarding replacement of the revenue lost.

Conservation Strategies

The following conservation strategies are among those available to ease the financial burden for owners of both natural and historic properties.

1. *Reduction in property tax assessments to the value of existing uses.* Instead of being assessed at its full cash or fair market value, property can be assessed at its value for current use, which often is lower. This solution, however, requires care in the definition of the property benefiting from preferential treatment. Also, in areas that are not under development pressure, this technique offers no tax relief since the fair market value *is* the use value. The principal attack on use-value assessment lies in its potential for confusion, especially where some properties are exempt and others are not. As of May 1979, there were at least 36 states with some form of use-value assessment or preferential treatment.[5]

2. *Reduction in potential property value.* While property would be assessed at its fair market value, its potential value for development could be reduced by a variety of government actions: (a) through regulation barring a more intensive use (usually by zoning); (b) through condemnation in which the government acquires by eminent domain the landowner's rights to alter the land and pays compensation;[6] (c) through transfer, by sale or donation, to a tax-exempt charitable entity; (d) through contracts with a governmental entity in which the landowners agree not to alter the land use in return for a fixed-period tax reduction;[7] or (e) through grant of a conservation easement to a governmental or private charitable entity. These techniques usually offer more opportunity to be site-specific than a broad use-value assessment law. They may also be less vulnerable to constitutional challenge because the land is assessed at existing rather than at its potential use value. A problem may arise, however, if the land is used as collateral and its ability to generate financing for farming or other purposes is dependent on a developmental value.

131

3. *Subisdy.* A subsidy is most often provided through "circuit-breaker" provisions for residential property backed financially through a state general fund. Payments from this fund allow tax relief to owners, not only elderly but also those of low income, and further extends benefits to tenants.[8] Unlike other techniques, a subsidy focuses more on personal need than on land use since it is usually tied to the income level of the claimant.

4. *Forgiveness.* The forgiveness technique is generally available in the case of unusual restrictions on land use. For example, New York municipalities are authorized "to provide by regulation, special conditions and restrictions, for the protection, enhancement, perpetuation, and use of places, districts, sites, buildings, structures, works of art, and other objects having a special character or a special historical or aesthetic interest or value." This statute has been used by New York cities and towns to protect significant properties and to exercise architectural controls over them. The enabling statute also provides that if controls constitute a taking of private property, such measures shall provide for "due compensation, which may include the limitation or remission of taxes."[9]

Problems with Conservation Strategies

Several problems arise when the various conservation strategies are actually practiced.

1. *Unevenness of property tax jurisdictions.* As has been indicated, the hydraulic and amputation relief strategies mean either an increased burden for nonqualifying taxpayers or revenue lost to the taxing jurisdiction. But jurisdictions with little change in land use, either because they are fairly well developed or because they are not currently subject to development pressure, suffer (and benefit) little from the effects of relief strategies. To assist those jurisdictions losing revenue from tax-relief measures, a bill was introduced in the Vermont legislature in 1975 to achieve a "circuit-breaker" effect on the municipal, but not the personal level. Each jurisdiction would set a maximum tax appraisal of 20 percent of the fair market value for "conservation land, farmland, forest land and homestead open land." Jurisdictions would then qualify for payments from the general state treasury so that the towns hardest hit (in terms of the percentage of taxes lost) would qualify for the most revenue. A complex formula was part of the scheme, but the aim was to equalize the relative tax income among jurisdictions when the process was complete.[10]

2. *Unrefusable offers.* Tax strategies that avoid the distress sale can fail to forestall a change in land use unless they address the problem of the unrefusable offer, which if accepted will cause an undesirable change of use. There are a variety of ways to approach this problem. First, freezing the use can obviate the unrefusable offer. Schemes that reduce value by regulation, by condemnation or by agreements granting easements can accomplish the same ends. The problem is that these approaches require either voluntary action by the landowner, compensatory payments or potentially unconstitutionally severe regulations by the government. In the latter category, some question exists about how much zoning actually freezes land uses, given the number of rezoning applications and variances approved.

Land value increment taxation is a second method to deter the unrefusable offer.[11] In 1973, Vermont enacted the Land Gains Tax, a special tax on gain derived from short-term sales of land.[12] This real estate transfer tax is collected by withholding at the time of sale and is measured by the extent of the seller's gain and the length of the holding period. For example, the tax rate could be as high as 60 percent if the seller earns a 200 percent profit and the sale occurs within a year of the seller's acquisition. The rate, however, decreases on a straight-line basis until the property has been held for seven years, at which point no tax is due. Gain from the sale of up to 10 acres of land is exempt if the property constitutes all or part of a primary residence or if it is sold to a purchaser who promises to build and occupy a structure as a principal residence within two years of acquisition. Most transfers resulting in no gain for federal income tax purposes are also exempt. The tax in general follows federal basis rules, although Vermont elected not to follow recent changes in federal tax law and retained a stepped-up basis at death.

The effects of the Vermont tax have not been studied empirically, although research is continuing. However, some potential purchasers of properties may withdraw from the market or deflate the prices they offer because they would be subject to the tax on resale after changing the land use intensity that produced much of the increase in land value. In Vermont the deterrent is more severe for subdividers than for builders because gain allocable to "buildings or other structures" is exempt. Similarly, some present short-term property owners may elect to postpone sales that would subject them to the tax.

A land value increment tax has also recently been applied to an urban residential jurisdiction, the District of Columbia, which has enacted a stiff gains tax on sales of non-owner-occupied residential property in order to discourage speculation in areas undergoing development and rehabilitation pressures.[13] Modifications of the Vermont scheme have also been proposed in Montana, Washington and Oregon. Related land value increment taxation is now in force in Ontario, Canada; New Zealand and Great Britain.[14]

Recapturing of long-term ill-gotten gains is a third approach to divert unrefusable offers. The Vermont Land Gains Tax includes some recapture of profits from short-term property owners. What about the long-term seller-owner? Many jurisdictions provide that conservation properties are subject to a tax upon sale that recaptures either some or all of the taxes abated, plus interest, if the use is changed.[15] Even so, the prospective purchaser's offer may still be too good to resist. Nonetheless, this method offers a way of making the tax shift seem less horizontal (i.e., to other property owners) and more vertical (i.e., to the current beneficiary sometime in the future).

3. *Tax windfalls.* Since most conservation strategies are use oriented, they may offer tax windfalls to wealthy owners of conservation properties or to owners of properties that are not subject to development pressure.[16] For example, the conservation tax programs of New Jersey and California have been criticized as providing investors who are not yet ready to develop properties with tax incentives to retain ownership until developing the land is financially advantageous.

4. *Colliding exemption strategies.* Imagine a municipality that has at its center a small historic district and is surrounded by unbroken green space. Busily at work in the legislature are advocates of both historic preservation and open space preservation. Each group achieves the object of its desire—property tax relief. Imagine the delight of the residents and property owners who do not live in old houses or on farms when they find out they have to assume the additional tax burden. Imagine tar and feathers for the environmental movement.

5. *Enhancement problems.* Alternatively, what if the aim is not conservation but a change in use, an enhancement, and the goal is to foster such a change using the tax system? Aside from the continuing discussion of site-value taxation, can tax exemptions offer an incentive for change in use or property improvement?

One method is to exempt, for a specified period, taxes attributable to renovation improvements. Several jurisdictions have adopted this type of exemption.[17] Another example of the use of taxation to enhance existing structures may be found in the Village of Great Neck Plaza, N.Y. In 1976 the village adopted an unusual zoning ordinance amendment that allowed the establishment of special "design districts" in the village, which would be subject to a "design development plan." The plan would describe in detail a scheme for

133

upgrading the appearance of all the properties in the district, with the benefits of each owner's investment reinforcing those of neighbors. In addition, the plan would require similar upgrading by the village of adjacent streets, sidewalks and other public areas. The village could then forego special assessments on property owners subject to the design development plan for all or part of this public improvement cost. This benefit would serve as an incentive for participation (or compensation for acquiescence) of property owners in the requirements of the plan, which would have to be met by all owners within a prescribed period.[18]

6. *Increased federal income tax.* Since property taxes constitute a deduction against federal income taxes, any tax abatement often means a lesser, but corresponding increase in federal taxes, partially offsetting the "benefits" of relief. This consideration is apart from the relative importance individual property owners may attach to federal, as opposed to state, tax considerations in planning their conduct.

7. *Constitutional issues.* Many state constitutions require taxes to be uniform upon the same class of subjects. To the extent that conservation tax relief violates these provisions it may be vulnerable.[19]

Arguably more vulnerable constitutionally might be land value increment taxation, which in the case of the Vermont Land Gains Tax included several specific exemptions and different tax rates. Nonetheless, the Vermont tax was upheld, primarily against an "equal protection of the laws" attack.[20] The Vermont Supreme Court viewed the equalization provisions of the Vermont constitution as essentially equivalent to those of the Fourteenth Amendment to the United States Constitution. Whether such a tax would survive a similar attack in a stricter jurisdiction is uncertain unless the tax were viewed as an excise, rather than a property, tax.

Considerations for Drafting Legislation

It may be difficult to draw lessons from open space conservation that will be directly applicable in the preservation of historic structures, but the following thoughts are offered for consideration during the drafting of legislation.

1. While focusing on tax relief, it is important not to forget the other significant factors that may affect a landowner's decision, such as an unrefusable offer or federal tax considerations.

2. It is helpful to recall that laws function like ecosystems; an intervention can produce unanticipated spillover effects. For example, a taxation scheme may deter enhancement yet promote conservation. Alternatively, taxation may deter important new construction, such as structures designed to utilize renewable energy sources such as wind and sunshine.

3. Within restrictions imposed by federal interstate commerce, by preemption and by equal protection constitutional restrictions, are there tax devices that states can enact to counter the anticonservation effects of federal taxation?

Finally, we are all only life tenants of this planet and are responsible to future generations for any waste we commit. This waste can include allowing our built environment to deteriorate or building on natural areas that should be preserved. Perhaps carefully drawn state tax devices can help avoid both.

134

NOTES

1. For general background on taxation and land-use control, see Hagman, *Urban Planning and Land Development Control Law* 345-69 (1971); *Urban Land Use Policy* 207-76 (Andrews, ed.)

(1972); Bab, "Taxation and Land Use Planning," 10 *Willamette Law Journal* 439 (1974); Currier, "Exploring the Role of Taxation in the Land Use Planning Process," 51 *Indiana Law Journal* 27 (1975); Delogu, "The Taxing Power as a Land Use Control Device," 45 *Denver Law Journal* 279 (1968); Zimmerman, "Tax Planning for Land Use Control," 5 *Urban Lawyer* 639 (1973) (hereafter cited as "Tax Planning").

For useful information on federal taxation in general, see Gurko, "Federal Income Taxes and Urban Sprawl," 48 *Denver Law Journal* 329 (1972). On the specific issue of federal taxation as a means of land conservation, see Browne and Van Dorn, "Charitable Gifts of Partial Interests in Real Property for Conservation Purposes," 29 *Tax Lawyer* 69 (1975); Browne, "Open Space and Estate Planning," *Trusts and Estates* (1976); K. Browne, ed., *Case Studies in Land Conservation* (Boston: New England Natural Resources Center, 1975-76). These case studies describe ways in which attorneys assisted their clients in preserving land through federal tax devices and are available for a nominal charge from the New England Natural Resources Center, 3 Joy Street, Boston, Mass. 02108.

Much of the discussion of property taxation impact on land use has focused on the issue of agricultural preservation. The Council on Environmental Quality has published a study of preferential assessment, *Untaxing Open Space,* which contains an extensive bibliography related to this area. Of additional interest is R.J. Gloudemans, *Use-Value Farmland Assessments: Theory, Practice, and Impact* (Chicago: International Association of Assessing Officers, 1974); see also Hagman, "Open Space Planning and Property Taxation: Some Suggestions," 1964 *Wisconsin Law Review* 628 (hereafter cited as "Open Space Planning"); and note, "Property Taxation of Agricultural and Open Space Land," 8 *Harvard Journal of Legislation* 158 (1970) (hereafter cited as "Property Taxation"). For a discussion of site-value taxation see Hagman, "The Single Tax and Land Use Planning: Henry George Updated," 12 *U.C.L.A. Law Review* 762 (1965); and note, "Site Value Taxation: Economic Incentives in Land Use Planning," 9 *Harvard Journal of Legislation* 115 (1971).

2. Massachusetts has passed a statute allowing local assessors to choose among one of the three alternative methods of property evaluation. See 1975 *Mass. Acts,* ch. 853.

3. The issue of when a tax can constitute an unconstitutional taking of private property without just compensation is explored in R.L. Baker, "Controlling Land Uses and Prices by Using Special Gain Taxation to Intervene in the Land Market: The Vermont Experiment," 4 *Environmental Affairs* 427 (1975) (hereafter cited as "Controlling Land Uses").

4. "Expenditure rises to meet income," set out in C.N. Parkinson, *The Law and the Profits* (Boston: Houghton Mifflin, 1960).

5. See discussion of preferential assessment in note 1.

6. See *Kamrowski v. State,* 31 Wis.2d 265. 142 N.W.2d 793 (1966).

7. See for example, "The Williamson Act," *Cal. Gov't. Code* § 51240-54 (West Supp. 1975); "Property Taxation," note 1 above, at 163, 174-79; "Tax Planning," note 1 above, at 660.

8. 1973 Vt. Acts No. 81 "Property Tax Circuit-Breakers," 3 *People and Taxes* No. 12 at 6 (December 1975); T. Hady and A. Sibold, "Property Tax Relief for Farmers: New Use for Circuit-Breakers," at 1 (Advisory Commission on Intergovernmental Relations, Information Bulletin No. 74-78) (1974).

9. *N.Y. Gen. Mun. Law* § 96-a (McKinney 1977).

10. See McGee, Mesches, and Johnson, "Property Taxes on Open Space Land in Vermont: A Study of the Practical Impact of Implementing House Bill 134" (Submitted to Tax Commissioner's Office, Agency of Administration, Montpelier, Vt., Sept. 5, 1975.)

11. "Controlling Land Uses," note 3 above; Harvith, "Subdivision Dedication Requirements and Alternatives: A Special Tax on Gain from Realty," 33 *Albany Law Review* 474 (1969); note, "State Taxation—Use of Taxing Power to Achieve Environmental Goals: Vermont Taxes Gains Realized from the Sale or Exchange of Land Held Less Than Six Years," 49 *Washington Law Review* 1159 (1974).

12. See *Vt. Stat. Ann.* §§ 10001-10.

13. "Residential Real Property Transfer Excise Tax of 1978," D.C. Law 2-91, effective July 13, 1978.

14. See "Controlling Land Uses," note 3 above.

15. See, for example, *Minn. Stat. Ann.* § 273.111(9) (West 1969); *Va. Code* § 258-769 (Supp. 1973); *Cal. Gov't Code* § 51283 (West Supp. 1975); *Mass Gen. Laws Ann.,* ch. 61A, § 12, 13 (West 1973); *Id.,* ch. 87, § 8 (West 1970); *Wash. Laws 2d Ex. Sess.* 705 (effective Jan. 1, 1971).

16. 3 *People and Taxes* No. 2 at 8 (February 1975).

17. See, for example, *Colo. Rev. Stat.* § 39-5-105; *Ill. Rev. Stat.,* ch. 120, § 500.23-3.

18. See Baker, "Enhancing the Visual Environment of the Twilight Commercial Zone: The Great Neck Plaza Experiment," 2 *Harvard Environmental Law Review* 389 (1977).

19. *Andrews v. Lathrop,* 315 A.2d 860 (1974).

20. See, generally, Newhouse, *Constitutional Uniformity and Equality in State Taxation* 603, 605-06 (1959). State constitutional provisions requiring uniformity and equality in taxation may determine what type of taxation alternative can be adopted. Statutes allowing for differential assessments of agricultural lands were struck down as being in violation of the uniformity clause in *Boyne v. State,* 80 Nev. 160, 390 P.2d 226 (1965), a statute allowing an owner of agricultural land to enter into a contract with an assessor for payment of taxes at value of land for agricultural use when value for other uses was higher; *Gottlieb v. City of Milwaukee,* 33 Wis.2d 408, 147 N.W.2d 633 (1967), statute allowing partial exemption for lands held by a redevelopment corporation; *State Tax Commission v. Wakefield,* 222 Md. 541, 161 A.2d 676 (1960), a statute allowing assessment of agricultural lands at use value. As indicated in Hagman, "Open Space Planning," note 1 above at 638-45, however, conflict with these constitutional provisions might be avoided by use of a general directive ordering assessors to presume that the application of a land-use control to a parcel of property is permanent in the absence of clear proof to the contrary and by subsequent enactment of a use restriction on the land.

Alexander Garvin

NEW YORK CITY'S J-51:
THE PROGRAM THAT RESTORED 700,000 APARTMENTS

Show a dilapidated building to a preservationist and you get an instant response: Rehabilitate! There then ensues a discussion of the quality of the building's design, the soundness of its structure, the life expectancy of its subsystems (heating, plumbing, wiring), the utility of its layout, the condition of finishes. . . . It's all physical. And it misses the point. There is no building that cannot be rehabilitated if you can pay for it.

Show the same building to an accountant and you hear: Tear it down. It has outlived its "useful" life. This too misses the point. Surely Chartres Cathedral ought not to be replaced because after more than 750 years it is a depreciated asset.

If we are to understand obsolescence we must get beyond both the preservationist's purely physical perspective and the accountant's purely fiscal approach. Obsolescence is a process that comes in two principal forms: economic and functional.

Economic obsolescence is caused by a change in demand usually as a result of changes in the size of the market area, the spendable income of that market or its spending patterns. This change can be both upward and downward. For example, if fewer households are willing or able to pay the price of maintaining a one-family townhouse it becomes economically obsolete and may be turned into a rooming house for which there is adequate demand. On the other hand, if young professionals in increasing numbers desire to live in older row-house neighborhoods they may price out the rooming houses.

Functional obsolescence occurs when a structure or location is no longer suited to its present use or when that use is no longer in demand. This process also goes in both directions. Warehouses that once were much in demand because of proximity to the waterfront may fall into disuse because shipping today demands huge port facilities that can accommodate container-truck cargoes. Later, the warehouses may again become desirable as the linchpin of bustling retail centers that attract tourists because of the historical seaport atmosphere.

If we are to preserve our valuable cultural patrimony we must understand these forms of obsolescence and find ways to intervene that either lower the cost of supply or increase the demand. Because it is unlikely that either local government or the federal government will artificially increase demand by paying people or businesses that use obsolete structures we must focus on the supply side.

In estimating rehabilitation costs a property owner must consider four items: profit, operating and maintenance expenses, debt service and real estate taxes.

Mr. Garvin is director, Office of Comprehensive Planning, Department of City Planning, City of New York.

Government cannot encourage restoration by reducing profit. Moreover, only when profit reaches a high enough level will a property owner consider reducing his price. Neither can there be preservation if operating and maintenance expenditures are reduced. This will only increase deterioration. But government can beneficially help to lower debt service and real estate taxes. Government can insure bank mortgages for preservation, encourage a lengthening of the term of amortization, subsidize interest rates or make outright grants to reduce debt service. There are public and private revolving preservation loan programs around the country. However, subsidized lending does not seem something government is about to support on a volume basis. That leaves real estate taxes.

The J-51 Program

New York City has a real estate tax incentive program that has worked on a volume basis to encourage the rehabilitation of more than 700,000 existing multiple dwellings. This program, called J-51 after its section number in the city's administrative code, was enacted in 1955. It originally provided tax incentives only for the elimination of unhealthy or unsafe housing conditions in tenements. Over the years, however, its scope was gradually expanded to include general upgrading (e.g., the replacement of plumbing, wiring, windows, heating systems, etc.) as well as the conversion of hotels, rooming houses and nonresidential space to multiple dwellings. Certain condominiums and cooperatives also have been made eligible for benefits under the program.

J-51 provides two kinds of benefits for eligible buildings—tax exemption and tax abatement. First, the program permits a 12-year exemption from any increase in tax resulting from improvements to the property. Thus, a property owner is not punished for improving his or her building by an increased real estate tax assessment. Second, it permits the abatement of property taxes equaling up to 90 percent of the reasonable construction costs for the improvement. The government, in effect, refunds 90 cents on every dollar spent on restoration. A limit of $8\frac{1}{3}$ percent of the certified reasonable cost of rehabilitation may be deducted from the property's real estate tax bill each year until the abatement is exhausted or 20 years pass, whichever is shorter (see examples on following pages).

138

To be eligible for J-51 benefits the building must comply with all building, zoning and safety laws, and all real estate, water and sewage taxes must be current. After construction is completed the building must be subject to rent control, rent stabilization or some other form of government rent regulation.

Two elements make J-51 effective: its certainty and its non-discretionary character. The law provides the certainty that any multiple dwelling that meets the requirements of the law will get benefits. Thus, banks are prepared to issue mortgages and developers are willing to risk their equity. Were the program not a non-discretionary guaranteed benefit, investors might be faced with an array of bureaucrats (perhaps highly skilled) whose review and approval could be subject to political pressure and graft.

Program Performance

The J-51 program has produced a number of benefits that are important to New York City. Most significant has been the program's ability to stimulate housing rehabilitation. Between 1961 and 1978, 19,000 buildings containing some 670,000 units have participated in the J-51 program. This number accounts for more than 35 percent of all private multiple dwelling units in the city and 55 percent of all such units built before World War II, the category of housing most frequently in need of J-51-type renovation. During the single program year of 1977-78, more than 48,000 units received benefits. In addition, through the program's conversion provisions, approximately 3,500 new

PROPERTIES RECEIVING J-51 BENEFITS IN 1977-78

	BUILDINGS	UNITS	DOLLARS
Major capital improvements and moderate rehabilitation	721	41,196	$10,521,700
Gut rehabilitation (residential)	169	3,532	22,246,400
Hotel conversion	49	1,671	11,894,700
Commercial conversion	33	1,593	24,257,500
Manufacturing conversion	8	169	2,468,200
TOTAL	980	48,161	$71,388,500

units were added to New York City's housing stock in 1977-78, a number particularly significant in light of the city's low level of new construction and its high rate of housing abandonment.

The work performed under the J-51 program falls into five general categories of activity:

1. *Major capital improvements*—the upgrading or replacement of a major building system, such as the installation of bathrooms, modernization of heating systems, roofing and wiring.

2. *Moderate rehabilitation*—the replacement and repair of building systems and the modernization of apartment interiors. This level of work is done with the building's tenants in occupancy.

(These two categories account for the great majority of activity taking place under the J-51 program. In 1977-78, for example, more than 41,000 apartments, or 85 percent of all units that qualified for the program that year, received either major capital improvements or underwent moderate rehabilitation.)

3. *Gut rehabilitation of multiple dwellings*—the complete renovation of a structure, during which everything but the building's foundation, its exterior walls and its main structural system is replaced. In 1977-78, more than 3,500 units, or 7 percent of all J-51 apartments, underwent gut rehabilitation.

4. *Hotel and single-room occupancy*—the conversion of a class B multiple dwelling, whose units are occupied on a transient or rooming house basis and/or are not separate self-contained apartments, to a class A multiple residential dwelling, whose units are intended for permanent residence and have their own bathroom and kitchen facilities. In 1977-78, 1,700 units, accounting for 4 percent of all J-51 activity in that year, were created through the conversion of hotels and single room occupancy units.

5. *Commercial and industrial conversions*—the conversion of nonresidential buildings such as lofts, offices, factories and warehouses to class A multiple dwellings. In 1977-78 about 1,800 units, accounting for 4 percent of the J-51 activity, were added to the city's housing stock through such conversions.

Another important benefit of the J-51 program is its ability to generate employment in New York City. The dollar value of rehabilitation costs certified under the program is a useful measure of the number of construction jobs it has created. A recent study of the J-51 program by New York's Citizens Budget Commission estimated that every $3 million in construction costs produced 100-150 jobs for a period of nine months. If this estimate is applied to $100 million* in construction receiving J-51 benefits, the resulting number of construction jobs ranges from 3,400-5,000. These numbers, moreover, do not include any indirect multiplier effect in construction-related industries.

139

The "certified reasonable cost" of renovation is usually about two-thirds of the actual cost of construction because some items are not eligible for benefits or exceed the allowable cost.

Beyond augmenting the city's stock of sound housing units and producing construction jobs, the J-51 program also has a direct impact on the city's tax base. While the city may initially lose tax revenues, it eventually will regain and even increase tax revenues as the exemptions and abatements expire. Also, since the average J-51 building's assessed valuation increases by approximately 12 percent after renovation (in the case of gut rehabilitation and conversions the assessments multiply several fold), the benefits that eventually will accrue to the city as a result of the program are considerable.

Moreover, this comparison does not take into account the positive, although indirect, impact that J-51 has on the city's tax base. First, there can be no question that the program has succeeded in reducing property tax arrearages in New York City. In order to qualify for J-51 benefits, both real estate taxes and water charges must be current. Many properties that are bought by developers for rehabilitation or conversion are several years delinquent in taxes. Through J-51 the city gains revenues by collecting back taxes that it would otherwise be unlikely to receive. In the same way, the prospect of future sales of older structures for renovation or conversion has encouraged many building owners to hold on to their properties and to continue to pay taxes in anticipation of sales.

There are other revenue-raising aspects of the J-51 program, but because

---

MAJOR CAPITAL IMPROVEMENT

Property: 24-unit, four-story walk-up
Pre-improvement assessed value: $60,000 (there is no increase in assessment in this case because of the small investment involved)
City-issued certificate of reasonable cost: $15,000
Post-improvement assessed value: $450,000
Assumed tax rate for duration of J-51 benefits: $8.775 for each $100

Year	Tax without exemption or abatement	Tax after exemption, before abatement	Tax abatement	Final tax bill
1	$5,265	$5,265	$1,250	$4,015
2	5,265	5,265	1,250	4,015
3	5,265	5,265	1,250	4,015
4	5,265	5,265	1,250	4,015
5	5,265	5,265	1,250	4,015
6	5,265	5,265	1,250	4,015
7	5,265	5,265	1,250	4,015
8	5,265	5,265	1,250	4,015
9	5,265	5,265	1,250	4,015
10	5,265	5,265	1,250	4,015
11	5,265	5,265	1,000	4,265
12	5,265	5,265	0	5,265
13	5,265	5,265	0	5,265
14	5,265	5,265	0	5,265
15	5,265	5,265	0	5,265
16	5,265	5,265	0	5,265
17	5,265	5,265	0	5,265
18	5,265	5,265	0	5,265
19	5,265	5,265	0	5,265
20	5,265	5,265	0	5,265

Source: N.Y.C. Department of Housing Preservation and Development

they are more indirect their benefits cannot be calculated easily. For example, the program has generated an estimated $515 million in construction costs since its inception in 1955. Furthermore, J-51 projects work to enhance the viability of surrounding properties and to encourage their owners to maintain and upgrade them. Clearly, the program has helped to reverse the process of neighborhood decline in such areas of Manhattan as Chelsea and the Upper West Side, where brownstone renovations are common; SoHo, where loft conversion has become increasingly popular; and Washington Heights, where more than 4,000 apartments received J-51 benefits during 1976-77. Finally, a new residential development that results from the J-51 conversion provision also stimulates investments in supporting commercial development, which in turn produces more tax revenues for the city.

Program Evaluation

A production level of 48,000 dwelling units in one year, 1977-78, is indeed dramatic. Few programs can match this level of effectiveness. J-51 is also an efficient program. Because the basic requirement for benefits is a legal certificate of occupancy on a completed violation-free renovation, the program costs very little to run. It is managed by two professionals, two clerks and the services of the city's housing inspection staff. This is an extremely low personnel cost for an annual housing investment of more than $100 million. The program

---

MODERATE REHABILITATION

Property: 19-unit, four-story walk-up
Pre-improvement assessed value: $46,000
City-issued certificate of reasonable cost: $85,000
Post-improvement assessed value: $102,000
Assumed tax rate for duration of J-51 benefits: $8.775 for each $100

Year	Tax without exemption or abatement	Tax after exemption, before abatement	Tax abatement	Final tax bill
1	$8,951	$4,037	$4,037	$0
2	8,951	4,037	4,037	0
3	8,951	4,037	4,037	0
4	8,951	4,037	4,037	0
5	8,951	4,037	4,037	0
6	8,951	4,037	4,037	0
7	8,951	4,037	4,037	0
8	8,951	4,037	4,037	0
9	8,951	4,037	4,037	0
10	8,951	4,037	4,037	0
11	8,951	4,037	4,037	0
12	8,951	4,037	4,037	0
13	8,951	8,951	7,081	1,870
14	8,951	8,951	7,081	1,870
15	8,951	8,951	7,081	1,870
16	8,951	8,951	6,813	2,138
17	8,951	8,951	0	8,951
18	8,951	8,951	0	8,951
19	8,951	8,951	0	8,951
20	8,951	8,951	0	8,951

Source: N.Y.C. Department of Housing Preservation and Development.

is also the most equitable of government housing interventions because all multiple dwellings in New York City are eligible and all buildings receive the same benefits.

Perhaps the most intriguing aspect of J-51's cost effectiveness lies in the creation of new apartments through conversion from nonresidential use. There is a flaw in calculating development cost simply on the basis of the cost to a developer. New housing costs more than that. It requires municipal investment in an elaborate infrastructure of streets, sewers, water supply systems, utility lines, transportation systems and schools. When a new community, such as Co-op City or Roosevelt Island, is added to an existing city, the municipality must spend millions on this infrastructure. When an existing nonresidential building is converted to housing it usually requires minimal additional municipal investment because that infrastructure is already in place.

While J-51 is an extraordinarily effective, economical and equitable program, it is not a panacea. When benefits are not sufficient to reduce a building's rent to the fair market level, the owner will not renovate. Nor does J-51 necessarily provide housing for poor people. If, after receiving J-51 benefits, the building's rent still exceeds a poor person's pocketbook, the city will still be without an increase in its supply of low-income housing.

The lesson of J-51 is that preservation of older buildings can be and has been achieved on a massive level. It has been achieved because of government in-

---

GUT REHABILITATION

Property: 35-unit, six-story elevator building
Pre-improvement assessed value: $150,000
City-issued certificate of reasonable cost: $400,000
Post-improvement assessed value: $450,000
Assumed tax rate for duration of J-51 benefits: $8.775 for each $100

Year	Tax without exemption or abatement	Tax after exemption, before abatement	Tax abatement	Final tax bill
1	$39,488	$13,163	$13,163	$0
2	39,488	13,163	13,163	0
3	39,488	13,163	13,163	0
4	39,488	13,163	13,163	0
5	39,488	13,163	13,163	0
6	39,488	13,163	13,163	0
7	39,488	13,163	13,163	0
8	39,488	13,163	13,163	0
9	39,488	13,163	13,163	0
10	39,488	13,163	13,163	0
11	39,488	13,163	13,163	0
12	39,488	13,163	13,163	0
13	39,488	39,488	33,320	6,168
14	39,488	39,488	33,320	6,168
15	39,488	39,488	33,320	6,168
16	39,488	39,488	33,320	6,168
17	39,488	39,488	33,320	6,168
18	39,488	39,488	33,320	6,168
19	39,488	39,488	2,124	37,364
20	39,488	39,488	0	39,488

Source: N.Y.C. Department of Housing Preservation and Development

tervention that ignores the specific problems of individual structures and instead aims directly at the economics of obsolescence.

Real estate tax exemption and abatement, whether following the specifics of J-51 or not ought to be part of every local preservationist's arsenal. Because many municipalities may be reticent about foregoing local taxes, even for so worthy a goal as housing preservation, I would propose that the federal government assume this burden and agree to reimburse municipalities for the annual cost of local tax exemption or abatement programs. Only then will we have any effective preservation effort on a national scale.

143

3. Tax Implications of Preservation Easements

Russell L. Brenneman and *Gregory E. Andrews*

PRESERVATION EASEMENTS AND THEIR TAX CONSEQUENCES

The subject of preservation easements and their tax consequences cannot be considered without defining at the outset what is meant by the word *easement*. In the context of this article a better term might be *recorded preservation agreement,* which carries better than does *easement* the concept of controls placed on property by an owner to assure its future for historic preservation purposes. It also suggests the bilateral character of the relationship in that there are two parties, the owner and another who has the right and perhaps the responsibility to enforce the control. Using the word easement brings in unnecessary and obsolete common law doctrines that can impede analysis of what this approach is intended to accomplish. Some statutes have abandoned the term entirely.[1] However, the nomenclature battle is byplay. Many people use the word easement to describe what others call a recorded preservation agreement; so long as everyone knows what is being discussed there is no real danger. When one looks closely at federal law on this point and at the regulations adopted by the Internal Revenue Service in connection with charitable contributions of this kind of interest, it may be helpful to stick closely to the term easement.

Kinds of Easements and Effect on Property Value

Easements for historic preservation have a variety of purposes. They may be scenic easements in the classical sense of providing controls to protect the visual amenities of a historic site.[2] They may be facade easements controlling the exterior physical features of a building or buildings.[3] They may govern interior features of buildings having historical or architectural significance.[4] They may combine several different purposes and in a single instrument protect a building or buildings and their surroundings.[5] The control may be imposed in a variety of forms, depending on the law and practice of the jurisdiction.

A key aspect of the tax implications of these easements is their effect on property values. Typically, an easement involves the surrender of some property right that an owner otherwise has, such as the right to modify a structure or use adjacent space in a way that would be harmful to the preservation of the historic site. The surrendered development right has a value. Its removal from the bundle of rights included within common law "title" should reduce the

Russell L. Brenneman is president of the Connecticut Resources Recovery Authority, Hartford, Conn. He serves as reporter for the Drafting Committee on the Uniform Conservation and Historic Preservation Agreements Act of the National Conference of Commissioners on Uniform State Laws. Mr. Andrews is an attorney in the Investment Division, Legal Department, Connecticut General Life Insurance Company, Bloomfield, Conn., and was formerly an attorney in the Office of Real Estate and Legal Services, National Trust for Historic Preservation.

value of the remaining rights in the bundle, at least in the abstract. Under federal income, gift and estate tax laws allowing deductions for charitable contributions of real property, one would think that the surrender of a valuable development right would support such a deduction. Under local laws that tax owners on the value of property, one would think that the reduction in value caused by the removal of the development right would be reflected in the amount of the property tax. To some extent the tax laws do bring about this result. But the way that it is reached depends on highly technical and often complex provisions of specific laws, which must be looked at with care. In the case of federal tax laws, the effect of charitable contributions of easements has changed much within recent years and still remains in flux. A brief look at this history is essential, therefore, in understanding their present and future tax consequences.

Easement Donations under Pre-1969 Federal Law

A gift of property by its owner to certain entities described in the Internal Revenue Code (including units of government and certain charitable organizations) entitles the owner to a charitable contribution income tax deduction. The amount is generally equal to the fair market value of the donated property at the time of the gift. There are certain limitations on the amount of the deduction and also special rules applicable to certain kinds of property. Comparable rules also apply under federal estate and gift taxes. Before 1969 it was clear that the gift of an interest in real property that was less than the whole bundle of the owner's rights would entitle the owner to deduct the value of the interest donated even though the owner did not give the whole property.[6] Of particular importance to those interested in using easements to control land use was a 1964 Internal Revenue Service ruling holding that a taxpayer could deduct the value of a restrictive easement granted to the United States for the scenic protection of a highway even though the United States received no affirmative rights for public use.[7] In this instance, the restrictions included limitations on the height and kind of buildings that could be constructed on the property. They also dealt with removal of vegetation, erection of signs, dumping of trash and other such materials. The ruling noted that these negative controls were a valid property interest under the applicable local law. It established the deductibility of "scenic" easements for federal income tax purposes. However, the Tax Reform Act of 1969 was to alter that picture.[8]

Easements under the Tax Reform Act of 1969

Largely because of problems with charitable contributions having nothing to do with land conservation or preservation easements,[9] the Tax Reform Act of 1969 included a provision that is now part of section 170(f)(3) of the Internal Revenue Code. That section provides that no deduction shall be allowed for federal income tax purposes for gifts of less than the taxpayer's "entire interest" in the gift property.[10] The Tax Reform Act of 1969 allowed only two exceptions to this rule, neither of which would appear to apply to scenic or historic preservation easements: A taxpayer could deduct the value of the gift of a remainder interest in a personal residence or farm[11] and could deduct the value of "an undivided portion of the taxpayer's entire interest in property."[12] While this language did not on its face give heart to those interested in continuing the traditional deductibility of scenic easements, the Internal Revenue Service, and indeed the Congress itself, took a more expansive view.

The congressional conference report on the Tax Reform Act of 1969 observed that "an open space easement in gross is to be considered a gift of an undivided interest in property (and therefore tax deductible) where the easement is in perpetuity."[13] It was this slender reed that supported the regulations adopted by the Internal Revenue Service governing the deductibility of gifts of such property restrictions. These regulations provided that:

For this purpose an easement in gross is a mere personal interest in, or right to use, the land of another; it is not supported by a dominant estate but is attached to, and vested in, the person to whom it is granted. Thus, for example, a deduction is allowed under section 170 for the value of a restrictive easement gratuitously conveyed to the United States in perpetuity whereby the owner agrees to certain restrictions on the use of his property, such as restrictions on the type and height of buildings that may be erected, the removal of trees, the erection of utility lines, the dumping of trash, and the use of signs.[14]

Authoritative writers cautioned, in the light of this history, that "so fragile an exception may be narrowly and strictly construed and if relied upon should be closely adhered to."[15] The tax deductibility of facade easements on historic structures, in particular, seemed questionable and the utility of this attractive technique for historic preservation doubtful. However, perhaps the reed was not so insubstantial as it seemed.

To be deductible, the donated interest had to be (1) an open space, (2) easement, (3) in perpetuity and (4) in gross. It evidently had to have all of these characteristics to qualify.

Open Space Requirement

The requirement that it be an open space easement suggested problems for easements restricting solely the physical aspects of historic buildings, while clearly an easement of the classical "scenic" type, controlling the spaces surrounding buildings, would meet the test. However, a 1975 ruling specifically involving the preservation of a historic building demonstrated a willingness on the part of the Internal Revenue Service to be expansive in interpreting what constitutes an "open space" easement.[16] In this instance the owner of a mansion that had been designated a state historic landmark granted to the state an easement restricting the owner's right to subdivide, mine or industrially develop the property or to alter the appearance or modify the architectural characteristics of the building. The state was given the right to inspect the property to require compliance, but the owner retained all other rights of use and enjoyment. After reciting language appearing in earlier rulings, this ruling noted that the arrangement constituted a restrictive scenic easement: "Furthermore, the easement is an open space easement within the meaning of section 1.170A-7(b)(1)(ii) of the regulations."[17]

149

Easement Requirement

The requirement that the eligible interest must be an easement raised other interesting questions. The easement in gross might not be recognized by the substantive law of a particular state, and the preservation lawyer would strive to fit the property control being imposed into a recognized legal niche. Some states have enacted statutes that, while they validate easements for conservation and historic preservation purposes, create a new nomenclature for these controls with such terms as *conservation restriction* and *historic preservation restriction*.[18] These statutes in a sense create an entirely new interest in land. There is also advocacy for other terms, such as *recorded preservation agreement*.[19] Would departing from the precise nomenclature of the regulation result in a denial of the deduction? The pattern of the rulings gave reason to hope that the Internal Revenue Service would allow substance, rather than form, to be determinative.

In-Perpetuity Requirement

A deductible interest also had to be in perpetuity. This requirement raised additional questions. While under traditional common law both negative and affirmative easements could be created in perpetuity, the laws of some states require periodic re-recording on the land records by the holder of the easement if it is to continue viable. In addition, such interests may be terminated by a variety of events, such as a release by the easement holder or merger of title.

The federal regulations specifically provided that a deduction would not be disallowed, on the ground that the interest is not in perpetuity, merely because it might be defeated by a later event or act if at the time of the gift "it appears that the possibility that such act or event will occur is so remote as to be negligible."[20] Did the possibility that the holder would fail to re-record meet that standard? The Internal Revenue Code regulations and rulings were silent on the point.

In-Gross Requirement

The requirement that a deductible easement be in gross has been charitably described as "perplexing."[21] The words were included, perhaps inadvertently, in the conference report on the 1969 Tax Reform Act; they were echoed in the IRS regulations and subsequent rulings. However, there would appear to be no sound tax policy for making the distinction suggested by these words. Under the law of some states, easements in gross simply do not exist conceptually,[22] and the law of other states, particularly regarding the assignability of such interests, is not at all settled.[23] This suggests to the careful legal practitioner that the transaction should be constructed to avoid the in-gross problem by creating either an appurtenant easement or by using a legal device that accomplishes the same end but avoids using an easement. However, by following a course that makes sense from the substantive law standpoint, it was possible to step outside the literal terms of the regulation. Yet the Internal Revenue Service might have ruled that the deductibility of an appurtenant easement follows a fortiori from the allowance of a deduction for an in-gross interest. This is a sensible and practical approach because appurtenant easements have always been considered by the U.S. legal system to have greater substance and probably are more valuable than easements in gross.[24]

The Internal Revenue Service generally was supportive of conservation and historic preservation in interpreting its regulations. All rulings on this point favored the taxpayer. As has been noted, neither the one ruling involving a historic preservation easement[25] nor others in analogous cases narrowly construed the open space requirement. The gift of an easement granting a right-of-way along an owner's property to be used by a donee charity for hiking and skiing purposes, in which the owner covenanted not to use the easement area for any purpose inconsistent with the grant, resulted in an approved deduction in a ruling that makes no distinction between affirmative and negative rights.[26] Another taxpayer owner was also successful, in a published ruling, in claiming a deduction where he granted a public agency 50 acres of vacant beachfront property to be used as a bathing beach and recreational area. The owner retained the mineral rights and also the right to have access over the easement property from open water to other land retained by him. The Internal Revenue Service ruled that the easement constituted an open space easement whose value was deductible under the regulations.[27]

Effects of the Tax Reform Act of 1976

Despite the Internal Revenue Service's generally supportive attitude toward conservation and historic preservation easements under the 1969 law and its regulations, concern about the deductibility of facade and scenic easements was responsible for efforts as early as 1972 to amend and clarify the law. A study by the President's Council on Environmental Quality and the U.S. Department of the Treasury was in large part responsible for the introduction in Congress that year of the proposed Environmental Protection Tax Act of 1972.[28] Congress enacted a revised form of that bill as part of the Tax Reform Act of 1976.[29] In addition to its innovative tax incentives for the preservation and rehabilitation of commercial and other income-producing historic structures,[30] section 2124 of this act considerably clarified the availability of tax deductions for preservation easements by adding a new section 170(f)(3)(B)(iii) to the Internal Revenue Code.[31]

This new provision recognized the deductibility of a charitable gift to a governmental or nonprofit organization of a lease, option to purchase or easement with respect to real property of not less than 30 years duration, or of a remainder interest in real property. This tax deduction is available for income, estate and gift tax purposes.[32] To qualify for the tax deduction, the grant of the property interest must be made exclusively for "conservation purposes." Section 170(f)(3)(C) defines conservation purposes as (1) the preservation of land areas for public outdoor recreation or education, or scenic enjoyment; (2) the preservation of historically important land areas or structures; or (3) the protection of natural environmental systems.

This 1976 amendment, and particularly the definition of "conservation purposes," clearly assures the tax deductibility of historic preservation easements. Qualifying easements need no longer be for "open space" purposes and "in gross." Donations of leases, options to purchase and otherwise qualifying remainder interests in any kind of real property, whether commercial or industrial, in addition to the previously recognized donations of remainder interests in personal residences or farms, are all now tax deductible and may be useful tools for historic preservation.

It is important to note, however, that the 1969 easement law and its accompanying regulations remain in effect. The 1976 provisions amend the earlier law but do not repeal it. Two bases for justifying tax deductions for preservation easements, therefore, now exist—the 1976 law, which is clearly stated, and the 1969 law, which is much less so.

1977 Amendment

The primary reason that the confusing 1969 provision was not repealed was that all of the historic preservation tax incentives in section 2124 of the Tax Reform Act of 1976 were enacted on a five-year trial basis and were intended to expire in 1981. The provisions affecting easements, however, were mistakenly written to apply only to contributions or transfers made before June 14, 1977. The Tax Reduction and Simplification Act of 1977 corrected this error and extended the life of the easements provision to 1981.[33] Unless Congress extends this provision beyond 1981, it will expire and the 1969 easements law and regulations will again be the sole legal basis for easement tax deductions.

Another result of the 1977 act was the reinstatement of the requirement that qualifying contributions of easements must be perpetual, rather than at least 30 years in duration.[34] The reasons for this latter change are not clear. Legislative history on this amendment is nonexistent. According to one commentator, the Treasury Department and the natural conservation community each objected to the 30-year provision and were among the prime backers of the change.[35]

Historic preservationists continue to be troubled by this reinstated requirement of perpetuity for several reasons in addition to those already discussed. Perpetual easements may effectively serve the purpose of natural conservation, which is to preserve forever land and other natural resources in a stable, static and ideally undeveloped state, but they do not necessarily best serve the goals of historic preservation. Significant structures should be preserved and protected, particularly when threatened with adverse change, but historic preservationists recognize that they change and deteriorate over time. It may not be possible to assure their preservation forever, at least not without unreasonable cost. In addition, a structure now thought significant may not be so at some future date. Development of the land on which these structures are situated in conjunction with, or in place of, the original structure itself, consequently may be reasonable at some future date. A perpetual easement in such a case, by imposing indefinite requirements to preserve a structure in a static condition, may well not be an effective treatment for a historic property. Instead, term easements arguably can better serve the purposes of historic preservation by guaranteeing the present preservation and maintenance of a property and by providing for a reevaluation of the property's condition and the desirability of an easement for its protection upon the expiration of the initial easement.

Another consideration is that many owners of significant structures will agree to impose term easements, but not perpetual easements, on their properties. People generally are less willing to impose restrictions on the use and development of property once it has been built on than if the property is still undeveloped. In the latter case a kind of positive inviolability is present and affects people's attitudes.

Finally, the requirement of perpetuity makes little sense with respect to leases and options to purchase. Few, if any, property owners will grant perpetual leases, even with the incentive of a tax break, and even fewer will be willing to encumber their property indefinitely with perpetual options to purchase. Donations of leases and options to purchase make sense in this regard only if they may be granted for finite terms. It is interesting to observe that the original 1972 statutory proposals required no more than 15-year terms for these partial interests in order to make their donation tax deductible.[36]

Several other changes would be helpful to improve and clarify these statutory provisions, either through administrative rulings, regulations or revisions of the Internal Revenue Code itself. Permanent reenactment in 1981 of an amended form of the current 1976 easements law may serve this purpose. It should be determined specifically that the possibility of the termination of a charitable grant of a partial property interest through failure on the part of the donee to re-record it periodically on the land records, as is required in some states, would not cause the property interest to lapse during its given term. The definition of a deductible easement should be interpreted to include those transfers or contributions that have the same effect although they are called something else, such as a conservation restriction. The "conservation purposes" requirement in the code also needs clarification. It is uncertain, for example, on what basis properties will be found of sufficient historical importance to qualify for the deduction. The conference report of the Tax Reduction and Simplification Act of 1977 gives some guidance in the direction by stating that "conservation purposes" should be liberally construed.[37]

The expiration in 1981 of the 1976 easements provisions offers Congress the opportunity to examine and refine this area of the law. The 1976 provisions should be reenacted permanently with the changes and corrections noted, particularly the reinstatement of the deductibility of term historic preservation easements. Retention of the perpetuity requirement for natural conservation easements, however, is justified. In addition, as part of this reenactment the "partial interests" provision originating in 1969 should be repealed in order to avoid the duplication and confusion it has caused.

Value of Deduction for Easement Donations

The amount of the income, estate and gift tax deduction that may be claimed for the charitable contribution of a qualifying easement or partial interest in property is the difference between the value of the gift property prior to the gift and its value afterward.[38] The donor's loss of value is the measure; the value of the benefit to the donee charity is not material. The basis of the underlying fee title should be reduced by the same proportion as the value of the easement bears to the prior value of the fee.[39] The importance of highly reliable appraisal work is obvious. Whether there is a diminution in value and, if so, the amount of diminution require sophisticated judgment, particularly in the case of a historic preservation easement.[40]

Easement Donations under Local Property Tax

When one considers taxes levied on property based on its value to the owner, such as the local property tax, the other side of the coin is apparent. Transferring valuable development rights from the "bundle" should result in a diminished value for the remaining bundle. The resulting tax based on the value of the restricted property should also be reduced. This reasoning is reinforced by the common requirement under state laws that assessments be based on "actual" or "fair" value.[41] Such laws clearly require that the assessment reflect the actual value in the marketplace, a value reflecting whatever restrictions may apply to the use of the property.[42]

Cases involving land-use restrictions for conservation purposes illuminate the rule as properly applied to property that is subject to historic preservation easements. In *Lochmoor Club* v. *City of Grosse Pointe Woods*,[43] for example, the assessor ignored restrictive open space covenants on land owned by a country club and valued it at its full development potential as a residential subdivision. The court held that the assessor had erred because the property legally could not be used for the "highest and best use," which was the premise of the valuation. The Maryland case of *Supervisor of Assessments of Anne Arundel County* v. *Bay Ridge Properties, Inc.*,[44] involved the valuation of a beach that was encumbered by a restrictive covenant prohibiting the erection of buildings. Rights to use the beach had been granted to owners of adjacent developed lots. An attempt to assess the beach at its "development" value was struck down by the Maryland Tax Court and the Maryland Court of Appeals, the latter observing that the "combination of the grants of easements for the recreational use of the beach and the imposition of restrictions against disposition and improvements deprived the beach, as the servient estate, of whatever value it might otherwise have had."[45] Cases such as these have clear applicability to reductions in value resulting from grants of easements for historic preservation as well as conservation purposes.

A number of states have enacted laws specifically dealing with the impact of historic preservation easements on the valuation of property for tax purposes. While not often specific about the formula to be followed, the purpose of these laws is to provide for the reduction, abatement, retardation or exemption of local property taxes on land or buildings burdened by historic preservation easements. The largest group of these statutes provides that the existence of the historic preservation restriction shall be taken into account in valuing the underlying fee.[46] In Missouri, for example, assessors are exhorted to "take due account of and assess private property interests with due regard to the limitation of future use of the land."[47] While such laws may be said simply to call the attention of the authorities to the significance of these controls when assessing property, they may also provide a more precise basis for legal challenge if the assessor ignores them.

While the legal basis for assessments based on a recognition of the impact of a preservation or conservation restriction is clear and while the economic theory is impeccable, it must be noted that predicting specific results in a given case is unreliable. The valuation of easements used to control the future of property has provided a perplexing problem surrounded by too much folklore and too little data.[48] The Internal Revenue Service has provided impetus for a "before-and-after" rule that is only common sense.[49] As experience increases in the application of the rule, it is hoped that greater clarity will develop.

153

Conclusion

There is a growing interest in the use of easements, recorded property agreements and other such approaches to control the future of historic properties.[50] A significant aspect of these controls is that they allow the retention and use of the historic property for private purposes while surrendering to a public body or charitable organization certain rights that, if exercised by an owner, might be harmful to historical values. Tax policy can provide incentives for owners to establish such controls, either by providing tax deductions for their contribution or by diminishing property values for "property" tax purposes. The federal, estate and gift tax laws now allow a deduction for historic preservation easements granted for conservation purposes, including those controlling the environs of historic buildings. However, these laws expire in 1981 and must be reenacted in order to avoid a return to the confusion under the 1969 law surrounding "open space easements in gross in perpetuity." The existing law needs further clarification and should be amended to remove the requirement of perpetuity for historic preservation easements. Valuation of the easement and valuation of the underlying fee, which may represent two sides of the same problem, also remain critical to predicting the tax result of a given transaction.

NOTES

1. For example, New Hampshire and Connecticut: *Conn. Gen. Stat.* § 47-42a-c (1978); *N.H. Rev. Stat. Ann.*, § 477: 45-47 (Supp. 1977).

2. Brenneman, 3 *Should Easements Be Used to Protect National Historic Landmarks? A Study for the National Park Service*, document D-32 (James River, Va.) (hereafter cited as *Should Easements*).

3. *Id.*, document D-51 (Reynolds Tavern, Annapolis, Md.).

4. *Id.*, document D-50 (6 Water Street, Ipswich, Mass.).

5. *Id.*, document D-53 (Historic Green Springs, Va.).

6. Benjamin Klopp, 19 *Tax Court Memorandum Decisions* (CCH) 973 (1960).

7. Revenue Ruling 64-205, 1964-2 *Cumulative Bulletin* 62.

8. Public Law No. 91-172, 83 Stat. 642 (1969).

9. These concerns included the proper allowable deduction for the charitable donation of the fair market value of a property's use. H.R. Report No. 91-413 (Part I), 91st Cong., 1st Sess. 57-58 (1969) *S. Report No. 552,* 91st Cong., 1st Sess. (1969); see Mattie Fair, 27 *Tax Court of the United States Reports* 866 (1957).

10. Comparable provisions were added to the estate and gift tax laws. Internal Revenue Code of 1954, §§ 2055, 2522.

11. Internal Revenue Code § 170(f)(3)(B)(i).

12. Internal Revenue Code § 170(f)(3)(B)(ii).

13. H.R. Report No. 782, 91st Cong., 1st Sess. 294 (1969).

14. Treasury Reg. § 1.170(A)-7(b)(1)(ii).

15. Browne and Van Dorn, "Charitable Gifts of Partial Interests in Real Property for Conservation Purposes," 29 *The Tax Lawyer* 75 (Fall 1975) (hereafter cited as "Charitable Gifts").

16. Revenue Ruling 75-358, 1975-2 *Cumulative Bulletin* 76.

17. *Id.*

18. See *Conn. Gen. Stat.* § 47-42-a-c (1978); *N.H. Rev. Stat. Ann.* 477:45-47 (Supp. 1977); *Mass. Gen. Laws Ann.,* ch. 184, §§ 31-33 (Supp. 1978).

19. *Should Easements,* note 2 above, at 71b.

20. Treasury Reg. § 1.170A-7(a)(3).

21. "Charitable Gifts," note 15 above, at 78.

22. *Loch Sheldrake Associates* v. *Evans,* 306 N.Y. 297, 118 N.E. 2d 444 (1954).

23. Brenneman, *Private Approaches to the Preservation of Open Land* 28-32 (Washington, D.C.: Conservation and Research Foundation, 1967); Brenneman, "Techniques for Controlling the Surroundings of Historic Sites," 36 *Law & Contemporary Problems* 416, 417-20 (1971).

24. "Charitable Gifts," note 15 above, at 79.

25. Revenue Ruling 75-358, 1975-2 *Cumulative Bulletin* 76.

26. Revenue Ruling 74-583, 1974-2 *Cumulative Bulletin* 80.

27. Revenue Ruling 75-373, 1975-2 *Cumulative Bulletin* 77.

28. Environmental Protection Tax Bill, H.R. 5584, 93rd Cong., 1st Sess. (1973).

29. Public Law No. 94-455, 90 Stat. 1916 (1976).

30. Public Law No. 94-455, §§ 2124(a)-(d), 90 Stat. 1916 (1976) (codified in Internal Revenue Code sections 167(o), 167(n), 191 and 280B).

31. Public Law No. 94-455, § 2124(e), 90 Stat. 1916 (1976).

32. See also Internal Revenue Code §§ 2055(e)(2) (estate tax) and 2522(c)(2) (gift tax).

33. Public Law No. 95-30, § 309(a) (1977).

34. Public Law No. 95-30, § 309(a) (1977) (codified in Internal Revenue Code section 170(f)(3)(B)(iii)).

35. Small, "The Tax Treatment of the Donation of Easements in Scenic and Historic Property," 9 *Environmental Law Reporter* 50009 (1979).

36. See note 28.

37. H.R. Report No. 95-263, 95th Cong., 1st Sess. 30 (1977).

38. Revenue Ruling 76-376, 1976-2 *Cumulative Bulletin* 53; Revenue Ruling 73-339, 1973-2 *Cumulative Bulletin* 68.

39. Revenue Ruling 64-205, 1964-2 *Cumulative Bulletin* 62; Revenue Ruling 73-339, 1973-2 *Cumulative Bulletin* 68; Revenue Ruling 76-376, 1976-2 *Cumulative Bulletin* 53.

40. Some of the nuances are discussed in "Charitable Gifts," note 15 above, at 86-88.

41. See, e.g., *Mass. Gen. Laws Ann.*, ch. 59 § 38 (Supp. 1978) ("Fair cash valuation").

42. *Lodge* v. *Inhabitants of Swampscott*, 216 Mass. 260, 103 N.E. 635 (1913).

43. 3 Mich. App. 524, 143 N.W. 2d 177 (1966). See also *Lockmoor Club* v. *City of Grosse Pointe Woods*, 10 Mich. App. 394, 159 N.W. 2d 756 (1968).

44. 270 Md. 216, 310 A.2d 733 (1973). See *Simon Distributing Corp.* v. *Bay Ridge Civic Assoc.*, 207 Md. 472, 114 A.2d 829 (1955).

45. 310 A.2d at 776. The case relied on *Macht* v. *Department of Assessments of Baltimore City*, 266 Md. 602, 296 A.2d 162 (1972).

46. 1 *Should Easements*, note 2 above, at 96.

47. *Mo. Ann. Stat.* § 67.870-910 (Vernon Cum. Supp. 1974).

48. For some observations about the folklore, see Whyte, *The Last Landscape* 98-99 (Garden City, N.Y.: Doubleday & Co., Inc., 1968). Some data are set forth in Sutte and Cunningham, "Scenic Easements: Legal, Administrative and Valuation Problems and Procedures," 56 *National Cooperative Highway Research Program Report* 76-81 (1968); Jordahl, "Conservation and Scenic Easements: An Experience Resume," *Land Economics No. 4* 39 (1963); Olson, "Progress and Problems in Wisconsin's Scenic and Conservation Easement Program," 1965 *Wisconsin Law Review* 352 (1965).

49. Revenue Ruling 73-339, 1973-2 *Cumulative Bulletin* 68. An interesting application of the rule in another setting (valuation of an easement in gross for condemnation purposes) will be found in *Hartford National Bank and Trust Company* v. *Redevelopment Agency of the City of Bristol*, 164 Conn. 337, 321 A.2d 469 (1973).

50. Wolfe, "Conservation of Historical Buildings and Areas: Legal Techniques," *Real Estate in Midcentury* 981, 990 (Chicago: American Bar Association, 1974).

Fred C. Forberg

EASEMENTS AND THE RESPONSE OF
THE VIRGINIA DEPARTMENT OF TAXATION

The Virginia Outdoors Plan, enacted in 1966, served as the initial means to authorize state action in the conservation and preservation of open space. This legislation established both the Virginia Outdoors Foundation and the Virginia Historic Landmarks Commission.

The Virginia Open Space Land Act of 1966 provided for the permanent preservation of open space areas for park, recreational, historical, scenic, natural resources and other purposes through acquisition by purchase, gift, devise, bequest, grant or other transmittal of full title or of any partial interest or rights in real property to the state or any other public body. The 1966 act further required "where an interest in real property less than the fee is held by a public body for the purpose of this act, assessments made on the property for taxation shall reflect any change in the market value of the property which may result from the interest held by the public body" [*Va. Code Ann.* § 10.155 (1950)].

The Virginia Historic Landmarks Commission, an agency of the Commonwealth of Virginia, was authorized to acquire by purchase, gift or lease real property and "to administer registered landmarks, sites and easements and interest therein" [*Va. Code Ann.* § 10.138 (1950)]. The Virginia Outdoors Foundation was established to promote the preservation of open space land and to encourage gifts for inclusion in natural, scenic, historical, scientific and recreational areas. It is appropriate, then, to discuss the assistance rendered by the Virginia Department of Taxation to the Virginia Historic Landmarks Commission and the Virginia Outdoors Foundation and several local government units in the matter of evaluating open space easements.

Virginia Property Tax Structure

Fifty years have passed since the commonwealth of Virginia last levied a state property tax on real and tangible personal property. In 1928 these two taxable subjects were segregated for, and made subject to, local property taxation only. The general assembly was still authorized, however, to determine the manner and rates at which such property was to be assessed or reassessed. Until December 31, 1975, local government units appraised the fair market value of all property subject to taxation but applied a percentage factor to convert estimates of fair market value to an assessed or taxable value. All localities are required periodically to reassess. Since January 1, 1976, all annual and general reassessments must be made at 100 percent of fair market value. During the ensuing five years, fractional assessments in Virginia will be phased out. In the conversion process from fractional assessments to assessments at 100 percent of fair market value, certain statutory restraints have been placed on governing

---

Mr. Forberg is director, Division of Real Estate Appraisal and Mapping, Virginia Department of Taxation, Richmond, Va.

bodies to prevent the conversion process from producing windfall revenues.

While some localities provide for annual assessments and reassessments by professionally qualified assessors who are usually appointed and employed by the governing body, the vast preponderance of localities use assessors appointed from among the citizen freeholders of the assessment area to make general reassessments of real estate. The state government provides aid and assistance with the preparation of real property identification maps and card record systems, and professional appraisal assistance when requested by any locality. Assessments and reassessments between general or periodic reassessments are the responsibility of an elected local commissioner of revenue who also may call on the state for similar professional guidance or assistance. This service to the Virginia assessing officers had been provided for 20 years before the adoption of the Virginia Open Space Land Act. State and local personnel have enjoyed a fine working relationship and have grown accustomed to solving assessment problems together.

Open Space Easements

Virginia now has a 12-year history with open space easements for the conservation of the built environment. The ink was barely dry on the Open Space Act of 1966 when the state tax commissioner was approached by the sponsor of the legislation with the request that the department prepare and publish guidelines for use by local assessing officers in their determination of what, if any, reduction of taxable values resulted from the granting of open space easements. Statutes required the cooperation of the Department of Taxation with public bodies authorized to undertake easement programs. The department carefully studied the legislation in light of the wide range of foreseeable easements before advising the sponsor that, in lieu of guidelines, it would be preferable to render assistance individually as requested.

Through the Virginia Outdoors Foundation and the Virginia Historic Landmarks Commission, the commonwealth had accepted about 150 open space easements by 1978. Not all of the easements were studied by the Department of Taxation, because requests to do so were not made in all instances by either the local assessing officer or the state agency acquiring the deed of easement. The department has, however, appraised the fair market values, both before and after the conveyances, for approximately half of the easements acquired.

157

Examples of Easements

Two widely different easements acquired by the Virginia Historic Landmarks Commission are in the tidewater area of Virginia and are useful examples of how to value such easements. One is Westover Plantation, the other Roaring Springs Farm, both manor houses dating from the 1730s. The two are excellent examples of the period, with Westover built on the river and Roaring Springs inland off navigable water.

Westover Plantation

Westover is located on the north bank of the James River halfway between Richmond and Williamsburg in Charles City County, one of the original Virginia shires. Its builder, William Byrd II, was also the founder of the city of Richmond. Westover is a designated National Historic Landmark for its noteworthy historical and architectural interest, and is listed in the Virginia Landmarks Register and the National Register of Historic Places. Both the owner and the commonwealth wish to assure the perpetuation and preservation of this plantation and that of the historic and architectural features that led to its national recognition.

The current owner conveyed a deed of perpetual easement on part of the entire plantation to the Virginia Historic Landmarks Commission on December 31, 1974. The role of the Department of Taxation in this transaction was: (1) to determine the fair market value of the entire parcel before the granting of the easement and, after the grant, to determine the fair market value of parcels A and B, subject to easement, and also the fair market value of parcels C and D, both unencumbered by the deed of easement, and (2) to recommend new assessed values to the local commissioner of revenue for the determination of the property tax.

Parcel A includes the manor house and its dependencies. The red brick house is considered by many architects to be one of the best examples of Georgian architecture in the United States. Several dependencies, including the original kitchen just west of the mansion, were constructed before the house itself. Brick walls flank the house and extend to the James River. The yard immediately north of the manor house is fenced and is worthy of special note for the stuccoed brick fence posts capped with finials of portland stone.

The perpetual open space deed of easement in gross specifies generally that no exterior changes to the structures or land, or to their use, can be made without the prior written approval of the grantee, the Virginia Historic Landmarks Commission. Interior alterations to the first and second floors of the central portion of the manor house are also prohibited, although certain interior changes may be made in the wings without the consent of the grantee. Leasing all or part of any building on parcels A or B is permitted. No additional structures are permitted on Parcel A except for a structure to cover the present ice house. Parcel A also may not be subdivided or mined. For all intents and purposes, therefore, Parcel A must remain intact as it existed on the date of easement grant to the Virginia Historic Landmarks Commission.

The opinion of the Department of Taxation was that the 10 acres in Parcel A suffered little, if any, reduction of value on December 31, 1974, from the granting of the easement. The appraisal of this parcel before the conveyance of the easement in gross remained unchanged afterwards at $710,000.

The effect of the easement on Parcel B was very different. This parcel, containing 611.25 acres, protects the immediate environs and vista of Westover's manor house. The conveyance by easement of the subdivision rights to the commonwealth had considerable measurable value. The grantor did reserve the right to carry on farming or to remove minerals (including sand and gravel), to construct four additional houses and to construct buildings and structures commonly or approximately incidental to residential dwellings and estates. The grantee's prior written approval is required only for the location and design of each of these four houses. In addition, no commercial or industrial activities, with the exception of tourist trade, are permitted without the prior written approval of the grantee. Farming, including timber and nursery activities appropriate to an 18th-century farm, is permitted.

Prior to the easement grant on December 31, 1974, Westover contained 1,024.25 acres and had a fair market value of $2,027,975. The estate was appraised as a whole, so it was necessary to appraise parcels C and D, neither of which was included in the deed of easement, to learn the loss in value to Parcel B. Parcel C, containing 30 acres situated on the James River and not fronting on a state-maintained road, was subject to local zoning requiring minimum lots of five acres each. Parcel D contained 373 acres, of which 158 acres were tidal marsh and 215 acres were high land well stocked with mature loblolly pine. The total fair market value appraisal of the entire 1,024.25 acres subject to the easement on parcels A and B was $1,624,375, a loss in value of $403,600.

Roaring Springs

Roaring Springs manor house, located in Gloucester County, stands serenely in the midst of a spacious yard with large magnificent trees. The house itself received its name from a large spring located southwest of the dwelling, which is said to have made a roaring sound from an underground cascade or waterfall.

The 18th-century manor house is considered typical of the informal "Old Virginia" homesteads that have been renovated and added to over the years. The weathered shingles on the gambrel roof and the parklike setting in the rolling countryside present quite a different appearance from the flat riverfront farms generally found in Gloucester County.

The farm is owned by a brother and sister who conveyed a deed of easement covering 88 acres to the Virginia Historic Landmarks Commission on March 1, 1974. In May 1978 they conveyed Roaring Springs to the Association for the Preservation of Virginia Antiquities, retaining a life interest.

It was deemed to be in the best interest of all parties to perpetuate and preserve the features of the manor house, the smokehouse, the renowned spring and their environs. The acreage covered by the easement in gross is the portion of the 192-acre farm lying east of State Route 616. The acreage lying west of this route, containing 104 acres, is not similarly protected by an easement. The grantors agreed in the easement that neither the manor house nor the smokehouse shall be changed, altered or enlarged without state approval, and that no building or structure shall be erected on the property other than outbuildings and structures commonly or appropriately incidental to a single-family dwelling, including without limitation a garage, swimming pool, tennis courts, guest house, servants quarters, farm laborers quarters and farm buildings or structures. In addition, the property may not be subdivided.

The owners also have agreed that the manor house and grounds shall be opened at no charge to small groups of persons designated by the state at such times and on such terms or conditions as may satisfy the two parties. The trees, which add significantly to the character of the farm and the manor house, may be cut only in accordance with the best tree-care practices. Other standing timber located on the property may be cut only for one of the following three reasons: if the trees are diseased, if cutting is necessary for safety purposes or if prior written approval of the grantee is obtained.

Roaring Springs Farm is located just beyond the village surrounding Gloucester County Courthouse. The area is currently undergoing rapid transition from agricultural to residential use. The quality of residential construction is good. Undeveloped land in the immediate vicinity of the farm and just before the granting of the easement on Roaring Springs commanded $1,000 to $1,200 per acre in quantities of 50 acres or more. The subdivision potential of the land was strong and development along Route 616 already had reached Roaring Springs. On March 1, 1974, it was determined that before the easement Roaring Springs Farm had a fair market value of $175,000, including land and buildings. The fair market value of the farm subject to the easement in gross fell to $147,600, a loss in value of $27,400. This change reflected the owner's forfeiture of the right to subdivide any portion of the land east of Route 616. The highest and best use under easement on March 1, 1974, was agricultural, but as the pressures of urbanization mount, the highest and best use will change from agriculture to use as a protected estate. The fair market value as a protected retreat or sanctuary in future years will overshadow the economic importance of the net productive earning power of the soil.

159

Overlook Farm

Another example of the impact of an easement is that of Overlook Farm in Fairfax County, Va. On January 30, 1969, the owners conveyed to the Virginia Outdoors Foundation a perpetual easement on the entire 59.3-acre tract in order to protect the scenic outlook from Gunston Hall, the home of George Mason. Some years before the gift of Gunston Hall to the commonwealth of Virginia, Overlook Farm was separated from it. A recorded right-of-way for ingress and egress to the county road leading to Overlook Farm, however, passes through the yard of Gunston Hall to the rear of the manor house.

The farm fronts not only on the Potomac River just a short distance down the river from Mount Vernon, but also has a long frontage on Gunston Cove. The entire parcel is strategically situated between Gunston Hall manor house and the Potomac River. The dwelling house located on Overlook Farm was built by Col. E.M. Lewis, a relative of George Washington. In addition to the main house there are two auxiliary dwellings, a garage, a swimming pool, a bathhouse, a barn and other small buildings normally associated with a farm.

At the time the easement was granted, Fairfax County was reported to be the most rapidly developing county in Virginia. Preservationists, however, were actively working in that part of the county near the farm to assure that certain areas remained open spaces for recreational and park purposes. The county had grown so rapidly that it could not keep up with demands for water, streets and other public services, and the commissioners placed a moratorium on additional sewer hookups until adequate treatment facilities could be installed. The area where Gunston Hall and Overlook Farm are located was included in the moratorium. County zoning permitted only single-family residences on no less than two-acre lots. The soil maps of the county indicated that a large amount of the 59.3 acres is not suitable for septic tanks, although nine sites within the total Overlook Farm would probably meet the requirements for percolation.

The deed of easement imposed restrictions on the use of the property for industrial, commercial and residential use other than the reserved right to construct an additional dwelling house, garage, swimming pool, guest house, servants' or farm laborers' quarters and other necessary farm-related structures. The property owner also forfeited the right to subdivide or develop the property as would otherwise be allowable under existing zoning.

The fair market value of the entire farm before the granting of the easement was appraised at $347,005; afterward, it was reduced to $199,317, indicating the value of the easement to be $147,688. Two other items require comment. To determine the highest and best use at the time the easement was granted to the Virginia Outdoors Foundation, it was necessary to take into consideration the zoning requirements and the physical capacity of the land to support residential development. Fairfax County had an abundance of sales of small, otherwise similar parcels off the water, but only a limited number of usable conveyances involving waterfront. A few sales that were a matter of public record and contained larger tracts having water frontage helped to establish the overall value.

Under the highest and best use concept of market value, it was necessary for the appraiser to discount the value of Overlook Farm's manor house and to disregard, for valuation purposes, the presence of the other structures. In effect, their presence did not add to the value of the land. Under the protection of the open space easement, however, these buildings appreciated in value because they are necessary to the operation of the only allowable use, farming.

Over time the effects of the easement on Overlook Farm are also noteworthy. Today, Overlook Farm has a fair market value substantially higher than its fair market value on January 30, 1969, before the granting of the easement to the state agency. The protection afforded by the easement cannot be ignored by the appraiser and has had a substantial effect on the farm's appreciation. An "oasis" such as this farm in an urbanizing area has measurable value.

Special Assessment

Virginia has not been oblivious to the supplemental protection afforded agricultural, horticultural, forest and open space land by assessing them based on their current use, rather than their fair market value. The general assembly has authorized any locality to adopt this technique by ordinance if it has first adopted a land-use plan. Four localities adopted ordinances in 1973, and two additional localities did so in 1974. By 1976, the number had grown to 31.

For the tax year 1978, 37 counties and 11 cities had such tax plans in force. Under this method, a State Land Evaluation Advisory Committee composed of the state tax commissioner, commissioner of agriculture and industry, director of the department of conservation and economic development, director of planning and community affairs, director of outdoor recreation and dean of the School of Agriculture of the Virginia Polytechnic Institute and State University are required to prepare and publish a range of suggested values for each of the eight soil conservation land capability classes. This publication then is used by the assessing office in each locality adopting an ordinance for use-value taxation.

This special assessment plan has given substantial support to preserving real estate devoted to agricultural, horticultural, forestry and open space use as a matter of vital public interest. The assessment plan is especially effective as a "back-up" to the Virginia Open Space Land Act of 1966, because assessments determined on the basis of use relieve the pressures stemming from the property tax increase necessitated by premature conversion from a low-intensity base. It is obvious in light of the changes taking place in rural land values that an assessor will no longer be able to limit consideration to the value of the residential area plus the value of the land for agricultural or related purposes. The selling price of rural land has reached new heights in dollar value. However, Virginia's suggested range of land-use values is based on a five-year average of net productive earnings. Unquestionably, this system will have a heavy impact on rural land valuation.

Since January 1, 1976, all annual and general reassessments have been required to be made at 100 percent of fair market value. This system applies equally to real property encumbered by easements—real estate so restricted must be assessed at 100 percent of fair market value subject to the easement. Where current land-use taxation applies, the owner is able to defer indefinitely from taxation the difference in taxes between the assessment at fair market value under easement and the value of the land assessment based on the productive earning power of the land at its current use. A "rollback" tax is imposed when the use changes to an ineligible classification. The rollback applies to the amount deferred from tax for the previous five years, with interest compounded at 6 percent. The owner who converts the land must pay these deferred taxes.

Because tax problems today in Virginia for historic and naturally important properties largely center on land taxation, the special assessment plan will go far in releasing pressure on them for the foreseeable future.

Virginia recently adopted legislation authorizing the establishment of agricultural and forested districts. This is a land option measure. At the present time only one Virginia county has authorized the establishment of such districts. This, too, should facilitate the easing of future land tax pressures.

4. Taxation of Private Preservation Organizations

Peter H. Brink

THE IMPACT OF TAXES ON A LOCAL HISTORIC PRESERVATION ORGANIZATION

The role tax considerations play in the historic preservation efforts of the Galveston Historical Foundation (GHF), with emphasis on the organization's experience since establishment of its revolving fund in 1973, is the subject of this article. Major considerations are: GHF's experience with Internal Revenue Code section 501(c)(3) tax-exempt status and the impact of tax incentives on for-profit undertakings to rehabilitate historic structures in Galveston.

Galveston is an island a mile off the Texas coast in the Gulf of Mexico, 45 miles southeast of Houston. In the 1800s the city and its port were the commercial hub of Texas, with cotton flowing out from much of the Southwest and immigrants and manufactured goods flowing in. Imposing commercial structures rose adjacent to the wharves on The Strand—"The Wall Street of the Southwest"—and residential structures, ranging from elegant mansions on grand boulevards to blocks of Victorian frame houses and raised cottages, crowded the eastern end of the island.

Today, more than 800 of these 19th-century structures have survived hurricanes, fires and economic changes. Indeed, the very absence of strong economic growth in the 1900s has enabled these structures to stand intact today, so that in recent years their beauty and economic worth could be rediscovered and utilized. The Galveston Historical Foundation is dedicated to the preservation, rehabilitation and active reuse of these 19th-century structures as part of our community, and to public understanding and appreciation of Galveston's history and architecture.

GHF is a community organization with more than 2,000 dues-paying members and is chartered as a nonprofit corporation under Texas law. Its activities, in addition to The Strand Revolving Fund, include restoration and administration of four historic properties (including an 1877 sailing ship), support for locally zoned historic districts and neighborhood organizations, historical research, tours, educational programs, public events and, always, a general watchdog role over historic Galveston.

Section 501(c)(3) Status

GHF is exempt from federal income tax under section 501(c)(3) of the Internal Revenue Code. This exemption is crucial to GHF's effective operation for several reasons.

Mr. Brink is executive director of the Galveston Historical Foundation and has lectured and written widely about historic preservation. He is a graduate of Harvard Law School and admitted to practice in New York and Washington, D.C. Special thanks are expressed to James L. Foutch and Michael J. Fieglein, attorneys with the firm of Dibrell, Dibrell, Greer, and Brown of Galveston, who reviewed drafts of this article.

First, by virtue of the exemption, GHF is relieved of the need to pay federal income tax so long as it does not profit from operations constituting "unrelated business." At present this consequence of 501(c)(3) status is not crucial to GHF in that almost none of GHF's income currently would be taxable even in the absence of exempt status. GHF's activities, such as operation of house museums, tours or its revolving fund are, at best, break-even operations. Little net income, and thus little taxable income, currently results. Money given to GHF by donation or grant, furthermore, constitutes a gift, which does not give rise to taxable income. GHF is, however, intent on generating within the next few years substantial net profit from its major public event, "Dickens's Evening on The Strand," and from tours of its nearly restored and opened 1877 square-rigged sailing vessel, with profits from those events used to support GHF's other historic preservation activities. Without exempt status, these efforts at self-sufficiency would be drastically hampered because net income generated by them would be taxable, even if it were used for other non-income-producing activities of GHF. Thus, for GHF or for any preservation organization seeking to be self-supporting and to carry on a broad preservation program, the exemption from paying income tax is critical.

Second, GHF's qualification under section 501(c)(3) of the code almost automatically means that donors may deduct for federal income tax purposes under section 170 of the code the value of cash, property or material donations to GHF. Such deductions provide donors with tax savings of as much as 50 percent of the value of their donations, depending on their tax brackets, thus greatly reducing the net cost to them of making such donations. Needless to say, without this major tax incentive to altruistic giving, the significant amount of donations to charitable organizations, including historic preservation organizations such as GHF, would be substantially reduced and the organizations badly hurt. (Qualification under section 501(c)(3) also assures that donations are deductible for federal estate tax purposes, but to date GHF has not received any bequests.)

Third, grants by private foundations to organizations that are not tax exempt under section 501(c)(3) will constitute a "taxable expenditure" of the foundation. GHF is dependent on foundation support for a significant part of both its operating and capital funds. Blanket denial of this support if GHF lacked tax-exempt status would drastically curtail GHF's historic preservation efforts. Similarly, other important grant programs, such as those of the National Trust for Historic Preservation and the National Endowment for the Arts, require that organizations qualify under section 501(c)(3) in order to be eligible for assistance. Even eligibility to obtain employees under the federal Comprehensive Employment Training Act (CETA) program appears closely tied to 501(c)(3) tax-exempt status. At one time GHF had 14 CETA employee positions, yet the local chamber of commerce, which does not qualify under section 501(c)(3), was having difficulty gaining eligibility to participate in CETA.

GHF's letter from the Internal Revenue Service granting exemption under section 501(c)(3) was issued in 1957. At that time GHF was engaged in historical research, public education (e.g., a booklet about historic landmarks in Galveston) and the restoration of a historic 1839 cottage as a museum. In 1969-70, GHF undertook the historical survey and development plan that resulted in the municipal establishment of a 40-block residential historic district. During 1969-73, GHF saved from demolition, and undertook the restoration and administration of, two additional house museums. Our records and the recollections of past officers indicate that GHF's exempt status was not questioned by the IRS during this period.

GHF's Strand Revolving Fund and Its Tax Implications

In 1973, GHF was granted funding from two Galveston-based foundations to establish a preservation revolving fund for The Strand, the 19th-century commercial center of Galveston. Funding totalled $215,000, with $165,000 as capital for the revolving fund and the remainder as operating funds to hire a full-time director (the author) and underwrite first-year program expenses.

The concept of the revolving fund had come to Galveston from the successful operation of such funds by the Historic Savannah Foundation and the Pittsburgh History and Landmarks Foundation. Drawing from their experience and advice, GHF (in cooperation with the Galveston County Cultural Arts Council) organized The Strand Revolving Fund and charted its mode of operation.

In these initial stages we generally assumed, because revolving funds were operating as part of broad-based section 501(c)(3) preservation organizations in Savannah, Charleston and Pittsburgh and were not being unduly questioned by the IRS, the GHF could operate a similar fund without endangering its exempt status. This assumption has been confirmed in several ways.

First, as a condition of the revolving fund grants, GHF was restructured and its bylaws rewritten in 1973 to establish an office of "Vice-President, Revolving Fund" and set forth that officer's responsibilities. As required, the bylaws were submitted to the IRS, which then notified GHF in 1973 that the changes did not adversely affect its tax-exempt status.

Second, GHF annually files the required Form 990, which includes full disclosure of purchases and sales of revolving fund properties. The IRS has not questioned or asked GHF to alter any of its activities.

Third, a grant from the National Endowment for the Arts in 1974 enabled GHF to contract with Tersh Boasberg, a Washington, D.C., attorney expert in exempt organizations, to undertake a case study of GHF entitled "Federal Tax Problems Arising from Real Estate Activities of Non-Profit Preservation Organizations."[1] This study concluded that the organization and operation of GHF's revolving fund were appropriate to its exempt status.

Fourth, in October 1976, the IRS audited GHF's operations for the calendar year 1974, which included substantial revolving fund transactions. The IRS notified GHF in January 1977 that, as a result of this examination, which will be discussed later, it would continue to recognize GHF as a tax-exempt 501(c)(3) organization.

Because these actions indicate that the IRS finds The Strand Revolving Fund acceptable to it as part of GHF's community-wide preservation efforts, it is appropriate to describe how the revolving fund is organized and operates and how it relates to the tax-exempt purposes required by section 501(c)(3).

The purpose of The Strand Revolving Fund and of its related activities has always been to provide a means to preserve and utilize the historic buildings within the 13-block Strand district so that their history and architecture will be more widely understood and appreciated. The revolving fund has functioned to assure that the structures are rehabilitated for active and economical uses and has helped transform The Strand from a run-down, derelict area to one revitalized with shops, restaurants, apartments and offices that are frequented and enjoyed by Galvestonians and visitors. GHF is thus working to preserve and use a valuable community asset in a way that contributes to the stability of the city's threatened downtown, adds a year-round attraction to Galveston's largely seasonal, beach-oriented tourist industry and provides much needed additional housing for the island.

To attain these goals, the GHF revolving fund purchases deteriorated Strand buildings and then typically sells them unrestored and subject to preservation deed restrictions and other conditions. The deed restrictions, which bind all subsequent owners, provide essentially that the building will not be demolished or its exterior modified without GHF approval and that it will be maintained in good condition. The purchaser usually is required to restore the exterior of the building in an agreed-upon manner and time period and to invest an agreed-upon sum in the development of the interior of the structure for active use. Alternatively, GHF achieves some of these results through the purchase of deed restrictions on certain buildings from the existing owners, without purchasing and reselling the entire structure. In addition, GHF has expended revolving fund monies to help fund planning work and capital improvements in the area, such as appropriate street lighting and linear parks.

GHF's revolving fund is the focal point for the Boasberg study's extensive analysis of the key section 501(c)(3) requirement that, in order to qualify for tax-exempt status, groups must be organized and operated exclusively for "charitable" purposes. In this analysis, the study relies principally on the IRS recognition that "charitable" purposes include those that are "educational" in nature, promote "social welfare" by "combating community deterioration," or "lessen the burdens of government." The study concludes that a revolving fund, if properly structured and operated, can qualify as being "in furtherance of and substantially related" to these exempt purposes, and that GHF's revolving fund should so qualify.

Several elements of GHF's revolving fund operations were identified in the Boasberg study or in subsequent work with our tax attorneys as being significant in the continued recognition by the IRS of our exempt status.

First and foremost, GHF is sincerely and sensibly working toward the historic preservation and public education goals of The Strand effort. Everything GHF does through its revolving fund, allowing for human judgment and error, is aimed at achieving these goals. A basic component of the IRS approach to revolving funds is that the exempt organization should always be able to distinguish its conduct from that of a non-tax-exempt, private real estate developer. A clear commitment to goals in line with tax-exempt purposes is thus the only sound basis upon which to initiate and operate a revolving fund.

This commitment to charitable goals is underlined in GHF's case by the continual financial losses the revolving fund suffers in order to achieve the preservation and rehabilitation of Strand buildings. Although GHF has made a profit on a few purchases and sales, it has depleted its initial capital of $165,000 in 1973 to less than $25,000 in 1979.

The commitment is likewise underlined by instances in which GHF fights seemingly impossible battles to save buildings of historical and architectural value from demolition. Thus, when a significant 19th-century building in The Strand was threatened, GHF waged a prolonged, intense and expensive effort, including litigation, to try to prevent demolition. This course of action was justified by GHF's historic preservation goals, but not by the goals of a for-profit real estate developer.

Second, revolving fund decisions are carried out with as much member and public participation as is feasible. Purchases and sales of properties are decided by GHF's elected board or 24-member executive committee in meetings open to the public (decisions to take options to purchase may be made by three officers acting together, however). Likewise, detailed financial records are maintained and an annual audit is done by a certified public accounting firm. Financial records are open for public inspection.

Third, revolving fund purchases are usually limited to property within the clearly defined Strand Historic District, which is listed in the National Register of Historic Places and designated a National Historic Landmark. Although most purchases are of 19th-century buildings, on occasion vacant lots within the district have been purchased for use with the adjacent buildings and to assure that any new construction is compatible. In one emergency, GHF tried to purchase through the revolving fund an individually listed National Register building some distance from The Strand to save it from imminent demolition.

Fourth, the general public directly benefits from the revolving fund activities because all buildings purchased are visible from public rights-of-way and the interiors of most are open regularly to the public in the normal course of business.

Fifth, revolving fund activities are carried out according to an overall plan for the preservation, restoration and revitalization of The Strand, although the plan does not list specific buildings to purchase. This "Action Plan for The Strand" by the architectural firm of Venturi and Rauch, with funding from the National Endowment for the Arts, was developed by qualified planners and architects working with a Strand planning committee.

Sixth, GHF's stringent deed restrictions and contractual requirements go far toward assuring that the goals for The Strand's preservation, restoration and active use will be carried out with regard to buildings purchased and sold. Other than for its own offices, GHF does not develop or retain ownership of Strand properties for investment or rental purposes. GHF economic involvement in real estate activities, therefore, does not go beyond what is reasonably necessary to attain its stated preservation goals.

Seventh, the revolving fund activities are part of a broad program of historic preservation and public education activities for The Strand that include regular free public walking tours; "building pictorial signs" with photos and text for visitors; a trompe l'oeil architectural mural; a magical "Dickens's Evening on The Strand" each December that draws 40,000 people; research to assist in restoration and tours; and articles for the news media about The Strand's history, architecture and current restoration and revitalization. For historic Galveston as a whole, GHF operates house museums for the public, provides tours of private historic structures and neighborhoods and carries on a strong public education effort through special events and the news media.

Last, the activities of the revolving fund are in fact succeeding in attaining the historic preservation goals for The Strand. Since its start, deed restrictions have been secured on 19 Strand properties, extensive restoration carried out on and adaptive use made of 18 and more than $5 million in for-profit investment attracted to purchase, restore, adapt and make use of Strand buildings.

GHF and the Internal Revenue Service

The IRS exempt organization specialist who conducted a 1976 audit of GHF's 1974 activities did not comment on the foregoing factors or explain the basis for the IRS conclusion that GHF's activities do not alter its tax-exempt status. Of note, however, was the thoroughness of the three-day examination and the concentration not only on GHF's financial records, but also on the content of its activities.

GHF was notified of the audit a few days in advance with a phone call from the IRS examiner, who emphasized that such audits are routine for exempt organizations and that GHF was not being singled out. Because GHF was associated with a citywide controversy over the fate of a historic landmark at that time, these assurances were welcome but did not completely assuage our fears. The examiner requested that GHF's financial records for 1974, and information about its programs and activities, be made available for his examination. We thus provided him with our 1974 monthly computer income and expense statements, audited annual financial statements, cancelled checks, deposit slips and budgets. We also furnished the complete minutes of GHF board and executive committee meetings, newsletters, annual activity reports, GHF brochures and publicity material, magazine and newspaper articles about GHF activities, membership solicitation material, Strand planning material and deed restrictions and contracts.

Although offered desk space with our accounting firm, the IRS examiner chose to work in the more hectic GHF offices, perhaps to get a feel for the flow of peole and activity in the organization. He met with our accounting firm and reviewed carefully GHF's financial material, about which he asked few questions other than to clarify the meaning of individual entries. He carefully reviewed the information about GHF activities, and showed a sincere desire to understand our historic preservation objectives and methods. He toured The Strand and was advised which buildings had been purchased and sold, how much restoration they had undergone and how the area had improved since the start of the revolving fund. Also included were visits to each historic property owned by GHF, perhaps to be sure they actually existed; a tour of our one property open to the public at that time (the 1859 Ashton Villa); and explanations of what kinds of activities comprised our special events such as the "Dickens's Evening."

The only transaction that required more documentation than that in our files was an income item of $12,000 from a private foundation and a corresponding expense item of $12,000 to a management company owned by the same foundation. The IRS examiner commented that such "in-out" transactions were usually a red flag. We explained, however, that the management company, without fee to GHF, had then spent this entire amount for exterior restoration of an important historic residential structure, and that in exchange the owners of the structure had subjected their property to a preservation deed restriction in favor of GHF. This subsidy was essential to prevent sale and demolition of the house because the real estate was worth more as commercial property without the structure. The examiner asked for back-up documentation of the transaction, and within a few days we mailed him evidence that the deed restriction had been given in exchange for expenditure of the full $12,000 on the house, the contract between GHF and the management company outlining a program to save key historic structures and material establishing the historical and architectural significance of the structure. We followed up with a phone call a week later to inquire if the material had cleared up any questions, and were told that it had and that we would be receiving notification soon of a "no-change" determination in our tax-exempt status. A few months later the formal notification arrived from the IRS stating that "as a result of our examinations for the above periods, we will continue to recognize your organization as tax-exempt."

Although we would not wish for an IRS audit, GHF is, as a result, reasonably confident that our real estate operations are an appropriate means of achieving our tax-exempt purposes and pleased that IRS appreciates the need for such activities by historic preservation organizations. Although great concern was caused by the IRS's initially adverse rulings in early 1977 regarding the incorporation exclusively as revolving funds of the Historic Preservation Fund of North Carolina, Inc., and of the Roslyn Preservation Corporation (N.Y.), these rulings were reversed by the IRS in November 1977. The rulings indicate that the factors found by GHF to be significant in assuring IRS approval of preservation revolving funds continue to remain valid.

It should be noted, however, that an organization recognized as exempt under section 501(c)(3) will nevertheless be subject to federal income tax on any net income derived from an "unrelated business." For example, if one of GHF's subsidiary activities were operation of a bowling alley, this would presumably be an "unrelated business," and GHF would have to pay taxes on the net income of the bowling alley even though that net income was used to help pay for historic preservation activities of GHF falling clearly within its exempt purposes. Similarly, if the revolving fund transactions of an exempt organization were carried out for purposes not substantially related to the organization's stated exempt purposes, but constituted only a small part of its otherwise tax-exempt activities, the IRS might leave the exempt status intact but determine that net income from the revolving fund was taxable as "unrelated business income." If the unrelated business is not generating any net income, after appropriate allocation of indirect cost, then there would be no income on which to pay taxes.

Much of the review undertaken in GHF's audit concerned whether GHF was operating an unrelated business as well as whether GHF should remain an exempt organization. The notification from IRS following the audit expressly indicated that GHF remains free from the unrelated business income tax.

Public Foundation Classification

It is important for a preservation organization, once it obtains a section 501(c)(3) exemption, to be classified by the IRS as a "public" foundation—that is, in IRS language, to be classified "as an organization that is not a private foundation as defined in section 509(a) of the Internal Revenue Code." Loss of public foundation classification would subject the organization to a matrix of special taxes and limiting rules. Loss would also mean that most grant-making foundations would be required to supervise closely the use of grants made to the organization, and this additional responsibility might deter the foundation from making a grant.

Essential to expeditious classification as a public foundation is a showing that "normally," typically a four-year average, at least one-third of the organization's support comes from public and/or governmental sources. The Internal Revenue Code provides two alternative mathematical formulas for calculating public support, with certain variations between them as to whether certain types of support can be counted as "public." Support from government units and relatively small donations or foundation grants (usually ones less than 2 percent of total support) count toward the one-third public support needed. Larger donations, foundation grants and gross receipts from activities related to the organization's exempt purposes generally, however, do not.

GHF received IRS notification in 1970 that it had been classified as a public foundation. Since then, GHF has relied heavily on its accounting firm to apply the public support formula to GHF's income on a quarterly basis and to warn GHF if it is in danger of not achieving the one-third public support needed.

To date, GHF has not been in such danger. Indeed, the allowable inclusion as public support of the substantial value of the government CETA positions assigned to GHF puts the organization well over the one-third public support requirement. What is disconcerting for the future, however, is that GHF hopes to increase substantially its exempt-purposes income from admissions to museums and from special events such as the "Dickens's Evening." To achieve such increases would seem an important and legitimate goal, since this would mean that GHF is carrying out its historic preservation activities and, in doing so, is generating income that can be used for other nonprofit preservation activities. Nevertheless, gross receipts from such historic preservation activities do not generally count toward the one-third public support needed—although under one formula they are excluded from both public and total support. As gross receipts rise, therefore, GHF's public-private support ratio could be altered adversely to the extent that GHF would be thrown into the private foundation classification, with all its negative consequences. The only apparent means available to insure against this would be to achieve a corresponding increase in government support or in relatively small donations and grants.

Political Intervention and Lobbying

Participation or intervention in a political campaign for public office or the use of a substantial part of the organization's resources to influence legislation violates specific prohibitions in the code and can cause the loss of a section 501(c)(3) organization's tax-exempt status.

GHF is careful to avoid this pitfall. Individual members of GHF are free to involve themselves politically as they choose, but, as an organization, GHF takes no part in election campaigns and uses only a modest amount of its staff time and resources to try to influence legislation. For example, GHF has written letters supporting higher funding by Congress for historic preservation programs and made public statements supporting the successful passage of a state constitutional amendment authorizing ad valorem tax assistance for historic properties.

GHF has not thoroughly investigated the option available under the Tax Reform Act of 1976 allowing greater lobbying activities if the organization agrees to detailed accounting and disclosure of these efforts. GHF believes it is well within the bounds of the current limitations, and thus would not choose to go through the additional administrative procedures required by this alternative arrangement.

Tax Incentives and For-Profit Undertakings

The preservation and rehabilitation of The Strand is taking place in large part because private purchasers of revolving fund properties have been persuaded to invest their funds in the development of individual Strand buildings. The hard test of a revolving fund is not primarily whether it is able to retain its capital intact, but whether it is convincing for-profit buyers to purchase and develop historic buildings.

Similarly, preservation and revitalization of Galveston's residential historic areas is succeeding only to the extent that existing or new owners are willing to invest in their properties, whether to live in them or rent them out.

In working in The Strand district, where GHF has had the most involvement, we have found a variety of motivations and considerations influencing potential purchasers to proceed or not to proceed.

During the five years of the revolving fund's operation, we have talked with nearly 200 prospective purchasers having more than a casual interest in buying. For those who decide *against* buying a Strand building, the predominant reasons are:

1. Doubt that The Strand will succeed as a whole, i.e., draw sufficient lessees for retail uses, offices and apartments or sufficient traffic to support retail uses. Thus, their undertakings would lose money.

2. Cost of rehabilitation is too high in relation to their estimates of achievable income to generate an adequate return on investment, even assuming the reasonable revitalization of the entire Strand.

3. Lack of buildings available with the right characteristics, especially ones large enough to allow development but not too large to overwhelm a new owner's financial capacity and level of acceptable risks. (After the first two or three years of the revolving fund, there is now a marked lack of buildings of 15,000 square feet or less for sale at a reasonable price.)

Of the many prospective purchasers, however, 14 have bought 18 Strand buildings (not all directly from us) and have completed or are in the process of developing them. Five more buildings have been purchased by nonprofit organizations. One category of purchaser has been the small-business owner who wants to operate a retail business as part of The Strand and to own, rather than lease, a building. These have been hard-working, imaginative entrepreneurs, personally managing their own businesses and providing The Strand with a delicatessen-sandwich-imported foods operation, an ice cream parlor-candy factory and a unique military surplus center.

The other major category of purchaser is more numerous and includes successful business people and persons of means who have bought buildings to develop and lease out space. These purchasers are almost always attracted personally to the beauty of Strand buildings and are willing to undertake an investment that initially may only break even, but whose value they expect to appreciate as The Strand develops over the coming five to ten years.

172

Virtually all Strand buyers have satisfied themselves before purchasing that the overall Strand revitalization can and probably will succeed sufficiently to support their individual undertaking. A significant factor in this judgment seems to be their assessment that GHF and others working for revitalization have sufficient effectiveness and staying power to complement their efforts. They believe they are part of an overall effort rather than proceeding solely by themselves. With 17 retail uses now open and a strong merchants association developing, buyers can satisfy themselves more easily on this point than in the initial years.

Also present in the decisions of most for-profit buyers of Strand buildings has been the incentive of obtaining some financial assistance in one or more of the following ways:

1. A break on the purchase price of revolving fund-owned properties because the fund is willing to take a loss, ranging from $1,000 to $15,000 each exclusive of holding costs, in order to achieve rehabilitation of a building.

2. Availability of long-term financing for commercial and residential rental properties on attractive terms through an arrangement worked out by GHF with six Galveston-based financial institutions. Typical terms provide for financing equal to 75 percent of the project cost, an interest rate set at .25 percent below the FHA multifamily rate at the date of the loan commitment and annual loan payments based on repayment over 25 years with a lump-sum balloon payment at the end of the 20th year to complete repayment.

3. The possibility of a matching grant for restoration from the Texas Historical Commission using U.S. Department of the Interior grant-in-aid funds. The imposition of a deed restriction requiring state or federal review of exterior and interior restoration and maintenance for a specified term is a condition of such assistance. From 1973 to 1979, Texas Historical Commission matching grants totalling $62,500 have been allocated to for-profit Strand owners. An additional $180,000 has been approved to assist nonprofit organizations with Strand buildings, including $50,000 to assist the revolving fund in acquiring a key building.

A final non-tax factor significant in at least four purchases, including one that triggered the $1 million development of a 30,000-square-foot building, was the feeling among these buyers, all holding prominent positions in the community, that such participation in The Strand was a civic responsibility and a source of favorable public recognition.

In terms of special tax factors affecting for-profit buyers of historic structures, there are now five potentials:

1. The right to deduct by amortization over five years the cost of rehabilitating income-producing historic buildings or, alternatively, to take accelerated depreciation tax deductions on such rehabilitated historic structures. Both of these rehabilitation incentives were created by the Tax Reform Act of 1976.

2. Disincentives under the Tax Reform Act of 1976 for the demolition or incompatible substantial alteration of historic structures.

3. A tax deduction for the donation of a facade or scenic easement on historic property to a governmental body or nonprofit preservation organization, also provided for in the Tax Reform Act of 1976.

4. A 10 percent investment tax credit for rehabilitating, for commercial or industrial purposes, structures in use for 20 years or more, as provided in the Revenue Act of 1978.

5. Some form of relief from ad valorem real and personal property taxes on historic properties.

(The often significant effect in Galveston of the Tax Reform Act's rehabilitation tax incentives is discussed in more detail in Mr. Brink's article on page 74.)

173

Deductions for Donations of Preservation Restrictions

Deductions are allowed under section 170 of the IRS code for the value of facade or scenic easements for historic preservation purposes that are donated to governmental bodies or to 501(c)(3) organizations so long as the easement is "in perpetuity." This provision was enacted as part of the Tax Reform Act of 1976 to resolve some confusion in the law and allowed this tax deduction for donations of easements of "not less than 30 years." However, this provision of the Tax Reform Act was amended in 1977 to require that qualifying easements must be perpetual.

Although the form of the deed restrictions GHF uses on Strand buildings is a mutual covenant, rather than an "easement" as stated in the code, GHF's attorneys are confident that a donation of these deed restrictions to GHF would qualify for a donation under section 170 so long as the restrictions are "in perpetuity." GHF is using covenants because our attorneys believe it is not certain, under Texas law, that facade easements will "run with the land" to bind subsequent owners, whereas they believe deed restrictions in the form of mutual covenants are certain to do so.

GHF has not, however, made an effective effort to obtain donations of deed restrictions. GHF has received the donation of only one deed restriction on a residential structure, although two owners of Strand buildings are now considering possible donations.

There are several reasons for the lack of donations of preservation deed restrictions to GHF:

1. Deed restrictions already have been placed on the buildings bought and sold by the revolving fund, so there is nothing left for the owner to donate.

2. The process of appraising the value of the donated deed restriction for purposes of the tax deduction is a difficult one. It entails valuing the building without any restrictions and then subtracting the value of the building with the restrictions in order to obtain the value of the donation. This difficulty creates uncertainty regarding the value that should be assigned the restriction. This uncertainty is further complicated by the requirement that the donor, not the donee, must pay the fee for any appraisal. Owners willing to consider donating a restriction hesitate to pay $500 or more when they are unsure if the resulting appraisal will justify their proceeding with the donation.

3. The value of deed restrictions on Strand buildings will, in fact, be less than that of restrictions on buildings in the middle of larger cities where development pressures are severe. Because the owner is giving up a right to certain types of development, such as demolition of the existing building and construction of a highrise, the value of this renunciation depends in large part on the economic potential of the types of development given up. Because there is no strong demand yet for construction of new structures on the sites of Strand buildings, the value of the restriction may not be high.

GHF is working to overcome these problems so that the donation of deed restrictions and the accompanying tax deductions can be another attractive feature of owning historic structures in Galveston.

Ad Valorem Tax Incentives

Since 1976, Texas statutory law has exempted from all ad valorem taxation real and personal property owned by nonprofit corporations that is "reasonably necessary for, and used for . . . restoration and preservation of historic houses, structures and landmarks."[2]

According to this provision, GHF, as a nonprofit Texas corporation, is currently exempt from ad valorem taxation on its three house museums and a Strand building being restored for GHF offices and public exhibits. In addition, the city of Galveston determined in 1973 that Strand buildings purchased by GHF through its revolving fund and placed on the market for resale subject to preservation deed restrictions and restoration requirements were exempt under this provision while they were actually owned by GHF. The county of Galveston, however, never made a decision regarding GHF's request with respect to revolving fund properties, and GHF did not force the matter in light of the small amount of county taxes at issue.

As soon as Strand buildings are resold for restoration and development, they are, of course, subject to ad valorem property taxation even though GHF continues to hold preservation deed restrictions on the buildings.

There is no doubt that this process of Strand development and revitalization under way in Galveston's historic residential areas has resulted in substantial increases in the amount of ad valorem taxes received by the city on these properties. Indeed, GHF has often cited actual and potential increases in the tax base of the city as one of the contributions being made by historic preservation efforts, and thus one of the reasons for public and city support of these efforts.[3]

The 1976 Galveston study "Historic Districts and Neighborhood Preservation" included a survey of changes in property values and tax levels in the 40-block residential East End Historic District. The study was undertaken by GHF under contract to the city with financial assistance from a HUD section 701 grant, and was coordinated by preservation consultant Ellen Beasley. Based on real estate sales data, the study concluded that values in the district increased 15 percent annually between 1971 and 1975, substantially higher than many other areas of the city. Assessed value for tax purposes increased 3 percent for the district during this same period, in contrast to an 11 percent *decrease* in assessed value in an adjacent non-historic district area.

GHF has not, however, made a survey of changes in assessed value with respect to The Strand. Although extensive rehabilitation is completed and in process for this area, tax authorities have not jumped on Strand owners as soon as rehabilitation is completed in order to raise their taxes abruptly to the full, new market value. Instead increases have been made with some restraint, such that over the past several years I have known of only one Strand owner who has complained strongly about inequitable tax increases caused by rehabilitation.

This situation is now undergoing a drastic change, however, with regard to both Strand and residential private owners. Recently the city's Tax Policy Committee completed a study of ad valorem taxation and, in line with this, the city and county, with pooled appraisal systems, have completed a reappraisal of all property in the city. The new valuations include significant increases especially in The Strand.

In a few rare instances these increased valuations may be offset by another major development. In November 1977, a statewide referendum approved Amendment Four to the Texas Constitution allowing possible ad valorem tax relief to private owners of residential and commercial historic structures. Enabling legislation passed by the state legislature pursuant to this constitutional amendment authorizes a city or county government to provide tax relief, if it so chooses, with respect to structures recognized as historic by the Texas Historical Commission or by city or county designation under a system approved by the state.[4] Austin, Tex., already has implemented this legislation by approving a flat percentage reduction in the ad valorem taxes of all property zoned historic by the city (56 such structures are privately owned).

Use of Amendment Four for ad valorem tax relief to private owners in Galveston is difficult in that such relief could affect hundreds of structures and further undermine the city's already inadequate tax base. An effort to obtain such widespread relief would be totally untenable. Thus, GHF's intention with regard to Amendment Four is to request relief only in return for appropriate rehabilitation work on designated buildings, and then only by freezing or slowing the increase of taxes based on the level applicable prior to the rehabilitation. This "quid pro quo" approach can be justified in that it would in no case lower taxes from their current level, it would be an incentive for additional rehabilitation of historic structures and it would provide tax relief only to the extent such rehabilitation has taken place.

Even with this restrictive approach to Amendment Four, GHF thinks that such tax relief would be tenable only where it could be shown that the rehabilitation of the historic structure could not reasonably occur in the absence of such relief. Given the present level of ad valorem taxes, this is not the case at this time with most Strand or residential structures, although it may already be the case with a few large landmark structures.

A second potential means for controlling the level of taxes on privately owned historic structures is one that should already be inherent in the existing appraisal system, and thus would not have to rely on implementation of Amendment Four. A deed restriction on any structure, whether or not obtained by donation, decreases to some extent the fair market value of that real estate. Thus, the existing deed restrictions on 19 Strand buildings should be taken into account in the normal appraisal process and should, to some extent, reduce the appraised value of the property and thus the ad valorem taxes assessed. As reasonable as this request is, however, GHF and individual property owners have not yet undertaken the intensive effort that will be necessary to obtain its recognition by city appraisers.

NOTES

1. A condensed version of this study appears under the same title in 8 *Urban Lawyer* 1 (Winter 1976).

2. *Tex. Rev. Civ. Stat. Ann.* art. 7151, § 22(a) (Vernon 1960).

3. Galveston is one of four historic communities examined in detail in *The Contribution of Historic Preservation to Urban Revitalization,* published January 1979 by the Advisory Council on Historic Preservation, Washington, D.C., and prepared for the council by Booz, Allen & Hamilton. Graphs in Exhibits B-5 to B-7 demonstrate that substantial increases in appraised property values and tax revenues have occurred between 1974 and 1977 in much of the property in Galveston's historic district.

4. *Tex. Rev. Civ. Stat. Ann.* art. 7150(i) (Vernon 1960).

Appendixes

Appendixes

Appendix A

HISTORIC PRESERVATION TAX PROVISIONS OF THE TAX REFORM ACT OF 1976

(As they appear in the Internal Revenue Code)

Reproduced with permission from *Internal Revenue Code*, published and copyrighted by Commerce Clearing House, Inc., 4025 West Peterson Avenue, Chicago, Ill. 60646.

Provisions Encouraging the Preservation and Rehabilitation of Certain Qualified Historic Structures and Discouraging Their Demolition (Sections 167(n)(o), 191 and 280B)

[Sec. 191]

SEC. 191. AMORTIZATION OF CERTAIN REHABILITATION EXPENDITURES FOR CERTIFIED HISTORIC STRUCTURES.

[Sec. 191(a)]

(a) ALLOWANCE OF DEDUCTION.—Every person, at his election, shall be entitled to a deduction with respect to the amortization of the amortizable basis of any certified historic structure (as defined in subsection (d)) based on a period of 60 months. Such amortization deduction shall be an amount, with respect to each month of such period within the taxable year, equal to the amortizable basis at the end of such month divided by the number of months (including the month for which the deduction is computed) remaining in the period. Such amortizable basis at the end of the month shall be computed without regard to the amortization deduction for such month. The amortization deduction provided by this section with respect to any month shall be in lieu of the depreciation deduction with respect to such basis for such month provided by section 167. The 60-month period shall begin, as to any historic structure, at the election of the taxpayer, with the month following the month in which the basis is acquired, or with the succeeding taxable year.

Source: New.

[Sec. 191(b)]

(b) ELECTION OF AMORTIZATION.—The election of the taxpayer to take the amortization deduction and to begin the 60-month period with the month following the month in which the basis is acquired, or with the taxable year succeeding the taxable year in which such basis is acquired, shall be made by filing with the Secretary, in such manner, in such form, and within such time as the Secretary may by regulations prescribe, a statement of such election.

Source: New.

[Sec. 191(c)]

(c) TERMINATION OF AMORTIZATION DEDUCTION.—A taxpayer who has elected under subsection (b) to take the amortization deduction provided in subsection (a) may, at any time after making such election, discontinue the amortization deduction with respect to the remainder of the amortization period, such discontinuance to begin as of the beginning of any month specified by the taxpayer in a notice in writing filed with the Secretary before the beginning of such month. The depreciation deduction provided under section 167 shall be allowed, beginning with the first month as to which the amortization deduction does not apply, and the taxpayer shall not be entitled to any further amortization deduction under this section with respect to such certified historic structure.

Source: New.

[Sec. 191(d)]

(d) DEFINITIONS.—For purposes of this section—

(1) CERTIFIED HISTORIC STRUCTURE.—The term "certified historic structure" means a

building or structure which is of a character subject to the allowance for depreciation provided in section 167 and which—

(A) is listed in the National Register, or

(B) is located in a registered historic district and is certified by the Secretary of the Interior to the Secretary as being of historic significance to the district.

(2) REGISTERED HISTORIC DISTRICT —The term "registered historic district" means—

(A) any district listed in the National Register, and

(B) any district—

(i) which is designated under a statute of the appropriate State or local government, if such statute is certified by the Secretary of the Interior to the Secretary as containing criteria which will substantially achieve the purpose of preserving and rehabilitating buildings of historic significance to the district, and

(ii) which is certified by the Secretary of the Interior to the Secretary as meeting substantially all of the requirements for the listing of districts in the National Register.

(3) AMORTIZABLE BASIS.—The term "amortizable basis" means the portion of the basis attributable to amounts expended in connection with certified rehabilitation.

(4) CERTIFIED REHABILITATION.—The term "certified rehabilitation" means any rehabilitation of a certified historic structure which the Secretary of the Interior has certified to the Secretary as being consistent with the historic character of such property or the district in which such property is located.

Source: New.

[Sec. 191(e)]

(e) DEPRECIATION DEDUCTION —The depreciation deduction provided by section 167 shall, despite the provisions of subsection (a), be allowed with respect to the portion of the adjusted basis which is not the amortizable basis.

Source: New.

[Sec. 191(f)]

(f) SPECIAL RULES FOR CERTAIN INTERESTS.—

(1) LIFE TENANT AND REMAINDERMAN.—In the case of property held by one person for life with remainder to another person, the deduction under this section shall be computed as if the life tenant were the absolute owner of the property and shall be allowable to the life tenant.

(2) CERTAIN LESSEES.—

180

(A) IN GENERAL.—In the case of a lessee of a certified historic structure who has expended amounts in connection with the certified rehabilitation of such structure which are properly chargeable to capital account, the deduction under this section shall be allowable to such lessee with respect to such amounts.

(B) AMORTIZABLE BASIS.—For purposes of subsection (a), the amortizable basis of such lessee shall not exceed the sum of the amounts described in subparagraph (A).

(C) LIMITATION.—Subparagraph (A) shall apply only if on the date the certified rehabilitation is completed, the remaining term of the lease (determined without regard to any renewal periods) extends—

(i) beyond the last day of the useful life (determined without regard to this section) of the improvements for which the amounts described in subparagraph (A) were expended, and

(ii) for not less than 30 years.

Source: New.

[Sec. 191(g)]

(g) CROSS REFERENCES.—

(1) For rules relating to the listing of buildings, structures, and historic districts in the National Register, see the Act entitled "An Act to establish a program for the preservation of additional historic properties throughout the Nation, and for other purposes", approved October 15, 1966 (16 U.S.C. 470 et seq.).

(2) For special rules with respect to certain gain derived from the disposition of property the adjusted basis of which is determined with regard to this section, see sections 1245 and 1250.

Source: New.

P.L. 95-600, § 701(f)(1):

Amended Code Sec. 191(d) by striking out paragraph (1), by redesignating paragraphs (2) and (3) as paragraphs (3) and (4), respectively, and by inserting new paragraphs (1) and (2) to read as above, effective as provided in P.L. 94-455, § 2124(a)(1). Prior to amendment, Code Sec. 191(d)(1) read as follows:

"(1) CERTIFIED HISTORIC STRUCTURE.—The term 'certified historic structure' means a building or structure which is of a character subject to the allowance for depreciation provided in section 167 which—

(A) is listed in the National Register,

(B) is located in a Registered Historic District and is certified by the Secretary of the Interior as being of historic significance to the district, or

(C) is located in an historic district designated under a statute of the appropriate State or local government if such statute is certified by the Secretary of the Interior to the Secretary as containing criteria which will substantially achieve the purpose of preserving and rehabilitating buildings of historic significance to the district."

P.L. 95-600, § 701(f)(2):

Amended Code Sec. 191(g) to read as above, effective as provided in P.L. 94-455, § 2124(a)(1). Prior to amendment, Code Sec. 191(g) read as follows:

"(g) CROSS REFERENCES.—

(1) For rules relating to the listing of buildings and structures in the National Register and for definitions of 'National Register' and 'Registered Historic District', see section 470 et seq. of title 16 of the United States Code.

(2) For special rule with respect to certain gain derived from the disposition of property the adjusted basis of which is determined with regard to this section, see section 1245."

P.L. 95-600, § 701(f)(7):

Amended Code Sec. 191(f) to read as above, effective as provided in P.L. 94-455, § 2124(a)(1). Prior to amendment, Code Sec. 191(f) read as follows:

"(f) LIFE TENANT AND REMAINDERMAN.—In the case of property held by one person for life with remainder to another person, the deduction under this section shall be computed as if the life tenant were the absolute owner of the property and shall be allowable to the life tenant."

P.L. 94-455, § 2124(a)(1):

Added Code Sec. 191 to read as above. Applicable to additions to capital account made after June 14, 1976, and before June 15, 1981.

[Sec. 167(n)]

(n) STRAIGHT LINE METHOD IN CERTAIN CASES.—

(1) IN GENERAL.—In the case of any property in whole or in part constructed, reconstructed, erected, or used on a site which was, on or after June 30, 1976, occupied by a certified historic structure (or by any structure in a registered historic district) which is demolished or substantially altered after such date—

(A) subsections (b), (j), (k), and (l) shall not apply, and

(B) the term "reasonable allowance" as used in subsection (a) means only an allowance computed under the straight line method.

The preceding sentence shall not apply if the last substantial alteration of the structure is a certified rehabilitation.

(2) EXCEPTIONS.—The limitations imposed by this subsection shall not apply—

(A) to personal property, and

(B) in the case of demolition or substantial alteration of a structure located in a registered historic district, if—

(i) such structure was not a certified historic structure,

(ii) the Secretary of the Interior certified to the Secretary that such structure is not of historic significance to the district, and

(iii) if the certification referred to in clause (ii) occurs after the beginning of the demolition or substantial alteration of such structure, the taxpayer certifies to the Secretary that, at the beginning of such demolition or substantial alteration, he in good faith was not aware of the requirements of clause (ii).

(3) DEFINITIONS.—For purposes of this subsection, the terms "certified historic structure", "registered historic district", and "certified rehabilitation" have the respective meanings given such terms by section 191(d).

Source: New.

P.L. 95-600, § 701(f)(4):

Amended Code Sec. 167(n) to read as above, effective as set forth in P.L. 95-600, § 701(f)(8). Prior to amendment, Code Sec. 167(n) read as follows:

"(n) STRAIGHT LINE METHOD IN CERTAIN CASES.—

(1) IN GENERAL.—In the case of any property in whole or in part constructed, reconstructed, erected, or used on a site which was, on or after June 30, 1976, occupied by a certified historic structure (as defined in section 191(d)(1)) which is demolished or substantially altered (other than by virtue of a certified rehabilitation as defined in section 191(d)(3)) after such date—

(A) subsections (b), (j), (k), and (l) shall not apply,

(B) the term "reasonable allowance" as used in subsection (a) shall mean only an allowance computed under the straight line method.

(2) EXCEPTION.—The limitations imposed by this subsection shall not apply to personal property."

181

(8) EFFECTIVE DATE.—The amendments made by this subsection shall take effect as if included in the respective provisions of the Internal Revenue Code of 1954 to which such amendments relate, as such provisions were added to such Code, or amended, by section 2124 of the Tax Reform Act of 1976.

P.L. 94-455, § 2124(c):

Redesignated former Code Sec. 167(n) to be Code Sec. 167(p) and added a new Code Sec. 167(n) to read as above. Applicable to that portion of the basis which is attributable to construction, reconstruction, or erection after December 31, 1975, and before January 1, 1981.

[Sec. 167(o)]

(o) SUBSTANTIALLY REHABILITATED HISTORIC PROPERTY.—

(1) GENERAL RULE.—Pursuant to regulations prescribed by the Secretary, the taxpayer may elect to compute the depreciation deduction attributable to substantially rehabilitated historic property (other than property with respect to which an amortization deduction has been allowed to the taxpayer under section 191) as though the original use of such property commenced with him. The election shall be effective with respect to the taxable year referred to in paragraph (2) and all succeeding taxable years.

(2) SUBSTANTIALLY REHABILITATED PROPERTY.—For purposes of paragraph (1), the term "substantially rehabilitated historic property" means any certified historic structure (as defined in section 191(d)(1)) with respect to which the additions to capital account for any certified rehabilitation (as defined in section 191(d)(4)) during the 24-month period ending on the last day of any taxable year, reduced by any amounts allowed or allowable as depreciation or amortization with respect thereto, exceeds the greater of—

(A) the adjusted basis of such property, or

(B) $5,000.

The adjusted basis of the property shall be determined as of the beginning of the first day of such 24-month period, or of the holding period of the property (within the meaning of section 1250(e)), whichever is later.

Source: New.

Amendments:	Sec. as amended effective:
P.L. 95-600, § 701(f)(6)(A)	....
P.L. 95-600, § 701(f)(6)(B)	....
P.L. 95-600, § 701(f)(8)	....
P.L. 94-455, § 2124(d)	....

182

P.L. 95-600, § 701(f)(6)(A):

Amended Code Sec. 167(o)(1) by inserting "(other than property with respect to which an amortization deduction has been allowed to the taxpayer under section 191)" after "substantially rehabilitated historic property", effective as set forth in P.L. 95-600, § 701(f)(8).

P.L. 95-600, § 701(f)(6)(B):

Amended Code Sec. 167(o)(2) by striking out "section 191(d)(3)" and inserting in lieu thereof "section 191(d)(4)" effective as set forth in P.L. 95-600, § 701(f)(8).

P.L. 95-600, § 701(f)(8):

(8) EFFECTIVE DATE.—The amendments made by this subsection shall take effect as if included in the respective provisions of the Internal Revenue Code of 1954 to which such amendments relate, as such provisions were added to such Code, or amended, by section 2124 of the Tax Reform Act of 1976.

P.L. 94-455, § 2124(d):

Added Code Sec. 167(o) to read as above. Applicable with respect to additions to capital account occurring after June 30, 1976, and before July 1, 1981.

[Sec. 280B]

SEC. 280B. DEMOLITION OF CERTAIN HISTORIC STRUCTURES.

[Sec. 280B(a)]

(a) GENERAL RULE.—In the case of the demolition of a certified historic structure (as defined in section 191(d)(1))—

(1) no deduction otherwise allowable under this chapter shall be allowed to the owner or lessee of such structure for—

(A) any amount expended for such demolition, or

(B) any loss sustained on account of such demolition; and

(2) amounts described in paragraph (1) shall be treated as properly chargeable to capital account with respect to the land on which the demolished structure was located.

Source: New.

Amendments:	Sec. as amended effective:
P.L. 94-455, § 2124(b)(1)	....

P.L. 94-455, § 2124(b)(1):

Added Code Sec. 280B(a) to read as above, effective for demolitions commencing after June 30, 1976, and before January 1, 1981.

(b) SPECIAL RULE FOR REGISTERED HISTORIC DISTRICTS.—For purposes of this section, any building or other structure located in a registered historic district (as defined in section 191(d)(2)) shall be treated as a certified historic structure unless the Secretary of the Interior has certified that such structure is not a certified historic structure, and that such structure is not of historic significance to the district, and if such certification occurs after the beginning of the demolition of such structure, the taxpayer has certified to the Secretary that, at the time of such demolition, he in good faith was not aware of the certification requirement by the Secretary of the Interior.

Source: New.

Amendments:	Sec. as amended effective:
P.L. 95-600, § 701(f)(5), (8) ...	....
P.L. 94-455, § 2124(b)(1)	....

P.L. 95-600, § 701(f)(5), (8):

Amended Code Sec. 280B(b) to read as above, effective as if such amendment was included in Code Sec. 280B(b) as added by P.L. 94-455, Sec. 2124(b)(1), below. Before amendment, such subsection read:

"(b) SPECIAL RULE FOR REGISTERED HISTORIC DISTRICTS.—For purposes of this section, any building or other structure located in a registered historic district shall be treated as a certified historic structure unless the Secretary of the Interior has certified, prior to the demolition of such structure, that such structure is not of historic significance to the district."

P.L. 94-455, § 2124(b)(1):

Added Code Sec. 280B(b) to read as above, effective for demolitions commencing after June 30, 1976, and before January 1, 1981.

Provisions on Charitable Deduction for Partial Interests in Historic Property (Section 170f)

[Sec. 170(f)]

(f) DISALLOWANCE OF DEDUCTION IN CERTAIN CASES AND SPECIAL RULES.—

(1) IN GENERAL.—No deduction shall be allowed under this section for a contribution to or for the use of an organization or trust described in section 508(d) or 4948(c)(4) subject to the conditions specified in such sections.

(2) CONTRIBUTIONS OF PROPERTY PLACED IN TRUST.—

(A) REMAINDER INTEREST.—In the case of property transferred in trust, no deduction shall be allowed under this section for the value of a contribution of a remainder interest unless the trust is a charitable remainder annuity trust or a charitable remainder unitrust (described in section 664), or a pooled income fund (described in section 642(c)(5)).

(B) INCOME INTERESTS, ETC.—No deduction shall be allowed under this section for the value of any interest in property (other than a remainder interest) transferred in trust unless the interest is in the form of a guaranteed annuity or the trust instrument specifies that the interest is a fixed percentage distributed yearly of the fair market value of the trust property (to be determined yearly) and the grantor is treated as the owner of such interest for purposes of applying section 671. If the donor ceases to be treated as the owner of such an interest for purposes of applying section 671, at the time the donor ceases to be so treated, the donor shall for purposes of this chapter be considered as having received an amount of income equal to the amount of any deduction he received under this section for the contribution reduced by the discounted value of all amounts of income earned by the trust and taxable to him before the time at which he ceases to be treated as the owner of the interest. Such amounts of income shall be discounted to the date of the contribution. The Secretary shall prescribe such regulations as may be necessary to carry out the purposes of this subparagraph.

(C) DENIAL OF DEDUCTION IN CASE OF PAYMENTS BY CERTAIN TRUSTS.—In any case in which a deduction is allowed under this section for the value of an interest in property described in subparagraph (B), transferred in trust, no deduction shall be allowed under this section to the grantor or any other person for the amount of any contribution made by the trust with respect to such interest.

(D) EXCEPTION.—This paragraph shall not apply in a case in which the value of all interests in property transferred in trust are deductible under subsection (a).

(3) DENIAL OF DEDUCTION IN CASE OF CERTAIN CONTRIBUTIONS OF PARTIAL INTERESTS IN PROPERTY.—

(A) IN GENERAL.—In the case of a contribution (not made by a transfer in trust) of an interest in property which consists of less than the taxpayer's entire interest in such property, a deduction shall be allowed under this section only to the extent that the value of the interest contributed would be allowable as a deduction under this section if such interest had been transferred in trust. For purposes of this subparagraph, a contribution by a taxpayer of the right to use property shall be treated as a contribution of less than the taxpayer's entire interest in such property.

(B) EXCEPTIONS.—Subparagraph (A) shall not apply to a contribution of—

(i) a remainder interest in a personal residence or farm,

(ii) an undivided portion of the taxpayer's entire interest in property,

(iii) a lease on, option to purchase, or easement with respect to real property granted in perpetuity to an organization described in subsection (b)(1)(A) exclusively for conservation purposes, or

(iv) a remainder interest in real property which is granted to an organization described in subsection (b)(1)(A) exclusively for conservation purposes.

(C) CONSERVATION PURPOSES DEFINED.—For purposes of subparagraph (B), the term "conservation purposes" means—

(i) the preservation of land areas for public outdoor recreation or education, or scenic enjoyment;

(ii) the preservation of historically important land areas or structures; or

(iii) the protection of natural environmental systems.

(4) VALUATION OF REMAINDER INTEREST IN REAL PROPERTY.—For purposes of this section, in determining the value of a remainder interest in real property, depreciation (computed on the straight line method) and depletion of such property shall be taken into account, and such value shall be discounted at a rate of 6 percent per annum, except that the Secretary may prescribe a different rate.

(5) REDUCTION FOR CERTAIN INTEREST.—If, in connection with any charitable contribution, a liability is assumed by the recipient or by any other person, or if a charitable contribution is of property which is subject to a liability, then, to the extent necessary to avoid the duplication of amounts, the amount taken into account for purposes of this section as the amount of the charitable contribution—

(A) shall be reduced for interest (i) which has been paid (or is to be paid) by the taxpayer, (ii) which is attributable to the liability, and (iii) which is attributable to any period after the making of the contribution, and

(B) in the case of a bond, shall be further reduced for interest (i) which has been paid (or is to be paid) by the taxpayer on indebtedness incurred or continued to purchase or carry such bond, and (ii) which is attributable to any period before the making of the contribution.

The reduction pursuant to subparagraph (B) shall not exceed the interest (including interest equivalent) on the bond which is attributable to any period before the making of the contribution and which is not (under the taxpayer's method of accounting) includible in the gross income of the taxpayer for any taxable year. For purposes of this paragraph, the term "bond" means any bond, debenture, note, or certificate or other evidence of indebtedness.

(6) DEDUCTIONS FOR OUT-OF-POCKET EXPENDITURES.—No deduction shall be allowed under this section for an out-of-pocket expenditure made by any person on behalf of an organization described in subsection (c) (other than an organization described in section 501(h)(5) (relating to churches, etc.)) if the expenditure is made for the purpose of influencing legislation (within the meaning of section 501(c)(3)).

184

Source: New.

Amendments: | **Sec. as amended effective:**

P.L. 95-30, § 309(a) . . . .
P.L. 94-455, § § 1307(c),
1901(a)(28), 1906(b)(13)(A),
2124(e) . . . .
P. L. 91-172, § 201(a)(1) . . . .
P. L. 88-272, § 209(e) . . . .

P.L. 95-30, § 309(a):

Amended clause (iii) of Code Sec. 170(f)(3)(B) to read as above, effective for contributions or transfers made after June 13, 1977, and before June 14, 1981. Prior to amendment, clause (iii) read as follows:

"(iii) a lease on, option to purchase, or easement with respect to real property of not less than 30 years' duration granted to an organization described in subsection (b)(1)(A) exclusively for conservation purposes, or".

P.L. 94-455, § § 1307(c), 1901(a)(28), 1906(b)(13)(A), 2124(e) (as amended by P.L. 95-30, § 309(b)(2)):

Amended Code Sec. 170(f) as follows:

§ 1901(a) repealed Code Sec. 170(f)(6) and § 1307(c) added a new paragraph (6) to read as above, effective for taxable years beginning after December 31, 1976. Prior to repeal, former Code Sec. 170(f)(6) read as follows:

(6) PARTIAL REDUCTION OF UNLIMITED DEDUCTION.—

(A) IN GENERAL.—If the limitations in subsections (b)(1)(A) and (B) do not apply because of the application of subsection (b)(1)(C), the amount otherwise allowable as a deduction under subsection (a) shall be reduced by the amount by which the taxpayer's taxable income computed without regard to this subparagraph is less than the transitional income percentage (determined under subparagraph (C)) of the taxpayer's adjusted gross income. However, in no case shall a taxpayer's deduction under this section be reduced below the amount allowable as a deduction under this section without the applicability of subsection (b)(1)(C).

(B) TRANSITIONAL DEDUCTION PERCENTAGE.—For purposes of applying subsection (b)(1)(C), the term "transitional deduction percentage" means—

(i) in the case of a taxable year beginning before 1970, 90 percent, and

(ii) in the case of a taxable year beginning in—

1970	80 percent
1971	74 percent
1972	68 percent
1973	62 percent
1974	56 percent.

HISTORIC PRESERVATION TAX PROVISIONS
OF THE TAX REFORM ACT OF 1976:
FEDERAL REGULATIONS

Title 36—Parks, Forests, and Public Property

CHAPTER I—NATIONAL PARK SERVICE, DEPARTMENT OF THE INTERIOR

PART 67—HISTORIC PRESERVATION CERTIFICATIONS PURSUANT TO THE TAX REFORM ACT OF 1976

AGENCY: National Park Service, Interior.

ACTION: Final rulemaking.

SUMMARY: This rule revises and makes final the interim regulations published for comment in the FEDERAL REGISTER of March 15, 1977 (42 FR 14121). The Tax Reform Act of 1976 requires the Secretary of the Interior to make certain certifications with respect to the historic character of buildings and structures and to the rehabilitation work undertaken on such buildings and structures.

EFFECTIVE DATE: November 7, 1977.

ADDRESS: Send comments to: Mr. Jerry L. Rogers, Chief, Office of Archeology and Historic Preservation, National Park Service, Department of the Interior, Washington, D.C. 20240 (202-523-5275).

SUPPLEMENTARY INFORMATION: On March 15, 1977, a notice of proposed rulemaking was published in the FEDERAL REGISTER (42 FR 14121) to amend Chapter I Title 36 of the Code of Federal Regulations by adding a new part 67 concerning historic preservation certifications pursuant to the Tax Reform Act of 1976 (Pub. L. 94–455 90 Stat. 1519) made by the Secretary of the Interior.

At that time, it was explained that under Section 2124, "Tax Incentives to Encourage the Preservation of Historic Structures," the Secretary of the Interior is required to make certain certifications with respect to the historic character of buildings and structures, the rehabilitation of historic buildings and structures, and the preservation criteria of State and Local statutes. The purpose of the proposed rulemaking was to regularize procedures, standards, and criteria for the making of such certifications. The Internal Revenue Service, pursuant to its regulatory authorities, has and will continue to issue all regulations necessary for implementation of Section 2124

of the Tax Reform Act of 1976 with respect to Federal income tax consequences, requirements, and procedures. However, the section 2124 tax incentive provisions are generally described as follows so as to permit a public understanding of the certifications required to be made by the Secretary:

1. Section 2124(a). (Section 191 of the Internal Revenue Code of 1954). Permits a 60-month amortization of certain rehabilitation expenses made in connection with qualified depreciable properties;

2. Section 2124(b). (Section 280B of the Internal Revenue Code of 1954). Disallows a deduction for demolition of qualified depreciable properties;

3. Section 2124(c). (Section 167(n) of the Internal Revenue Code of 1954). Generally precludes accelerated depreciation for structures built on the site of qualified depreciable properties;

4. Section 2124(d). (Section 167(o) of the Internal Revenue Code of 1954). Provides special depreciation rules for qualified rehabilitated property;

5. Section 2124(e). (Sections 170(f)(3), 2055(e)(2) and 2522(c)(2) of the Internal Revenue Code of 1954). Amends charitable contribution deductions on income, estate, and gift taxes to liberalize deductions for conservation purposes (including historic preservation).

The term "depreciable properties" as used above generally means those properties subject to the allowance for depreciation under Section 167 of the Internal Revenue Code of 1954 and generally excludes owner-occupied homes.

Sections (a)–(d) of Section 2124 as briefly described above require the Secretary of the Interior to make the following classes of certifications:

a. *Certified Historic Structures.* All the tax provisions described above (except subsection 2124(e)) are related to so-called "Certified Historic Structures," which, generally, are defined as qualified depreciable properties of historic character which are either listed in the National Register, or are located within a historic district listed in the National Register or created by or pursuant to a certified State or local Statute. The Secretary, as a general rule, must certify that such structures are in fact "Certified Historic Structures" before the described tax consequences accrue.

b. *Certified Rehabilitation.* In order for the tax consequences described above relating to rehabilitation to accrue, the Secretary must determine not only that the rehabilitation was done to a certified historic structure but also that it meets certain standards with respect to the historic integrity of the rehabilitation work.

c. *Certified Statutes.* Qualified historic structures located in historic districts designated under a statute of the appropriate State or local government are subject to the tax consequences discussed above if located within a historic district created by or pursuant to a statute of local or State government certified by the Secretary as containing criteria which will substantially achieve the purposes of preserving and rehabilitating buildings of historic significance to the district. This rulemaking is developed under the authority of Section 101(a)(1) of the National Historic Preservation Act of 1966 U.S.C. 470a–1(a) (1970 ed.), as amended, and Section 2124 of the Tax Reform Act of 1976, 90 Stat. 1519. In compliance with the National Environmental Policy Act of 1969 (42 U.S.C. 4331, et seq.) the National Park Service has prepared an environmental assessment of these regulations. Based on this assessment, it is determined that implementation of the regulations is not a major Federal action that would have a significant effect on the quality of the human environment and that an environmental impact statement is not required. The assessment, on file in the office of the Chief, Office of Archeology and Historic Preservation, National Park Service, Department of the Interior, Washington, D.C. 20240, is available for public inspection. It has been administratively determined that this proposed rulemaking is not "major" within the intent of Section 2124 of the Tax Reform Act of 1976 and that an inflationary impact certification is therefore not required.

Changes have been incorporated in this final rulemaking both in response to the comments that were received and based upon National Park Service review. Consistent with the discussions below, no major changes in the certification process have been necessary. The minor changes are as follows:

1. Recognizing that active State participation in the certification process may not be possible at this time, Section 67.3 has been expanded to explain how in certain situations owners of record may apply for certifications directly to the Secretary and bypassing the State preservation office.

2. Recognizing that some completed rehabilitation projects may not require an onsite inspection, the revised regulations (Section 67.7) require the owner to provide photographs of the completed rehabilitation to the State Historic Preservation Officer and to attest that in the owner's opinion, the rehabilitation is consistent with the Secretary's "Standards for Rehabilitation." In some cases, this documentation will be sufficient to enable the Secretary to certify the rehabilitation without an onsite inspection being necessary.

3. In the interim regulations, reference was made to three application forms: "Application for Evaluation of Significance;" "Application for Certified Rehabilitation;" and "Request for Inspection" form. In an attempt to simplify the certification process, the decision was made to consolidate the information required by these three forms into a single application form. The resulting "Historic Preservation Certification Application" eliminates some of the duplication present in the three forms yet provides sufficient space for documentation on the historic character of the building and the nature of the rehabilitation work.

4. The Secretary's "Standards for Rehabilitation," set forth in Section 67.7, have been modified slightly and renumbered, reflecting the comments from State Historic Preservation Officers and others. The revised standards set forth herein have been reviewed and approved by the Committee on Rules and Regulations of the National Conference of State Historic Preservation Officers. There was some concern that the National Park Service was restricting the range of rehabilitation projects by requiring that all rehabilitated structures be used for their originally intended purpose. This was not the intent of the Secretary's "Standards for Rehabilitation," and to clarify this point, the Standards were reworded to encourage compatible and creative adaptive use provided that the architectural and historical integrity of the structure is not irrevocably impaired.

Two new standards have been added, one dealing with the surface cleaning of structures, the other concerned with the protection of archaeological resources affected by rehabilitation projects. Both standards articulate concerns implied in the earlier set of standards.

5. Under temporary income tax regulations published on April 6, 1977 by the Department of the Treasury (26 CFR Part 7, 42 FR 18275), taxpayers may elect to amortize expenditures incurred in rehabilitating a structure prior to actual certification of the project by the Secretary, provided the taxpayer has requested certification in accord with these regulations. Sections 67.4 and 67.6 have been amended to enable owners of such structures to obtain a preliminary determination whether their structure contributes to the historic significance of the district in which it is included and a preliminary determination whether the rehabilitation work will meet the Secretary of Interior's "Standards for Rehabilitation." The regulations make it clear that taxpayers owning structures not yet determined to be "certified historic struc-

tures" will be proceeding at their own risk.

On August 10, 1977, Section 67 of the interim rules was amended by adding a new Section 67.9 entitled "Certification of State or Local Statutes." This particular section will remain as an interim regulation until such time as it may be amended and published in final. The originators of these regulations are Carol Shull, Ward Jandl, and Katherine Cole, National Park Service.

Accordingly, with minor changes and additions, and in consideration of the foregoing comments and the reasons given in the preamble to the proposed rulemaking on March 15, 1977, which is specifically hereto by reference, the proposed new part 67.1 through 67.8 of Chapter I of Title 36 of the Code of Federal Regulations is hereby adopted, effective November 7, 1977, as follows:

AUTHORITY: Sec. 101(a)(1). 80 Stat. 915 as amended. (16 U.S.C. 470–1(a)): Sec. 2124. 90 Stat. 1519.

§ 67.1   The Tax Reform Act of 1976.

The Tax Reform Act of 1976, 90 Stat. 1519, requires the Secretary to make certifications of historic significance and certifications of rehabilitation in connection with certain tax incentives involving historic preservation. The procedures for obtaining such certifications are set forth below. The Internal Revenue Service is responsible for all procedures, legal determinations and rules and regulations concerning the tax consequences of the historic preservation incentives of the Tax Reform Act of 1976. Any certifications made by the Secretary pursuant to this part shall not be considered as binding upon the Internal Revenue Service with respect to tax consequences or interpretations of the Internal Revenue Code of 1954. Certifications made by the Secretary do not constitute determinations that a structure is of the type subject to the allowance for depreciation under Section 167 of the Internal Revenue Code of 1954.

§ 67.2   Definitions.

As used in these procedures:

(a) "Certified Historic Structure" means a structure which is of a character subject to the allowance for depreciation provided in Section 167 of the Internal Revenue Code of 1954 which is either (1) listed in the National Register; or (2) located in a National Register historic district and certified by the Secretary of the Interior as being of historic significance to the district; or (3) located in a historic district designated under a statute of the appropriate State or local government if such a statute is certified by the Secretary to the Secretary of the Treasury pursuant to 36 CFR 67.9

(b) "Certified Rehabilitation" means any rehabilitation of a certified historic structure occurring after June 14, 1976, and prior to June 15, 1981, which the Secretary has certified to the Secretary of the Treasury as being consistent with the historic character of such property or the district in which such property is located.

(c) "Historic District" means a geographically definable area, urban or rural, possessing a significant concentration, linkage, or continuity of sites, buildings, structures, or objects which are united by past events or aesthetically by plan or physical development.

(d) "Inspection" means a visit by an authorized representative of the Secretary of the Interior to a certified historic structure for the purposes of reviewing and evaluating the significance of the structures and the completed rehabilitation work.

(e) "National Register" means the national register of districts, sites, buildings, structures, and objects significant in American history, architecture, archeology, and culture that the Secretary is authorized to expand and maintain pursuant to Section 101(a)(1) of the National Historic Preservation Act of 1966.

(f) "National Register Program" means the survey, planning, and registration program that has evolved under the Secretary's authority pursuant to 101(a)(1) of the National Historic Preservation Act of 1966. The procedures of the National Register program appear in 36 CFR Part 60.

(g) "Registered Historic District" means any district listed in the National Register or any district designated under a State or local statute which has been certified by the Secretary as containing criteria which will substantially achieve the purpose of preserving and rehabilitating buildings of historic significance to the district.

(h) "Rehabilitation" means the process of returning a property to a state of utility, through repair or alteration, which makes possible an efficient contemporary use while preserving those portions and features of the property which are significant to its historic, architectural and cultural values.

(i) "Secretary" means the Secretary of the Interior or the designee authorized to carry out his responsibilities.

(j) "Standards for Rehabilitation" mean the Secretary of the Interior's "Standards for Rehabilitation" as set forth in § 67.7. hereof.

(k) "State Historic Preservation Officer" means the official within each State, or his designated representative, authorized by the State at the request of the Secretary to act as liaison for purposes of implementing the requirements of the National Historic Preservation Act of 1966.

(I) "Structure" means a specific piece of real estate, including building(s) and other site improvements.

§ 67.3 How to apply.

(a) Ordinarily, only the record owner of the property in question may apply for the certifications described in §§ 67.4 and 67.6 hereof. However, upon request of a State Historic Preservation Officer, the Secretary may determine whether or not a particular structure located within a Registered Historic District qualifies as a certified historic structure. The Secretary shall do so, however, only after notifying the property owner of record of the request, informing such owner of the possible tax consequences of such decision, and permitting the property owner to submit written comments to the Secretary prior to decision.

(b) Requests for certifications shall be made through the appropriate State Historic Preservation Officer except in those cases when that official chooses not to participate in the certification process. The recommendations of the State Historic Preservation Officer are generally accepted and supported by the Secretary. If, however, a State Historic Preservation Officer has indicated to the Secretary his inability to participate in the certification process or is unable to make recommendations to the Secretary within the period of time specified herein, the property owner may apply directly to the Secretary. In all other situations, requests for certification are to be made through the appropriate State Historic Preservation Officer.

§ 67.4 Certifications of historic significance.

(a) Requests for evaluation of historic significance as required by sections 2124(a), (b), (c), and (d) of the Tax Reform Act of 1976 should be made by the owner in accordance with respective procedures for the following categories of certifications: (1) That a structure is listed in the National Register; (2) that a structure is located within a Registered Historic District but is or is not of historic significance to such district.

(b) If the property is individually listed in the National Register:

(1) To determine whether or not a property is individually listed in the National Register, the owner should consult the listing of National Register properties in the FEDERAL REGISTER (found in most large libraries). This listing generally appears the first Tuesday of February each year, with regular monthly updates. If access to the FEDERAL REGISTER is difficult, the owner shall contact the appropriate State Historic Preservation Officer for this information.

(2) If the property is individually listed in the National Register and the owner believes it has lost the characteristics which caused it to be nominated

and therefore wishes it delisted, the owner should refer to the procedures outlined in 36 CFR 60.17.

(c) If the property is located within the boundaries of a Registered Historic District and the owner wishes the Secretary to certify as to whether the structure is of historic significance to the district, the owner must make written application to the appropriate State Historic Preservation Officer and provide the following minimum documentation to the State Historic Preservation Officer, upon his request:

(1) Name of owner;

(2) Name and address of structure;

(3) Name of historic district;

(4) Current photographs of structure;

(5) Brief description of appearance including alterations, distinctive features and spaces, and date(s) of construction;

(6) Brief statement of significance (architectural and/or historical); and

(7) Signature of property owner requesting the evaluation.

(d) The State Historic Preservation Officer will forward the information listed in paragraph (c) of this section, along with his written recommendation as to the significance of the structure, to the Keeper of the National Register. Part I of an "Historic Preservation Certification Application" shall be used in requesting an evaluation from the Secretary. Applicantion forms are supplied to the State Historic Preservation Officers by the Keeper of the National Register at the address given above.

(e) The State Historic Preservation Officer shall forward Part 1 of the "Historic Preservation Certification Application" to the Keeper of the National Register within 45 days after the owner has submitted the required information. If this period has expired without such actions being taken the owner may request an evaluation of significance directly from the Keeper of the National Register pursuant to § 67.3(c) above.

(f) Structures within Registered Historic Districts will be evaluated for conformance with the Secretary's "Standards for Evaluating within Historic Districts" as set forth in § 67.5 hereof. Once the significance of the structure has been determined by the Secretary, written notification will be sent directly to the property owner in the form of a Certification of Significance or as a notice that the structure does not contribute to the historic significance of the district. Written notification will be made within 30 days of receipt of Part 1 of an "Historic Preservation Certification Application."

(g) Owners of structures which (1) appear to meet National Register criteria (36 CFR 60.6) but are not yet listed in the National Register; or (2) are located within a historic district which appears to meet National Register criteria but has not yet been listed in the National Register may request preliminary determinations, through the State Historic Preservation Officer, as to whether such

188

structures may qualify as certified historic structures when and if the property or district is listed in the National Register. Any such determinations are preliminary only and will be reconsidered upon further review by the Secretary at the time the individual property or district is nominated to the National Register.

§ 67.5 Standards for evaluating structures within Registered Historic Districts.

Structures located within Registered Historic Districts are reviewed by the Secretary for conformance to the following "Standards for Evaluating Structures within Registered Historic Districts." These standards shall be used by the State Historic Preservation Officer in making recommendations to the Secretary.

(a) A structure contributing to the historic significance of a district is one which by location, design, setting, materials, workmanship, feeling and association adds to the district's sense of time and place and historical development.

(b) A structure not contributing to the historic significance of a district is one which detracts from the district's sense of time and place and historical development intrinsically; or when the integrity of the original design or individual architectural features or spaces have been irretrievably lost.

(c) Ordinarily structures that have been built within the past 50 years shall not be considered eligible unless a strong justification concerning their historical or architectural merit is given or the historical attributes of the district are considered to be less than 50 years old.

§ 67.6 Certification of rehabilitation.

Property owners desirous of having rehabilitations of certified historic structures certified by the Secretary as being consistent with the historic character of the structure or district in which the structure is located, thus qualifying as "certified rehabilitations," shall comply with the following procedures:

(a) Obtain from the appropriate State Historic Preservation Officer or from the Technical Preservation Services Division, National Park Service, Washington, D.C. 20240, an "Historic Preservation Certification Application" and a copy of the Secretary's "Standards for Rehabilitation" and guidelines for applying these standards.

(b) Complete part 2 of the application form and submit it to the State Historic Preservation Officer. The application may be for proposed rehabilitation or completed rehabilitation.

(c) If the work described in part 2 of the application form has not commenced, the appropriate State Historic Preservation Officer shall review the proposed project as to whether or not the project is likely to meet the Secretary of the Interior's "Standards for Rehabilitation" and forward the application and recommendations to the Secretary within 45 days of receipt of the application and any additional information the State Historic Preservation Officer may request.

(d) Upon receipt of the application describing the proposed project and the recommendation of the State Historic Preservation Officer, the Secretary shall determine, normally within 45 days, if the proposed project is consistent with the "Standards for Rehabilitation." If the proposed project does not meet the "Standards for Rehabilitation," the owner shall be advised of necessary revisions to meet such standards.

(e) Upon completion of the rehabilitation project, the owner shall notify the appropriate State Historic Preservation Officer in writing of the project completion date and shall sign a statement that, in the owner's opinion, the completed rehabilitation meets the Secretary's "Standards for Rehabilitation" and is consistent with the work described in part 2 of the "Historic Preservation Certification Application." At this time the owner will be requested to provide photographs of the completed rehabilitation project and other documentation that the State Historic Preservation Officer believes is necessary to make a recommendation to the Secretary. The completed project may be inspected by an authorized representative of the Secretary to determine if the work meets the "Standards for Rehabilitation." Inspections, if made, will normally be completed within 30 days of receipt by the State Historic Preservation Officer of the project completion date. The Secretary reserves the right to make inspections at any time after completion of the rehabilitation and to withdraw certification of the rehabilitation upon determining that the project does not meet the Secretary's "Standards for Rehabilitation" as proposed and/or completed.

(f) The State Historic Preservation Officer shall forward his recommendations as to certification to the Secretary within 30 days of receipt of the project completion date and documentation described in paragraph (e) of this section.

(g) Notification as to certification shall be in writing and will normally be made by the Secretary within 15 days of receipt of the State Historic Preservation Officer's recommendations.

(h) In the event that the completed rehabilitation project does not meet the "Standards for Rehabilitation," an explanatory letter will be sent to the owner. An appeal from this decision may be made by the owner pursuant to § 67.8.

(i) Although parts 1 and 2 of the "Historic Preservation Certification Application" may be submitted concurrently to the Secretary, no certifications of rehabilitation will be issued until the structure has been designated a "certified historic structure."

(j) (1) A determination that a rehabilitation project is consistent with the Secretary's "Standards for Rehabilitation" may be made for structures not yet designated "certified historic structures." Such determinations will be made only if the owner has requested certification in accord with these regulations and has obtained confirmation from the appropriate State Historic Preservation Officer (i) that the structure appears to meet National Register Criteria for Evaluation and will likely be nominated to the National Register in accordance with National Park Service procedures (36 CFR 60); or (ii) that the structure is located within a historic district that appears to meet National Register Criteria for Evaluation, will likely be nominated to the National Register in accordance with National Park Service procedures (36 CFR 60), and appears to contribute to the character of said district, in accordance with § 67.5 above.

(2) Taxpayers should understand that confirmation of intent to nominate does not constitute listing in the National Register nor does it constitute an evaluation of significance as required under Section 2124 (a), (b), (c), and (d) of the Tax Reform Act of 1976.

(3) Taxpayers should be aware that they are proceeding at their own risk, for when additional research on the structure is completed, it may become clear that the property does not meet National Register Criteria for Evaluation.

(4) Owners of record should fill out Parts 1 and 2 of the "Historic Preservation Certification Application" and submit the completed form to the State Historic Preservation Officer. Review of rehabilitation work undertaken on such a structure will be made in accord with procedures set forth above. Issuance of a certification of rehabilitation, however, will be made only for "certified historic structures." A determination that rehabilitation of a structure not yet designated a "certified historic structure" meets the Secretary's "Standards for Rehabilitation" does not constitute a certification of rehabilitation.

§ 67.7 Standards for rehabilitation.

(a) The following "Standards for Rehabilitation" shall be used by the Secretary to determine if rehabilitation of a certified historic structure qualifies as "certified rehabilitation." With respect to certified historic structures located within districts designated by State or local Statutes certified by the Secretary, the rehabilitated structure must be consistent with the historic character of the district in which it is located to qualify as "certified rehabilitation."

(1) Every reasonable effort shall be made to provide a compatible use for a property which requires minimal alterations of the building structure, or site and its environment, or to use a property for its originally intended purpose.

(2) The distinguishing original qualities or character of a building structure or site and its environment shall not be destroyed. The removal or alteration of any historic material or distinctive architectural features should be avoided when possible.

(3) All buildings, structures, and sites shall be recognized as products of their own time. Alterations that have no historical basis and which seek to create an earlier appearance shall be discouraged.

(4) Changes which may have taken place in the course of time are evidence of the history and development of a building, structure, or site and its environment. These changes may have acquired significance in their own right, and this significance shall be recognized and respected.

(5) Distinctive stylistic features or examples of skilled craftsmanship which characterize a building, structure, or site shall be treated with sensitivity.

(6) Deteriorated architectural features shall be repaired rather than replaced, wherever possible. In the event replacement is necessary, the new material should match the material being replaced in composition, design, color, texture, and other visual qualities. Repair or replacement of missing architectural features should be based on accurate duplications rather than on conjectural designs or the availability of different architectural elements from other buildings or structures.

(7) The surface cleaning of structures shall be undertaken with the gentlest means possible. Sandblasting and other cleaning methods that will damage the historic building materials shall not be undertaken.

(8) Every reasonable effort shall be made to protect and preserve archaeological resources affected by, or adjacent to any rehabilitation project.

(9) Contemporary design for alterations and additions to existing properties shall not be discouraged when such alterations and additions do not destroy significant historical, architectural, or cultural material, and such design is compatible with the size, scale, color, material, and character of the property, neighborhood or environment.

(10) Wherever possible, new additions or alterations to structures shall be done in such a manner that if such additions or alterations were to be removed in the future, the essential form and integrity of the structure would be unimpaired.

(b) Guidelines to help property owners formulate plans for the rehabilitation, preservation, and continued use of historic properties consistent with the intent of the Secretary's "Standards for Rehabilitation," are available from the Technical Preservation Services Division,

National Park Service, Washington, D.C. 20240.

§ 67.8 Appeals.

An appeal may be made from any of the certifications or denials of certifications made pursuant to this part. Such appeals must be in writing and received by the Chief, Office of Archaeology and Historic Preservation, National Park Service, Department of the Interior, Washington, D.C. 20240 within 30 days of receipt by the appellant of the decision which is the subject of the appeal. The Chief, Office of Archaeology and Historic Preservation, will review such appeals and the written record of the decision in question and shall advise the appellant within 30 days of its receipt unless the appellant is required to submit additional information. The decision of the Chief, Office of Archaeology and Historic Preservation, shall be the final administrative decision on the matter. Appeals pursuant hereto should be mailed to the address noted above.

Dated: September 29, 1977.

ERNEST ALLEN CONNALLY,
Acting Director,
National Park Service.

[FR Doc.77–29459 Filed 10–6–77; 8:45 am]

[26 CFR Parts 1 and 7]

[LR–199–76]

INCOME TAX

Amortization of Certain Rehabilitation Costs for Certified Historic Structures

AGENCY: Internal Revenue Service, Treasury.

ACTION: Notice of proposed rulemaking.

SUMMARY: This document contains proposed regulations relating to amortization of certain rehabilitation expenditures for certified historic structures. Changes to the applicable tax law were made by the Tax Reform Act of 1976. These regulations affect all persons desiring to amortize such rehabilitation expenditures and provide them with the guidance needed to comply with the law.

DATES: Written comments and requests for a public hearing must be delivered or mailed by October 30, 1978. The amendments are proposed to be effective for costs incurred after June 14, 1976, and before June 15, 1981.

ADDRESS: Send comments and requests for a public hearing to: Commissioner of Internal Revenue, Attention: CC:LR:T (LR–199–76), Washington, D.C. 20224.

FOR FURTHER INFORMATION CONTACT:

H. B. Hartley of the Legislation and Regulations Division, Office of Chief Counsel, Internal Revenue Service, 1111 Constitution Avenue NW., Washington, D C. 20224, 202-566-6624 (not a toll-free number).

SUPPLEMENTARY INFORMATION:

BACKGROUND

This document contains proposed amendments to the Income Tax Regulations (26 CFR Part 1) and the Temporary Income Tax Regulations under the Tax Reform Act of 1976 (26 CFR Part 7), all under section 191. The amendments are proposed to conform the regulations to section 2124 (a) (1) and (3) (B) of the Tax Reform Act of 1976 (90 Stat. 1916). They are issued under the authority contained in sections 191 and 7805 of the Internal Revenue Code of 1954 (90 Stat. 1916, 68A Stat. 917; 26 U.S.C. 191, 7805).

PROVISIONS OF THE REGULATIONS

Under section 191, owners of historic structures certified by the Secretary of the Interior may elect to amortize the amortizable basis attributable to costs incurred in certified rehabilitations of these structures. If this election is made, the rehabilitation costs are amortized over a 60-month period rather than depreciated over their actual useful life. Amortization deductions under section 191 may not be claimed if any part of the costs of the certified rehabilitation are deducted under any other provision of the Internal Revenue Code. However, allowable depreciation deductions on the basis of the historic structure, exclusive of the rehabilitation costs, may be continued during the amortization period. If an election involving the historic structure is made under section 191, no election may be made under section 167 (o).

The election is available only to owners (or life tenants) of certified historic structures. Lessees and other persons owning less than a fee simple interest are not treated as owners of certified historic structures for purposes of section 191. In general, owners may amortize only those expenditures made while they own the property and only those expenditures for rehabilitation.

In the event of a disposition of the property, part or all of the amounts deducted under section 191 may be recaptured as ordinary income. In addition, the difference between rapid amortization and straight-line depreciation may be subject to the minimum tax.

191

All costs of a certified rehabilitation are generally amortizable. However, costs attributable to nondepreciable portions of a certified historic structure only part of which is used in a trade or business or for the production of income and costs of new construction associated with a certified rehabilitation, are not amortizable.

To elect the 60-month amortization, the taxpayer attaches a statement to the taxpayer's return for the taxable year in which falls the first month of the amortization period chosen pursuant to section 191(a). The election may be made after a request has been made for, but before, certification of the project by the Department of the Interior. In such a case, proof of certification is to be submitted with the first tax return filed by the taxpayer after receipt of the certification. If a certification is not submitted within 30 months after commencement of the amortization period, the taxpayer may be asked to agree to an extension of time for assessment of additional tax for the period for which deductions are claimed.

Once made, the election may be discontinued by filing written notice with the Internal Revenue Service at any time before the month in which amortization is to cease.

DRAFTING INFORMATION

The principal author of these regulations was H. B. Hartley of the Legislation and Regulations Division of the Office of Chief Counsel, Internal Revenue Service. However, personnel from other offices of the Internal Revenue Service and Treasury Department participated in developing the regulations, both on matters of substance and style.

PROPOSED AMENDMENTS TO THE REGULATIONS

The proposed amendments to 26 CFR Parts 1 and 7 are as follows:

INCOME TAX REGULATIONS

(26 CFR PART 1)

PARAGRAPH 1. The following new sections are added immediately after § 1.187-2.

§ 1.191-1. **Amortization of certain rehabilitation costs for certified historic structures.**

(a) *In general.* Section 191 allows an owner of a certified historic structure who rehabilitates that structure to elect to amortize over a 60-month period certain expenditures attributable to certified rehabilitation. The election may be made only if the certified historic structure (as defined in § 1.191-2(a)) and the improvements made are otherwise of a character subject to depreciation under section 167 of the Internal Revenue Code. Only those rehabilitation expenditures which result in additions to capital account after June 14, 1976, and before June 15, 1981, are eligible for this special amortization procedure. To qualify for the election, the rehabilitation must be certified by the Secretary of the Interior to the Internal Revenue Service as consistent with the historic character of the structure. See § 1.191-2(d) for the definition of certified rehabilitation. Along with the amortization deductions, the taxpayer may continue otherwise allowable depreciation deductions of the basis of the structure, exclusive of rehabilitation costs which are a part of the amortizable basis (as defined in § 1.191-2(e)).

(b) *Allowance of deduction*—(1) *Determination of amortization period*—(i) *General rule.* The taxpayer may elect to begin the 60-month amortization period with the month following the month in which the amortizable basis is acquired, or with the first month of the succeeding taxable year. For purposes of this section, the month in which the amortizable basis is acquired is the latter of the month in which both the work is completed and the expenditure is actually made or the month in which depreciation deductions under section 167 would be first allowable with respect to the structure. Therefore, no amortization deductions may be claimed before a building is used in a trade or business or for the production of income.

(ii) *Multiple amortization periods.* After a structure is eligible for depreciation, a separate amortization period may be established for each month's expenditures and completed work as that portion of the rehabilitation is placed in service in a depreciable use. The completed work for which a separate amortization period is established must, however, be an identifiable separate component of the entire project and not simply progress payments upon partial completion of overal rehabilitation activities. For example, a single structure could have a series of amortization periods based upon the work completed and expenditures made during each month in which the certified rehabilitation is in progress if the structure were already depreciable before completion of the rehabilitation activities. Alternatively, the taxpayer may treat his entire amortizable basis as acquired upon completion of the entire rehabilitation project rather than allocating amounts to each month in which component parts could have been added to basis. This treatment applies although a project

192

extends over more than one taxable year, if there is no interruption in rehabilitation activities.

(2) *Amount of deduction.* The allowable deduction for each month is determined by dividing the amortizable basis as of the last day of the month by the number of months (including the current month) which remain in the 60-month amortization period. This calculation is repeated for each month of the 60-month period to determine each month's allowable amount of amortization deduction.

(3) *Relation to section 167(o) and other depreciation provisions.* If an election involving a certified historic structure is made under section 191, no election may be made under section 167(o). Additionally, no election is permitted under section 191 if depreciation deductions or credits against tax based upon any part of the costs qualifying for amortization under section 191, are at any time claimed under any depreciation or other provision (including section 38) of the Internal Revenue Code of 1954.

(4) *Depreciation upon notice to discontinue amortization deductions.* If the taxpayer chooses to discontinue amortization deductions, the unamortized rehabilitation costs are added to the adjusted basis of the structuture as of the first day of the month for which the notice to discontinue amortization deductions is effective. Deductions for depreciation of the structure under section 167 may then be computed on the resulting adjusted basis beginning at that time and are based on the estimated remaining useful life of the rehabilitated structure.

(5) *Examples.* The provisions of this paragraph (b) may be illustrated by the following examples:

Example (i) A, a calendar-year taxpayer, secured the necessary certifications from the Secretary of the Interior and began rehabilitation of a 100-year old townhouse previously rented as a one-family dwelling, in order to convert it into two equaly-sized apartments. In June 1977, the exterior work was completed, and A paid his contractor the cost of $20,000. Apartment #1 was completed and rented in September, and the cost of $40,000 was paid. In November, Apartment #2 was finished and rented, and A paid the cost of $47,500. A elects to use the 60-month amortization allowed under section 191. A chooses to establish separate amortization periods for each of these phases of the work, each period beginning at the earliest possible date. these periods and the amortizable basis for each period are as follows:

Apartment No. 1, beginning October 1, 1977, $50,000 basis and Allocable Portion of Exterior.

Apartment No. 2, beginning December 1, 1977, $57,500 basis and Allocable Portion of Exterior.

If A had chosen to do so, A could have selected an amortization period for an entire amortizable basis of $107,500 beginning on December 1, 1977, or January 1, 1978.

Example (ii). B owns a 19th Century warehouse building which is listed on the National Register. In a certified rehabilitation B converted the building into a small shopping mall at a cost of $480,000. The rehabilitation was begun in January 1977, and was completed, placed in service, and paid for in November 1977. B elected to claim amortization deductions under section 191 and to begin the amortization period in December 1977. B's allowable amortization deductions are $8,000 per month, computed as follows:

December 1977: $480,000 amortizable basis/60 months in period = $8,000 deduction.

January 1978: $472,000 amortizable basis/59 months in period = $8,000 deduction.

(c) *Person to claim deduction—(1) In general.* Except as otherwise provided in this paragraph (c)—

(i) Only the owner of a fee-simple interest in a certified historic structure and the site on which the structure is located may elect to amortize certified rehabilitation costs;

(ii) The electing owner must have acquired ownership of the property before commencement of rehabilitation activities, the costs of which are to be amortized; and

(iii) An owner need not have owned the property before commencement of all rehabilitation activities; however, only those costs subsequent to its acquistion of ownership of the structure may be considered for purposes of amortization deductions under section 191.

(2) *Exceptions and special rules—(i) Life tenant and remainderman.* For purposes of section 191, the holder of a life estate in property is considered to own the property. A remainderman taking the property on the death of the life tenant is permitted to amortize only those rehabilitation costs which are incurred for improvements begun following termination of all preceding interests in the property and paid by that remainderman.

(ii) *Owners of joint or undivided interests in historic structures.* Joint tenants, tenants by the entirety, tenants in common, and owners of other joint ჟ undivided interests in a certified historic structure may, under section 191, amortize expenditures made for certified rehabilitation. The right of any one such owner to make an election under section 191 is not dependent upon any other coowner making such an election. Each electing owner's amortizable basis consists of the full amount of expenditures made by that individual owner for certified rehabilitation. See paragraph (c)(2)(v) of this section for rules on partnerships.

(iii) *Certain transferees of historic structures.* If expenditures for certified rehabilitation are in fact made by the owner of a certified historic structure, and if one or more transferees then acquire the ownership of the rehabilitated structure directly from that owner before the structure is placed in service, the transferees, solely for purposes of section 191, may be treated as having made the rehabilitation expenditures at the later of the time the structure is placed in service or the rehabilitation is completed. The amount of rehabilitation expenditures treated as made by the transferees under this subdivision (iii) is the lesser amount of—

(A) The rehabilitation expenditures actually made before the date on which the transferee acquired ownership of the structure, or

(B) The portion of the transferee's cost or other basis for the property which is attributable to rehabilitation expenditures made before the date on which the transferee acquired ownership of the structure.

(iv) *Estates and trusts.* The amortization deduction provided by section 191 is allowable to estates and trusts; see sections 642(f) and 1.642(f)-1.

(v) *Partnerships.* Partnerships owning certified historic structures may elect to amortize expenditures for certified rehabilitations made by the partnerships. See however, section 465 and the regulations thereunder for limitations on deductions to amounts at risk.

(vi) *Concessionaires from the United States Park Service.* For purposes of section 191 and this section, holders of concession contracts under the act of October 9, 1965 (79 Stat. 969, 16 U.S.C. 20) for structures in U.S. National Parks are considered to be lessees and not owners of the structure and are not eligible to elect the application of section 191 with respect to amortization of the costs of certified rehabilitations of those structures.

(d) *Recapture.* If a taxpayer disposes of property for which the taxpayer has claimed amortization deductions under section 191, part or all of any gain on the disposition may be recaptured as ordinary income under the applicable provisions of the code.

§ 1.191-2 Definitions and special rules.

(a) *Certified historic structure.* A certified historic structure is a building or other structure which is of a character subject to depreciation under section 167 and is either,

(1) Listed in the National Register of Historic Places,

(2) Located in an historic district which is listed in the National Register of Historic Places and certified by the Secretary of the Interior as being of historic significance to the district, or

(3) Located in an historic district which is designated under a stature (including an ordinance) of a State or local government, but only if the State or local stuatue authorizing establishment of the district is certified by the Secretary of the Interior as containing criteria which substantially achieve the purpose of preserving and rehabilitating historic buildings.

(b) *Registered historic district.* [Reserved]

(c) *Structure.* A structure is a specific building or other man made construction which constitutes depreciable real property under section 167 of the Code. The term structure also includes ships and other vessels which are permanently anchored and used in a depreciable use. The term structure does not include site work or other related items associated with the build ing or other construction. Examples of structures include rental housing, office buildings, lighthouses, hotels, and bridges.

(d) *Certified rehabilitation.* A certified rehabilitation consists of improvements to or restoration of a certified historic structure, which the Secretary of the Interior certifies to be consistent with Interior Department standards for rehabilitation. The specific improvements or restoration must enhance the historic nature of the building or other structure and, where applicable, the character of the historic district in which the structure is located. Thus, for example, the reconstruction (as opposed to restoration) of an historic structure is not a certified rehabilitation even in cases where the reconstruction is listed on the National Register upon its completion since it does not enhance the historic value of an existing building or other structure.

(e) *Amortizable basis—(1) In general.* The amortizable basis of a certified historic structure consists of any otherwise depreciable additions to the capital account of the structure during the effective period of section 191. Only amounts expended by the electing property owner directly for rehabilitation of existing historic structures are part of amortizable basis. Amortizable basis does not include new construction even though the certification of rehabilitation by the Secretary of the Interior may apply to an entire project. Amortizable basis also does not include certain additions which do not meet the requirements of paragraphs (d) and (e) of this section even though such additions are considered under local law to be rehabilitation. For purposes of section 191, architectural and engineering fees, real estate commissions, site survey fees, legal expenses, insurance premiums (including title insurance), developers' fees, and other construction-related costs are a part of amortizable basis. Any costs for which a deduction is claimed under any other section of the Code or for which specific provision is made in another section of the Code (such as section 189 on construction period interest and taxes or section 266 on carrying charges) are not a part of amortizable basis. Any costs which must be added to the basis of land associated with the historic structure, rather than depreciated under section 167, are not a part of the amortizable basis.

(2) *Partially depreciable property.* A certified historic structure may be depreciable only in part, as, for example, a private residence which includes a separate rental apartment. In such case, only that portion of the costs of the certified rehabilitation which is attributable to the portion of the total structure that is depreciable property under section 167 is a part of amortizable basis. The determination of the portion of the expenditures which is included in amortizable basis is made according to the rules of section 167. The remaining certified rehabilitation costs must be added to the nondepreciable portion of the basis of the historic structure.

(3) *Rehabilitations which include new construction.* If a rehabilitation project only partially qualifies for amortization deductions because a portion of the project is new construction (as defined in paragraph (e)(5) of this section), the apportionment rules of paragraph (e)(2) of this section apply to determine the amount of the taxpayer's amortizable basis. For example, the cost of a single heating system used both for a rehabilitated historic structure; and for a nonhistoric new wing added thereto would be apportioned between the amortizable rehabilitation costs and nonamortizable new construction costs.

(4) *Modernization of existing structure included.* Expenditures for structural modernization of an existing historic structure, which are made in a rehabilitation certified by the Secretary of the Interior to be consistent with the historic nature of the structure, are a part of amortizable basis. Examples of such expenditures include the costs of modern plumbing and electrical wiring and fixtures, heating and air conditioning systems, elevators, escalators, and other improvements required by local building

or fire codes. The addition of an attached facility exclusively for elevators, fire stairs, or barrier-free access will also be considered rehabilitation, if the construction of elevators, fire stairs, or barrier-free access within the existing structure is prohibited by the Secretary of the Interior as destructive of the historic character of the structure. Carpeting, draperies, office equipment, furniture (even where it is built in), nonpermanent (demountable) walls or partitions, and other similar items are not a part of amortizable basis.

(5) *New construction excluded.* Expenditures attributable to new construction associated with a certified rehabilitation are not a part of amortizable basis. Whether expenditures are attributable to the rehabilitation of an existing structure, or are attributable to new construction, will be determined upon the basis of all the facts and circumstances. Expenditures will generally be considered attributable to rehabilitation if the foundation and outer walls of the existing building are retained and the costs are attributable to work done within that existing framework. Except as provided to the contrary in this paragraph (e)(3) and paragraph (e)(2) of this section, any expansion of the existing structure will be considered new construction. For example, the addition of a new story to an existing building is new construction. Likewise, related construction such as a garage, sidewalk, or parking lot (or the addition of landscaping) will not be considered rehabilitation even though the related construction may be physically attached to the historic structure.

(6) *Time when amounts are added to capital account.* Under section 191, expenditures are treated as added to capital account (and to amortizable basis) only at the time they are actually made (paid or accrued) and only after the improvements are completed. Therfore, expenditures for improvements completed after June 14, 1981, are not a part of the taxpayer's amortizable basis even though they may have been paid or accrued prior to that date. In the case of a single and continuous rehabilitation project all of which is certified by the Secretary of the Interior, expenditures for rehabilitation begun before June 14, 1976, but completed and charged thereafter, are a part of the taxpayer's amortizable basis. However, even where there is a single and continuous rehabilitation project, expenditures made for any separable part of the improvements completed and charged before June 14, 1976, are not a part of the taxpayer's amortizable basis.

195

§ 1.191–3 Time and manner of making election.

(a) *In general.* Under section 191(b), an election by the taxpayer to claim amortization deductions with respect to a certified historic structure is made by a statement to that effect filed with the taxpayer's return for the taxable year in which falls the first month of the 60-month amortization period selected pursuant to § 1.191–1(b). The statement claiming the deduction shall include the following information:

(1) A description clearly identifying each certified rehabilitation and each certified historic structure (including the address) for which an amortization deduction is claimed;

(2) The date on which the amortizable basis, as defined in § 1.191–2(d), was acquired;

(3) The date the amortization period is to begin;

(4) The total amount of amortizable basis claimed for the rehabilitation of the historic structure, as of the first month for which the amortization deduction provided for by section 191(a) is elected;

(5) Either (i) a statement that the historic structure and the rehabilitation have been certified by the Secretary of the Interior along with the dates of those certifications; or (ii) if certifications of the historic structure and the rehabilitation have been applied for, but have not been issued, the dates on which requests for the certifications were made.

(b) *Special rules*—(1) *Letters of certification.* The letters of certification issued by the Secretary of the Interior qualifying the historic structure and the rehabilitation are not to be submitted with the statement electing to amortize rehabilitation expenses but must be submitted later if specifically requested by the Internal Revenue Service.

(2) *Certifications not issued or failure to submit proof of certification.* If paragraph (a)(5)(ii) of this section applies, the taxpayer must submit a statement showing receipt of the certifications required by section 191 and the dates of the certifications with the first income tax return filed after the receipt by the taxpayer of the certifications. If the required notice of certifications is not received by the Internal Revenue Service within 30 months after the date of the commencement of the 60-month amortization period, the electing taxpayer may be requested to consent to an agreement under section 6501(c)(4) extending the period of assessment for any tax relating to the time for which amortization deductions are claimed.

(3) *Election of multiple amortization periods for a single structure.* If the taxpayer elects a separate amortization period for each month in which rehabilitation expenditures are made and work completed, the taxpayer must combine all such elections for periods beginning in one taxable year in a single statement. The information requested in paragraphs (a) (2), (3), and (4) of this section must be separately identified for each amortization period chosen, and the nature of the expenditures included for each such amortization period shown.

(c) *Notice to discontinue amortization*—(1) *In general.* A notice to discontinue the amortization deduction as provided by section 191(c) may be made at any time during the amortization period. This notice is made by a statement attached to the return of the taxpayer filed for the taxable year in which falls the first month for which the election terminates. The statement must specify the month as of the beginning of which the taxpayer chooses to discontinue the amortization deductions. The statement must be filed before the beginning of that month. In addition, the statement must contain a description clearly identifying the certified historic structure and rehabilitation with respect to which the taxpayer elects to discontinue the amortization deduction. In the case of multiple amortization periods relating to the same structure, a single election to discontinue amortization deductions is effective for all amortization periods that have been established. If certifications of the structure and rehabilitation have been issued, their dates shall be shown. Copies of the letters of certification are not, however, to be submitted unless later specifically requested by the Internal Revenue Service. If, at the time of the election to discontinue amortization deductions, certifications have not been issued, the taxpayer must report the dates of their issuance with the next succeeding tax return after their receipt. If the required certifications have not been issued and 30 months or more have elapsed since the original section 191 elections was made, the taxpayer may be requested to consent to an agreement under section 6501(c)(4) extending the period of assessment for any tax relating to the time for which amortization deductions were claimed.

(2) *Notification by Secretary of the Interior.* For purposes of this paragraph (c), notification to the Secretary or his delegate from the Secretary of the Interior that the historic structure

or the rehabilitation no longer meet the requirements for certification has the same effect as notice from the taxpayer electing to terminate amortization deductions as of the first day of the month following the month that the structure or rehabilitation ceased to meet the requirements of section 191.

PAR. 2. Section 1.642(f)-1 is amended to read as follows:

§ 1.642(f)-1 Amortization deductions.

An estate or trust is allowed amortization deductions with respect to an emergency facility as defined in section 168(d), with respect to a certified pollution control facility as defined in section 169(d), with respect to qualified railroad rolling stock as defined in section 184(d), with respect to certified coal mine safety equipment as defined in section 187(d), with respect to on-the-job training and child-care facilities as defined in section 188(b), and with respect to certain rehabilitations of certified historic structures as defined in section 191, in the same manner and to the same extent as in the case of an individual. However, the principles governing the apportionment of the deductions for depreciation and depletion between fiduciaries and the beneficiaries of an estate or trust (see sections 167(h) and 611(b) and the regulations thereunder) shall be applicable with respect to such amortization deductions.

TEMPORARY INCOME TAX REGULATIONS UNDER THE TAX REFORM ACT OF 1976

(26 CFR PART 7)

§ 7.191-1 [Deleted]

PAR. 3. Section 7.191-1 is deleted.

JEROME KURTZ,
*Commissioner of
Internal Revenue.*

[FR Doc. 78-24435 Filed 8-29-78; 8:45 am]

Title 36—Parks, Forests, and Public Property

CHAPTER I—NATIONAL PARK SERVICE, DEPARTMENT OF THE INTERIOR

PART 67—HISTORIC PRESERVATION CERTIFICATIONS PURSUANT TO THE TAX REFORM ACT OF 1976

Certification of State or Local Statutes

AGENCY: National Park Service, Interior.

ACTION: Additional interim procedures.

SUMMARY: This rule supplements the previous interim regulations by adding a new section in the certification process. The Tax Reform Act of 1976 requires the certification of State and local statutes by the Secretary of the Interior, so that an owner of a structure in a historic district created by legislation certified under these regulations may be able to take advantage of the provisions of the Act.

DATE: Effective: August 10, 1977. Comments by September 9, 1977.

ADDRESS: Send comments to: Mr. Jerry L. Rogers, Chief, Office of Archeology and Historic Preservation, National Park Service, Department of the Interior, Washington, D.C. 20240, 202-523-5275.

SUPPLEMENTARY INFORMATION: The Tax Reform Act of 1976, Pub. L. 94-455, 90 Stat. 1519, included among its many provisions section 2124, "Tax Incentives to Encourage the Preservation of Historic Structures," under which the Secretary of the Interior is required to make certain certifications with respect to the historic character of buildings and structures, the rehabilitation of historic buildings and structures, and the preservation criteria of State and local statutes.

Regulations for certifying the historic significance of structures and certification of rehabilitations were published as interim regulations and for comment in the FEDERAL REGISTER on March 15, 1977 (42 FR 14121). These interim regulations are still in effect. These regulations for certifying State and local statutes under section 2124(a) will be an addition to 36 CFR Part 67 as published on March 15, 1977. They are published separately in the interim but will be fully integrated when the regulations are published in final.

Since certification of a State or local statute under this process provides significant tax benefits for historic structures in districts designated thereunder, certification is likely to be a significant and beneficial impetus to rehabilitation and upgrading of properties in historic districts. The Department of the Interior urges State and local governments to evaluate the social implications of improvements in such districts to assure that the residents in these districts are provided for, as appropriate.

When the certification of State statutes will have an impact on districts in specific localities, the Department of the Interior urges State governments to notify and consult with appropriate local officials prior to submitting a request for certification of the statute.

For structures in State or locally designated historic districts where the statute has been certified, requests for certification of the historic significance or rehabilitation of individual structures within such districts should be made in accord with the interim regulations of March 15, 1977, 36 CFR Part 67. The certification of significance of such structures will be made or denied upon an evaluation of whether the strucure contributes to the significance of the State or locally designated district, based upon the documentation submitted on the structure and the district in which it is located. Certifications of rehabilitation will be based on whether or not the rehabilitation is consistent with the historic character of the structure or the district in which the structure is located.

It is the policy of the Department of the Interior, whenever practicable, to offer the public an opportunity to participate in the rulemaking process. Accordingly, interested persons may submit written comments, suggestions, or objections regarding the proposed regulations to the Chief, Office of Archeology and Historic Preservation, National Park Service, Department of the Interior, Washington, D.C. 20240, on or before September 8, 1977. However, inasmuch as taxpayers are already requesting that certifications be made under the Tax Reform Act, the process set forth below will be utilized as interim regulations until such time as the proposed regulations, as they may be amended, are published in final.

This rulemaking is developed under the authority of section 101(a)(1) of the National Historic Preservation Act of 1966, 16 U.S.C. 470a–1(a) (1970 ed.), as amended, and section 2124 of the Tax Reform Act of 1976, 90 Stat. 1519. In compliance with the National Environmental Policy Act of 1969 (42 U.S.C. 4331, et seq.) the National Park Service has prepared an environmental assessment. of these proposed regulations. Based on this assessment, it is determined that implementation of the proposed regulations is not a major Federal action that would have a significant effect on the quality of the human environment and that an environmental impact statement is not required. The assessment, which is on file in the office of the Chief, Office of Archeology and Historic Preservation, National Park Service, Department of the Interior, Washington, D.C. 20240, is available for public inspection, and will be available for public comment for a period running concurrently with the comment period for these proposed regulations.

The originator of these regulations is Carol Shull, Historian, National Register of Historic Places (202–523–5483).

Accordingly, section 67 is amended by adding a new § 67.9 entitled Certification of State or Local Statutes. These regulations are in interim effect as of this date of publication to read as follows:

§ 67.9 Certification of State or Local Statutes.

(a) State or local statutes which will be certified by the Secretary of the Interior. For the purpose of this regulation, a State or local statute is a law of the State or local government designating a historic district or districts, including any by-laws or ordinances pertaining to the district or districts designated thereunder. Such statutes must contain criteria which will substantially achieve the purpose of preserving and rehabilitating buildings of historic significance to the district. To be certified by the Secretary of the Interior, the statute generally must provide for a duly designated review body, such as a review board or commission, with power to review proposed alterations to structures within the boundaries of the district or districts designated under the statute. State enabling legislation for the creation of historic districts not containing the minimum criteria above will not be certified. When the certification of State statutes will have an impact on districts in specific localities, the Department of the Interior urges States governments to notify and consult with appropriate local officials prior to submitting a request for certification of the statute.

(b) Who may apply. Requests for certification of State or local statutes may be made only by the duly authorized representative of the government which enacted the statute. The applicant shall certify that he or she is authorized by the governing body to apply for certification.

(c) Certification process. Requests for certification of statutes as required under section 2124(a) of the Tax Reform Act of 1976 shall be made as follows:

(1) Requests for certifications of statutes shall be submitted to the appropriate State Historic Preservation Officer and accompanied by the following:

(i) A written request from the authorized representative of the government that enacted the statute(s) including the certification required by paragraph (b) of this section.

(ii) A copy of the statute or statutes for which certification is requested, including by-laws and/or ordinances, if any, which pertain to district(s) already designated under the statute(s).

(iii) Local governments shall submit a copy of the State enabling legislation, if any, authorizing the designation of historic districts.

(2) Documentation on each district designated under the statute shall be submitted in duplicate, including a:

(i) Description;

(ii) Statement of significance;

(iii) Map defining boundaries of district;

(iv) Representative photographs of the district including streetscape photographs.

One copy of the documentation will be forwarded to the Keeper of the National Register. Where practical the documentation on each district should accompany the request for certification. If not, the documentation must be submitted to the State Historic Preservation Officer and the Keeper of the National Register before the Secretary of the Interior will process requests for certification of an individual structure within the district or districts for which the request for certification of statute(s) has been made. This also applies to documentation on additional districts designated under State or local statutes certified prior to the designation of such districts.

(3) The State Historic Preservation Officer shall review the statute(s) and the documentation on the district(s) protected thereunder and make an assessment of whether the statute(s) contain criteria which will substantially achieve the purposes of preserving and rehabilitating buildings of historic significance to the district(s) based upon the standards set out above in paragraph (a) of this section. If the statute(s) contain such a provision and if, in the opinion of the State Historic Preservation Officer, this and other provisions in the statute will substantially achieve the purpose of preserving and rehabilitating buildings of historic significance to the district, the State Historic Preservation Officer should recommend that the statute be certified.

(4) The State Historic Preservation Officer shall forward the request with the accompanying documentation as specified in paragraph (c) of this section with his written recommendation as to whether the statute should be certified to the Keeper of the National Register, Office of Archeology and Historic Preservation, National Park Service, Department of the Interior, Washington, D.C. 20240. The State Historic Preservation Officer shall forward the request with his recommendation within 45 days of receipt of the request by the duly authorized representative: *Provided,* The request is submitted in accord with paragraph (c) of this section. If this period has expired without such actions being taken the duly authorized representative of the State or local government may submit the request for certification of the statute(s) directly to the Keeper of the National Register in accord with paragraph (c) of this section.

(5) The Keeper of the National Register shall review the request and the recommendation of the State Historic Preservation Officer and make a decision as to certification. If, in the opinion of the Keeper of the National Register, the statute(s) contain criteria which will substantially achieve the purpose of preserving and rehabilitating buildings of historic significance to the district, the Secretary will certify the statute(s).

(6) The Keeper of the National Register shall provide written notification to the applicant and the appropriate State Historic Preservation Officer when certification of the statute is given or denied within 45 days of receipt of the request for certification. If certification is denied, the notification will provide a justification for such denial.

(d) Certification of such statutes under this regulation in no way constitutes certification of significance of individual structures within the district or of the rehabilitation by the Secretary for purposes of section 2124. Regulations for obtaining certifications of significance and rehabilitation pursuant to section 2124 are contained in 36 CFR 67.4 through 67.7. The Secretary of the Interior will certify the significance of individual structures within such districts after an evaluation of whether the structure contributes to the significance of the State or locally designated district based upon the documentation submitted on the structure and the district in which it is located. Certifications of rehabilitation will be based on whether or not the rehabilitation is consistent with the historic character of the structure or the district in which it is located.

(e) For appeals, refer to 36 CFR 67.8, Appeals, Historic Preservation Certifications Pursuant to the Tax Reform Act of 1976.

(f) State or local governments, as appropriate, must notify the Secretary of the Interior and the Secretary of the Treasury, in the event that certified statutes are amended in any respect or repealed.

Approved: July 27, 1977.

WILLIAM J. WHALEN,
Director, National Park Service.

[FR Doc.77–23010 Filed 8–9–77; 8:45 am]

199

INVESTMENT TAX CREDIT PROVISIONS FOR REHABILITATION IN THE REVENUE ACT OF 1978

(As they appear in the Internal Revenue Code)

Reproduced with permission from *Internal Revenue Code*, published and copyrighted by Commerce Clearing House, Inc., 4025 West Peterson Avenue, Chicago, Ill. 60646.

Section 315 of Public Law No. 95-600, the Revenue Act of 1978, signed into law by President Carter on November 6, 1978, created an investment tax credit for the rehabilitation of certain qualified buildings. Reproduced in this appendix are those provisions of the Internal Revenue Code that were created or amended by section 315, together with selected other code provisions that are key to understanding the operation of this tax credit.

Part IV of the Internal Revenue Code: "Credits Against Tax"

Subpart A: "Credits Allowable" (Sections 31-42, of which only section 38 is reproduced in this appendix)

[Sec. 38]
SEC. 38. INVESTMENT IN CERTAIN DEPRECIABLE PROPERTY.

[Sec. 38(a)]

(a) GENERAL RULE.—There shall be allowed, as a credit against the tax imposed by this chapter, the amount determined under subpart B of this part.
Source: New.

[Sec. 38(b)]

(b) REGULATIONS.—The Secretary shall prescribe such regulations as may be necessary to carry out the purposes of this section and subpart B.
Source: New.

Amendments:	Sec. as amended effective:	P. L. 87-834, § 2:
P. L. 87-834, § 2	. . . .	Sec. 2 amended part IV of subchapter A of chapter 1 by redesignating Sec. 38 as Sec. 39 and by inserting after Sec. 37 a new Sec. 38 to read as above.

Subpart B: "Rules for Computing Credit for Investment in Certain Depreciable Property" (Sections 46-50, of which only section 46 and parts of section 48 are reproduced in this appendix)

SEC. 46. AMOUNT OF CREDIT.

(a) GENERAL RULE.—

(1) FIRST-IN-FIRST-OUT RULE.—The amount of the credit allowed by section 38 for the taxable year shall be an amount equal to the sum of—

(A) the investment credit carryovers carried to such taxable year,

(B) the amount of the credit determined under paragraph (2) for such taxable year, plus

(C) the investment credit carrybacks carried to such taxable year.

(2) AMOUNT OF CREDIT.—

(A) IN GENERAL.—The amount of the credit determined under this paragraph for the taxable year shall be an amount equal to the sum of the following percentages of the qualified investment (as determined under subsections (c) and (d)):

(i) the regular percentage,

(ii) in the case of energy property, the energy percentage, and

(iii) the ESOP percentage.

[*] *(B)* REGULAR PERCENTAGE.—*For purposes of this paragraph, the regular percentage is—*

(i) 10 percent with respect to the period beginning on January 21, 1975, and ending on December 31, 1980, or

(ii) 7 percent with respect to the period beginning on January 1, 1981.

(C) ENERGY PERCENTAGE.—*For purposes of this paragraph, the energy percentage is—*

(i) 10 percent with respect to the period beginning on October 1, 1978, and ending on December 31, 1982, or

(ii) zero with respect to any other period.

(D) SPECIAL RULE FOR CERTAIN ENERGY PROPERTY.—*For purposes of this paragraph, the regular percentage shall not apply to any energy property which, but for section 48(l)(1), would not be section 38 property.*

(E) ESOP PERCENTAGE.—*For purposes of this paragraph, the ESOP percentage is—*

(i) with respect to the period beginning on January 21, 1975, and ending on December 31, 1983, 1 percent, and

(ii) with respect to the period beginning on January 1, 1977, and ending on December 31, 1983, an additional percentage (not in excess of ½ of 1 percent) which results in an amount equal to the amount determined under section 48(n)(1)(B).

This subparagraph shall apply to a corporation only if it meets the requirements of section 409A and only if it elects (at such time, in such form, and in such manner as the Secretary prescribes) to have this subparagraph apply.

(3) LIMITATION BASED ON AMOUNT OF TAX.—*Notwithstanding paragraph (1), the credit allowed by section 38 for the taxable year shall not exceed—*

(A) so much of the liability for tax for the taxable year as does not exceed $25,000, plus

(B) the following percentage of so much of the liability for tax for the taxable year as exceeds $25,000:

If the taxable year ends in:	The percentage is:
1979	60
1980	70
1981	80
1982 or thereafter	90.

(4) LIABILITY FOR TAX.—For purposes of paragraph (3), the liability for tax for the taxable year shall be the tax imposed by this chapter for such year, reduced by the sum of the credits allowable under—

(A) section 33 (relating to foreign tax credit), and

(B) section 37 (relating to credit for the elderly).

201

For purposes of this paragraph, any tax imposed for the taxable year by section 56 (relating to minimum tax for tax preferences), section 72 (m)(5)(B) (relating to 10 percent tax on premature distributions to owner-employees), section 402(e) (relating to tax on lump sum distributions), section 408(f) (relating to additional tax on income from certain retirement accounts), section 531 (relating to accumulated earnings tax), section 541 (relating to personal holding company tax), or section 1378 (relating to tax on certain capital gains of subchapter S corporations) and any additional tax imposed for the taxable year by section 1351(d)(1) (relating to recoveries of foreign expropriation losses), shall not be considered tax imposed by this chapter for such year.

(5) MARRIED INDIVIDUALS.—In the case of a husband or wife who files a separate return, the amount specified under subparagraphs (A) and (B) of paragraph (3) shall be $12,500 in lieu of $25,000. This paragraph shall not apply if the spouse of the taxpayer has no qualified investment for, and no unused credit carryback or carryover to, the taxable year of such spouse which ends within or with the taxpayer's taxable year.

(6) CONTROLLED GROUPS.—In the case of a controlled group, the $25,000

---

[*] **Note:** Revenue Act Sec. 311(a) at ¶ 1126, enacted 11-6-78, amended Code Sec. 46(a)(2)(B) to set the investment tax credit rate at 10% permanently. However, Energy Act Sec. 301(a)(1) at ¶ 1426, enacted 11-9-78, amended Code Sec. 46(a)(2)(B) to read as shown above.

amount specified under paragraph (3) shall be reduced for each component member of such group by apportioning $25,000 among the component members of such group in such manner as the Secretary shall by regulations prescribe. For purposes of the preceding sentence, the term "controlled group" has the meaning assigned to such term by section 1563(a).

(7) ALTERNATIVE LIMITATION IN THE CASE OF CERTAIN UTILITIES.—

(A) IN GENERAL.—If, for the taxable year ending in 1979—

(i) the amount of the qualified investment of the taxpayer which is attributable to public utility property is 25 percent or more of his aggregate qualified investment, and

(ii) the application of this paragraph results in a percentage higher than 60 percent,

then subparagraph (B) of paragraph (3) of this subsection shall be applied by substituting for "60 percent" the taxpayer's applicable percentage for such year.

(B) APPLICABLE PERCENTAGE.—The applicable percentage for any taxpayer for any taxable year ending in 1979 is—

(i) 50 percent, plus

(ii) that portion of 20 percent which the taxpayer's amount of qualified investment which is public utility property bears to his aggregate qualified investment.

If the proportion referred to in clause (ii) is 75 percent or more, the applicable percentage of the taxpayer for the year shall be 70 percent.

(C) PUBLIC UTILITY PROPERTY DEFINED.—For purposes of this paragraph, the term "public utility property" has the meaning given to such term by the first sentence of subsection (c)(3)(B).

(8) ALTERNATIVE LIMITATION IN THE CASE OF CERTAIN RAILROADS AND AIRLINES.—

(A) IN GENERAL.—If, for a taxable year ending in 1979 or 1980—

(i) the amount of the qualified investment of the taxpayer which is attributable to railroad property or to airline property, as the case may be, is 25 percent or more of his aggregate qualified investment, and

(ii) the application of this paragraph results in a percentage higher than 60 percent (70 percent in the case of a taxable year ending in 1980),

then subparagraph (B) of paragraph (3) of this subsection shall be applied by substituting for "60 percent" ("70 percent" in the case of a taxable year ending in 1980) the taxpayer's applicable percentage for such year.

(B) APPLICABLE PERCENTAGE.—The applicable percentage of any taxpayer for any taxable year under this paragraph is—

(i) 50 percent, plus

(ii) that portion of the tentative percentage for the taxable year which the taxpayer's amount of qualified investment which is railroad property or airline property (as the case may be) bears to his aggregate qualified investment.

If the proportion referred to in clause (ii) is 75 percent or more, the applicable percentage of the taxpayer for the taxable year shall be 90 percent (80 percent in the case of a taxable year ending in 1980).

(C) TENTATIVE PERCENTAGE.—For purposes of subparagraph (B), the tentative percentage shall be determined under the following table:

If the taxable year ends in:	The tentative percentage is:
1979	40
1980	30

(D) RAILROAD PROPERTY DEFINED.—For purposes of this paragraph, the term "railroad property" means section 38 property used by the taxpayer directly in connection with the trade or business carried on by the taxpayer of operating a railroad (including a railroad switching or terminal company).

(E) AIRLINE PROPERTY DEFINED.—For purposes of this paragraph, the term "airline property" means section 38 property used by the taxpayer directly in connection with the trade or business carried on by the taxpayer of the furnishing or sale of transportation as a common carrier by air subject to the jurisdiction of the Civil Aeronautics Board or the Federal Aviation Administration.

(9) [Repealed]

(10) SPECIAL RULES IN THE CASE OF ENERGY PROPERTY.—Under regulations prescribed by the Secretary—

(A) In general.—This subsection and subsection (b) shall be applied separately—

(i) first with respect to so much of the credit allowed by section 38 as is not attributable to the energy percentage,

(ii) second with respect to so much of the credit allowed by section 38 as is attributable to the application of the energy percentage to energy property (other than solar or wind energy property), and

(iii) then with respect to so much of the credit allowed by section 38 as is attributable to the application of the energy percentage to solar or wind energy property.

(B) Rules of application for energy property other than solar or wind energy property.—In applying this subsection and subsection (b) for taxable years ending after September 30, 1978, with respect to so much of the credit allowed by section 38 as is described in subparagraph (A) (ii)—

(i) paragraph (3)(C) shall be applied by substituting "100 percent" for "50 percent",

(ii) paragraphs (7), (8), and (9) shall not apply, and

(iii) the liability for tax shall be the amount determined under paragraph (4) reduced by so much of the credit allowed by section 38 as is described in subparagraph (A)(i).

(C) Refundable credit for solar or wind energy property.—In the case of so much of the credit allowed by section 38 as is described in subparagraph (A)(iii)—

(i) paragraph (3) shall not apply, and

(ii) for purposes of this title (other than section 38, this subpart, and chapter 63), such credit shall be treated as if it were allowed by section 39 and not by section 38.

(b) Carryback and Carryover of Unused Credits.—

(1) In general.—If the sum of the amount of the investment credit carryovers to the taxable year under subsection (a)(1)(A) plus the amount determined under subsection (a)(1)(B) for the taxable year exceeds the amount of the limitation imposed by subsection (a)(3) for such taxable year (hereinafter in this subsection referred to as the "unused credit year"), such excess attributable to the amount determined under subsection (a)(1)(B) shall be—

(A) an investment credit carryback to each of the 3 taxable years preceding the unused credit year, and

(B) an investment credit carryover to each of the 7 taxable years following the unused credit year,

and, subject to the limitations imposed by paragraphs (2) and (3), shall be taken into account under the provisions of subsection (a)(1) in the manner provided in such subsection. The entire amount of the unused credit for an unused credit year shall be carried to the earliest of the 10 taxable years to which (by reason of subparagraphs (A) and (B)) such credit may be carried and then to each of the other 9 taxable years to the extent, because of the limitations imposed by paragraphs (2) and (3), such unused credit may not be taken into account under subsection (a)(1) for a prior taxable year to which such unused credit may be carried. In the case of an unused credit for an unused credit year ending before January 1, 1971, which is an investment credit carryover to a taxable year beginning after December 31, 1970 (determined without regard to this sentence), this paragraph shall be applied—

(C) by substituting "10 taxable years" for "7 taxable years" in subparagraph (B), and by substituting "13 taxable years" for "10 taxable years," and "12 taxable years" for "9 taxable years" in the preceding sentence, and

(D) by carrying such an investment credit carryover to a later taxable year (than the taxable year to which it would, but for this subparagraph, be carried) to which it may be carried if, because of the amendments made by section 802(b)(2) of the Tax Reform Act of 1976, carrying such carryover to the taxable year to which it would, but for this subparagraph, be carried would cause a portion of an unused credit from an unused credit year ending after December 31, 1970 to expire.

(2) Limitation on carrybacks.—The amount of the unused credit which may be taken into account under subsection (a)(1) for any preceding taxable year shall not exceed the amount by which the limitation imposed by subsection (a)(3) for such taxable year exceeds the sum of—

(A) the amounts determined under subparagraphs (A) and (B) of subsection (a)(1) for such taxable year, plus

(B) the amounts which (by reason of this subsection) are carried back to such taxable year and are attributable to taxable years preceding the unused credit year.

(3) LIMITATION ON CARRYOVERS.—The amount of the unused credit which may be taken into account under subsection (a)(1)(A) for any succeeding taxable year shall not exceed the amount by which the limitation imposed by subsection (a)(3) for such taxable year exceeds the sum of the amounts which, by reason of this subsection, are carried to such taxable year and are attributable to taxable years preceding the unused credit year.

(c) QUALIFIED INVESTMENT.—

(1) IN GENERAL.—For purposes of this subpart, the term "qualified investment" means, with respect to any taxable year, the aggregate of—

(A) the applicable percentage of the basis of each new section 38 property (as defined in section 48(b)) placed in service by the taxpayer during such taxable year, plus

(B) the applicable percentage of the cost of each used section 38 property (as defined in section 48(c)(1)) placed in service by the taxpayer during such taxable year.

(2) APPLICABLE PERCENTAGE.—For purposes of paragraph (1), the applicable percentage for any property shall be determined under the following table:

If the useful life is—	The applicable percentage is—
3 years or more but less than 5 years..........	33⅓
5 years or more but less than 7 years..........	66⅔
7 years or more	100

For purposes of this subpart, the useful life of any property shall be the useful life used in computing the allowance for depreciation under section 167 for the taxable year in which the property is placed in service.

(3) PUBLIC UTILITY PROPERTY.—

(A) To the extent that the credit allowed by section 38 with respect to any public utility property is determined at the rate of 7 percent, in the case of any property which is public utility property, the amount of the qualified investment shall be 4/7 of the amount determined under paragraph (1). The preceding sentence shall not apply for purposes of applying the energy percentage.

(B) For purposes of subparagraph (A), the term "public utility property" means property used predominantly in the trade or business of the furnishing or sale of—

(i) electrical energy, water, or sewage disposal services,

(ii) gas through a local distribution system or

(iii) telephone service, telegraph service by means of domestic telegraph operations (as defined in section 222(a)(5) of the Communications Act of 1934, as amended; 47 U. S. C. 222(a)(5)), or other communication services (other than international telegraph service),

if the rates for such furnishing or sale, as the case may be, have been established or approved by a State or political subdivision thereof, by an agency or instrumentality of the United States, or by a public service or public utility commission or other similar body of any State or political subdivision thereof. Such term also means communication property of the type used by persons engaged in providing telephone or microwave communication services to which clause (iii) applies, if such property is used predominantly for communication purposes.

(C) In the case of any interest in a submarine cable circuit used to furnish telegraph service between the United States and a point outside the United States of a taxpayer engaged in furnishing international telegraph service (if the rates for such furnishing have been established or approved by a governmental unit, agency, instrumentality, commission, or similar body described in subparagraph (B)), the qualified investment shall not exceed the qualified investment attributable to so much of the interest of the taxpayer in the circuit as does not exceed 50 percent of all interests in the circuit.

(4) COORDINATION WITH SUBSECTION (d).—The amount which would (but for this paragraph) be treated as qualified investment under this subsection with respect to any property shall be reduced (but not below zero) by any

amount treated by the taxpayer or a predecessor of the taxpayer (or, in the case of a sale and leaseback described in section 47(a)(3)(C), by the lessee) as qualified investment with respect to such property under subsection (d), to the extent the amount so treated has not been required to be recaptured by reason of section 47(a)(3).

(5) APPLICABLE PERCENTAGE IN THE CASE OF CERTAIN POLLUTION CONTROL FACILITIES.—

(A) IN GENERAL.—Notwithstanding paragraph (2), in the case of property—

(i) with respect to which an election under section 169 applies, and

(ii) the useful life of which (determined without regard to section 169) is not less than 5 years,

100 percent shall be the applicable percentage for purposes of applying paragraph (1) with respect to so much of the adjusted basis of the property as (after the application of section 169(f)) constitutes the amortizable basis for purposes of section 169.

(B) SPECIAL RULE WHERE PROPERTY IS FINANCED BY INDUSTRIAL DEVELOPMENT BONDS.—To the extent that any property is financed by the proceeds of an industrial development bond (within the meaning of section 103(b)(2)) the interest on which is exempt from tax under section 103, subparagraph (A) shall be applied by substituting "50 percent" for "100 percent."

(6) SPECIAL RULE FOR COMMUTER HIGHWAY VEHICLES.—

(A) IN GENERAL.—Notwithstanding paragraph (2), in the case of a commuter highway vehicle the useful life of which is 3 years or more, the applicable percentage for purposes of paragraph (1) shall be 100 percent.

(B) DEFINITION OF COMMUTER HIGHWAY VEHICLE.—For purposes of subparagraph (A), the term "commuter highway vehicle" means a highway vehicle—

(i) the seating capacity of which is at least 8 adults (not including the driver),

(ii) at least 80 percent of the mileage use of which can reasonably be expected to be (I) for purposes of transporting the taxpayer's employees between their residences and their place of employment, and (II) on trips during which the number of employees transported for such purposes is at least one-half of the adult seating capacity of such vehicle (not including the driver),

(iii) which is acquired by the taxpayer on or after the date of the enactment of the Energy Tax Act of 1978, and placed in service by the taxpayer before January 1, 1986, and

(iv) with respect to which the taxpayer makes an election under this paragraph on his return for the taxable year in which such vehicle is placed in service.

205

(d) QUALIFIED PROGRESS EXPENDITURES.—

(1) IN GENERAL.—In the case of any taxpayer who has made an election under paragraph (6), the amount of his qualified investment for the taxable year (determined under subsection (c) without regard to this subsection) shall be increased by an amount equal to his aggregate qualified progress expenditures for the taxable year with respect to progress expenditure property.

(2) PROGRESS EXPENDITURE PROPERTY DEFINED.—

(A) IN GENERAL.—For purposes of this subsection, the term "progress expenditure property" means any property which is being constructed by or for the taxpayer and which—

(i) has a normal construction period of two years or more, and

(ii) it is reasonable to believe will be new section 38 property having a useful life of 7 years or more in the hands of the taxpayer when it is placed in service.

Clauses (i) and (ii) of the preceding sentence shall be applied on the basis of facts known at the close of the taxable year of the taxpayer in which construction begins (or, if later, at the close of the first taxable year to which an election under this subsection applies).

(B) NORMAL CONSTRUCTION PERIOD.—For purposes of subparagraph (A), the term "normal construction period" means the period reasonably expected to be required for the construction of the property—

(i) beginning with the date on which physical work on the construction begins (or, if later, the first day of the first taxable year to which an election under this subsection applies), and

(ii) ending on the date on which it is expected that the property will be available for placing in service.

(3) QUALIFIED PROGRESS EXPENDITURES DEFINED.—For purposes of this subsection—

(A) SELF-CONSTRUCTED PROPERTY.—In the case of any self-constructed property, the term "qualified progress expenditures" means the amount which, for purposes of this subpart, is, properly chargeable (during such taxable year) to capital account with respect to such property.

(B) NON-SELF-CONSTRUCTED PROPERTY.—In the case of non-self-constructed property, the term "qualified progress expenditures" means the lesser of—

(i) the amount paid during the taxable year to another person for the construction of such property, or

(ii) the amount which represents that proportion of the overall cost to the taxpayer of the construction by such other person which is properly attributable to that portion of such construction which is completed during such taxable year.

(4) SPECIAL RULES FOR APPLYING PARAGRAPH (3).—For purposes of paragraph (3)—

(A) COMPONENT PARTS, ETC.—Property which is to be a component part of, or is otherwise to be included in, any progress expenditure property shall be taken into account—

(i) at a time not earlier than the time at which it becomes irrevocably devoted to use in the progress expenditure property, and

(ii) as if (at the time referred to in clause (i)) the taxpayer had expended an amount equal to that portion of the cost to the taxpayer of such component or other property which, for purposes of this subpart, is properly chargeable (during such taxable year) to capital account with respect to such property.

(B) CERTAIN BORROWINGS DISREGARDED.—Any amount borrowed directly or indirectly by the taxpayer from the person constructing the property for him shall not be treated as an amount expended for such construction.

(C) CERTAIN UNUSED EXPENDITURES CARRIED OVER.—In the case of non-self-constructed property, if for the taxable year—

(i) the amount under clause (i) of paragraph (3)(B) exceeds the amount under clause (ii) of paragraph (3)(B), then the amount of such excess shall be taken into account under such clause (i) for the succeeding taxable year, or

(ii) the amount under clause (ii) of paragraph (3)(B) exceeds the amount under clause (i) of paragraph (3)(B), then the amount of such excess shall be taken into account under such clause (ii) for the succeeding taxable year.

(D) DETERMINATION OF PERCENTAGE OF COMPLETION.—In the case of non-self-constructed property, the determination under paragraph (3)(B)(ii) of the proportion of the overall cost to the taxpayer of the construction of any property which is properly attributable to construction completed during any taxable year shall be made, under regulations prescribed by the Secretary, on the basis of engineering or architectural estimates or on the basis of cost accounting records. Unless the taxpayer establishes otherwise by clear and convincing evidence, the construction shall be deemed to be completed not more rapidly than ratably over the normal construction period.

(E) NO QUALIFIED PROGRESS EXPENDITURES FOR CERTAIN PRIOR PERIODS.—In the case of any property, no qualified progress expenditures shall be taken into account under this subsection for any period before January 22, 1975 (or, if later, before the first day of the first taxable year to which an election under this subsection applies).

(F) NO QUALIFIED PROGRESS EXPENDITURES FOR PROPERTY FOR YEAR IT IS PLACED IN SERVICE, ETC.—In the case of any property, no qualified progress expenditures shall be taken into account under this subsection for the earlier of—

(i) the taxable year in which the property is placed in service, or

(ii) the first taxable year for which recapture is required under section 47(a)(3) with respect to such property,

or for any taxable year thereafter.

(5) OTHER DEFINITIONS.—For purposes of this subsection—

(A) SELF-CONSTRUCTED PROPERTY.—The term "self-constructed property" means property more than half of the construction expenditures for which it is reasonable to believe will be made directly by the taxpayer.

(B) NON-SELF-CONSTRUCTED PROPERTY.—The term "non-self-constructed property" means property which is not self-constructed property.

(C) CONSTRUCTION, ETC.—The term "construction" includes reconstruction and erection, and the term "constructed" includes reconstructed and erected.

(D) ONLY CONSTRUCTION OF SECTION 38 PROPERTY TO BE TAKEN INTO ACCOUNT.—Construction shall be taken into account only if, for purposes of this subpart, expenditures therefor are properly chargeable to capital account with respect to the property.

(6) ELECTION.—An election under this subsection may be made at such time and in such manner as the Secretary may by regulations prescribe. Such an election shall apply to the taxable year for which made and to all subsequent taxable years. Such an election, once made, may not be revoked except with the consent of the Secretary.

(7) TRANSITIONAL RULES.—The qualified investment taken into account under this subsection for any taxable year beginning before January 1, 1980, with respect to any property shall be (in lieu of the full amount) an amount equal to the sum of—

(A) the applicable percentage of the full amount determined under the following table:

For a taxable year beginning in:	The applicable percentage is:
1974 or 1975	20
1976	40
1977	60
1978	80
1979	100;
plus	

(B) in the case of any property to which this subsection applied for one or more preceding taxable years, 20 percent of the full amount for each such preceding taxable year.

For purposes of this paragraph, the term "full amount", when used with respect to any property for any taxable year, means the amount of the qualified investment for such property for such year determined under this subsection without regard to this paragraph.

(e) LIMITATIONS WITH RESPECT TO CERTAIN PERSONS.—

(1) IN GENERAL.—In the case of—

(A) an organization to which section 593 applies, *and*

(B) a regulated investment company or a real estate investment trust subject to taxation under subchapter M (sec. 851 and following),

the qualified investment and the $25,000 amount specified under subparagraphs (A) and (B) of subsection (a)(3) shall equal such person's ratable share of such items.

(2) RATABLE SHARE.—For purposes of paragraph (1), the ratable share of any person for any taxable year of the items described therein shall be—

(A) in the case of an organization referred to in paragraph (1)(A), 50 percent thereof, *and*

(B) in the case of a regulated investment company or a real estate investment trust, the ratio (i) the numerator of which is its taxable income and (ii) the denominator of which is its taxable income computed without regard to the deduction for dividends paid provided by section 852(b)(2)(D) or 857(b)(2)(B), as the case may be.

For purposes of subparagraph (B) of the preceding sentence, the term "taxable income" means in the case of a regulated investment company its investment company taxable income (within the meaning of section 852(b)(2)), and in the case of a real estate investment trust its real estate investment trust taxable income (within the meaning of section 857(b)(2)) determined without regard to any deduction for capital gains dividends (as defined in section 857(b)(3)(C)) and by excluding any net capital gain.

(3) NONCORPORATE LESSORS.—A credit shall be allowed by section 38 to a

person which is not a corporation with respect to property of which such person is the lessor only if—

(A) the property subject to the lease has been manufactured or produced by the lessor, or

(B) the term of the lease (taking into account options to renew) is less than 50 percent of the useful life of the property, and for the period consisting of the first 12 months after the date on which the property is transferred to the lessee the sum of the deductions with respect to such property which are allowable to the lessor solely by reason of section 162 (other than rents and reimbursed amounts with respect to such property) exceeds 15 percent of the rental income produced by such property.

In the case of property of which a partnership is the lessor, the credit otherwise allowable under section 38 with respect to such property to any partner which is a corporation shall be allowed notwithstanding the first sentence of this paragraph. For purposes of this paragraph, an electing small business corporation (as defined in section 1371) shall be treated as a person which is not a corporation.

(f) LIMITATION IN CASE OF CERTAIN REGULATED COMPANIES.—

(1) GENERAL RULE.—Except as otherwise provided in this subsection, no credit shall be allowed by section 38 with respect to any property which is public utility property (as defined in paragraph (5)) of the taxpayer—

(A) COST OF SERVICE REDUCTION.—If the taxpayer's cost of service for ratemaking purposes is reduced by reason of any portion of the credit allowable by section 38 (determined without regard to this subsection); or

(B) RATE BASE REDUCTION.—If the base to which the taxpayer's rate of return for ratemaking purposes is applied is reduced by reason of any portion of the credit allowable by section 38 (determined without regard to this subsection).

Subparagraph (B) shall not apply if the reduction in the rate base is restored not less rapidly than ratably. If the taxpayer makes an election under this sentence within 90 days after the date of the enactment of this paragraph in the manner prescribed by the Secretary, the immediately preceding sentence shall not apply to property described in paragraph (5)(B) if any agency or instrumentality of the United States having jurisdiction for ratemaking purposes with respect to such taxpayer's trade or business referred to in paragraph (5)(B) determines that the natural domestic supply of the product furnished by the taxpayer in the course of such trade or business is insufficient to meet the present and future requirements of the domestic economy.

(2) SPECIAL RULE FOR RATABLE FLOW-THROUGH.—If the taxpayer makes an election under this paragraph within 90 days after the date of the enactment of this paragraph in the manner prescribed by the Secretary, paragraph (1) shall not apply, but no credit shall be allowed by section 38 with respect to any property which is public utility property (as defined in paragraph (5)) of the taxpayer—

(A) COST OF SERVICE REDUCTION.—If the taxpayer's cost of service for ratemaking purposes or in its regulated books of account is reduced by more than a ratable portion of the credit allowable by section 38 (determined without regard to this subsection), or

(B) RATE BASE REDUCTION.—If the base to which the taxpayer's rate of return for ratemaking purposes is applied is reduced by reason of any portion of the credit allowable by section 38 (determined without regard to this subsection).

(3) SPECIAL RULE FOR IMMEDIATE FLOW-THROUGH IN CERTAIN CASES.—In the case of property to which section 167(1)(2)(C) applies, if the taxpayer makes an election under this paragraph within 90 days after the date of the enactment of this paragraph in the manner prescribed by the Secretary, paragraphs (1) and (2) shall not apply to such property.

(4) LIMITATION.—

(A) IN GENERAL.—The requirements of paragraphs (1), (2), and (9) regarding cost of service and rate base adjustments shall not be applied to public utility property of the taxpayer to disallow the credit with respect to such property before the first final determination which is inconsistent with paragraph (1), (2), or (9) (as the case may be) is put into effect with respect to public utility property (to which this subsection applies) of the taxpayer. Thereupon, paragraph (1), (2), or (9) shall apply to disallow the credit with respect to public utility property (to which this subsection applies) placed in service by the taxpayer—

(i) before the date that the first final determination, or a subsequent determination, which is inconsistent with paragraph (1), (2), or (9) (as the case may be) is put into effect, and

(ii) on or after the date that a determination referred to in clause (i) is put into effect and before the date that a subsequent determination thereafter which is consistent with paragraph (1), (2), or (9) (as the case may be) is put into effect.

(B) DETERMINATIONS—For purposes of this paragraph, a determination is a determination made with respect to public utility property (to which this subsection applies) by a governmental unit, agency, instrumentality, or commission or similar body described in subsection (c)(3)(B) which determines the effect of the credit allowed by section 38 (determined without regard to this subsection)—

(i) on the taxpayer's cost of service or rate base for ratemaking purposes, or

(ii) in the case of a taxpayer which made an election under paragraph (2) or the election described in paragraph (9), on the taxpayer's cost of service for ratemaking purposes or in its regulated books of account or rate base for ratemaking purposes.

(C) SPECIAL RULES—For purposes of this paragraph—

(i) a determination is final if all rights to appeal or to request a review, a rehearing, or a redetermination, have been exhausted or have lapsed,

(ii) the first final determination is the first final determination made after the date of the enactment of this subsection, and

(iii) a subsequent determination is a determination subsequent to a final determination.

(5) PUBLIC UTILITY PROPERTY.—For purposes of this subsection, the term "public utility property" means—

(A) property which is public utility property within the meaning of subsection (c)(3)(B), and

(B) property used predominantly in the trade or business of the furnishing or sale of (i) steam through a local distribution system or (ii) the transportation of gas or steam by pipeline, if the rates for such furnishing or sale are established or approved by a governmental unit, agency, instrumentality, or commission described in subsection (c)(3)(B).

(6) RATABLE PORTION.—For purposes of determining ratable restorations to base under paragraph (1) and for purposes of determining ratable portions under paragraph (2)(A), the period of time used in computing depreciation expense for purposes of reflecting operating results in the taxpayer's regulated books of account shall be used.

(7) REORGANIZATIONS, ASSETS ACQUISITIONS, ETC.—If by reason of a corporate reorganization, by reason of any other acquisition of the assets of one taxpayer by another taxpayer, by reason of the fact that any trade or business of the taxpayer is subject to ratemaking by more than one body, or by reason of other circumstances, the application of any provisions of this subsection to any public utility property does not carry out the purposes of this subsection, the Secretary shall provide by regulations for the application of such provisions in a manner consistent with the purposes of this subsection.

(8) PROHIBITION OF IMMEDIATE FLOWTHROUGH.—An election made under paragraph (3) shall apply only to the amount of the credit allowable under section 38 with respect to public utility property (within the meaning of *subsection (a)(7)(D)*) determined as if the Tax Reduction Act of 1975, *the Tax Reform Act of 1976, the Energy Act of 1978, and the Revenue Act of 1978* had not been enacted. Any taxpayer who had timely made an election under paragraph (3) may, at his own option and without regard to any requirement imposed by an agency described in subsection (c)(3)(B), elect within 90 days after the date of the enactment of the Tax Reduction Act of 1975 (in such manner as the Secretary shall prescribe) to have the provisions of paragraph (3) apply with respect to the amount of the credit allowable under section 38 with respect to such property which is in excess of the amount determined under the preceding sentence. If such taxpayer does not make such an election, paragraph (1) or (2) (whichever paragraph is applicable without regard to this paragraph) shall apply to such excess credit, except that if neither paragraph (1) nor (2) is applicable (without regard to this paragraph), paragraph (1) shall apply unless the taxpayer elects (in such manner as the Secretary shall prescribe) within 90 days after the date of the enactment of the Tax Reduction Act of 1975 to have

the provisions of paragraph (2) apply. The provisions of this paragraph shall not be applied to disallow such excess credit before the first final determination which is inconsistent with such requirements is made, determined in the same manner as under paragraph (4).

(9) SPECIAL RULE FOR ADDITIONAL CREDIT.—If the taxpayer makes an election under subparagraph (B) of subsection (a)(2), for a taxable year beginning after December 31, 1975, then, notwithstanding the prior paragraphs of this subsection, no credit shall be allowed by section 38 in excess of the amount which would be allowed without regard to the provisions of subparagraph (B) of subsection (a)(2) if—

(A) the taxpayer's cost of service for ratemaking purposes or in its regulated books of account is reduced by reason of any portion of such credit which results from the transfer of employer securities or cash to an employee stock ownership plan which meets the requirements of section 301(d) of the Tax Reduction Act of 1975;

(B) the base to which the taxpayer's rate of return for ratemaking purposes is applied is reduced by reason of any portion of such credit which results from a transfer described in subparagraph (A) to such employee stock ownership plan; or

(C) any portion of the amount of such credit which results from a transfer described in subparagraph (A) to such employee stock ownership plan is treated for ratemaking purposes in any way other than as though it had been contributed by the taxpayer's common shareholders.

(g) 50 PERCENT CREDIT IN THE CASE OF CERTAIN VESSELS.—

(1) IN GENERAL.—In the case of a qualified withdrawal out of the untaxed portion of a capital gain account or out of an ordinary income account in a capital construction fund established under section 607 of the Merchant Marine Act, 1936 (46 U. S. C. 1177), for—

(A) the acquisition, construction, or reconstruction of a qualified vessel, or

(B) the acquisition, construction, or reconstruction of barges or containers which are part of the complement of a qualified vessel and to which subsection (f)(1)(B) of such section 607 applies,

for purposes of section 38 there shall be deemed to have been made (at the time of such withdrawal) a qualified investment (within the meaning of subsection (c)) or qualified progress expenditures (within the meaning of subsection (d)), whichever is appropriate with respect to property which is section 38 property.

(2) AMOUNT OF CREDIT.—For purposes of paragraph (1), the amount of the qualified investment shall be 50 percent of the applicable percentage of the qualified withdrawal referred to in paragraph (1), or the amount of the qualified progress expenditures shall be 50 percent of such withdrawal, as the case may be. For purposes of determining the amount of the credit allowable by reason of this subsection for any taxable year, the limitation of subsection (a)(3) shall be determined without regard to subsection (d)(1)(A) of such section 607.

(3) COORDINATION WITH SECTION 38.—The amount of the credit allowable by reason of this subsection with respect to any property shall be the minimum amount allowable under section 38 with respect to such property. If, without regard to this subsection, a greater amount is allowable under section 38 with respect to such property, then such greater amount shall apply and this subsection shall not apply.

(4) COORDINATION WITH SECTION 47.—Section 47 shall be applied—

(A) to any property to which this subsection applies, and

(B) to the payment (out of the untaxed portion of a capital gain account or out of the ordinary income account of a capital construction fund established under section 607 of the Merchant Marine Act, 1936) of the principal of any indebtedness incurred in connection with property with respect to which a credit was allowed under section 38.

For purposes of section 47, any payment described in subparagraph (B) of the preceding sentence shall be treated as a disposition occurring less than 3 years after the property was placed in service; but, in the case of a credit allowable without regard to this subsection, the aggregate amount which may be recaptured by reason of this sentence shall not exceed 50 percent of such credit.

(5) DEFINITIONS.—Any term used in section 607 of the *Merchant Marine Act, 1936*, shall have the same meaning when used in this subsection.

(6) NO INFERENCE.—Nothing in this subsection shall be construed to infer that any property described in this subsection is or is not section 38 property, and any determination of such issue shall be made as if this subsection had not been enacted.

(h) SPECIAL RULES FOR COOPERATIVES.—In the case of a cooperative organization described in section 1381(a)—

(1) that portion of the credit allowable to the organization under section 38 which the organization cannot use for the taxable year to which the qualified investment is attributable because of the limitation contained in subsection (a)(3) shall be allocated to the patrons of the organization,

(2) section 47 (relating to certain dispositions, etc., of section 38 property) shall be applied as if any allocated portion of the credit had been retained by the organization, and

(3) the rules necessary to carry out the purposes of this subsection shall be determined under regulations prescribed by the Secretary.

SEC. 48. DEFINITIONS; SPECIAL RULES.

(a) SECTION 38 PROPERTY.—

(1) IN GENERAL.—Except as provided in this subsection, the term "section 38 property" means—

(A) tangible personal property (other than an air conditioning or heating unit), or
(B) other tangible property (not including a building and its structural components) but only if such property—

(i) is used as an integral part of manufacturing, production, or extraction or of furnishing transportation, communications, electrical energy, gas, water, or sewage disposal services, or

(ii) constitutes a research facility used in connection with any of the activities referred to in clause (i), or

(iii) constitutes a facility used in connection with any of the activities referred to in clause (i) for the bulk storage of fungible commodities (including commodities in a liquid or gaseous state), or

(C) elevators and escalators, but only if—

(i) the construction, reconstruction, or erection of the elevator or escalator is completed by the taxpayer after June 30, 1963, or

(ii) the elevator or escalator is acquired after June 30, 1963, and the original use of such elevator or escalator commences with the taxpayer and commences after such date, *or*

(D) single purpose agricultural or horticultural structures; or

(E) in the case of a qualified rehabilitated building, that portion of the basis which is attributable to qualified rehabilitation expenditures (within the meaning of subsection (g)).

Such term includes only property with respect to which depreciation (or amortization in lieu of depreciation) is allowable and having a useful life (determined as of the time such property is placed in service) of 3 years or more.

---

(3) PROPERTY USED FOR LODGING.—Property which is used predominantly to furnish lodging or in connection with the furnishing of lodging shall not be treated as section 38 property. The preceding sentence shall not apply to—

(A) nonlodging commercial facilities which are available to persons not using the lodging facilities on the same basis as they are available to persons using the lodging facilities,

(B) property used by a hotel or motel in connection with the trade or business of furnishing lodging where the predominant portion of the accommodations is used by transients, and

(C) coin-operated vending machines and coin-operated washing machines and dryers.

---

(8) Amortized property.—Any property with respect to which an election under section 167(k), 184, *188, or 191* applies shall not be treated as section 38 property.

(d) Certain Leased Property.—

(1) General rule.—A person (other than a person referred to in section 46(e)(1)) who is a lessor of property may (at such time, in such manner, and subject to such conditions as are provided by regulations prescribed by the Secretary) elect with respect to any new section 38 property (other than property described in paragraph (4)) to treat the lessee as having acquired such property for an amount equal to—

(A) except as provided in subparagraph (B), the fair market value of such property, or

(B) if the property is leased by a corporation which is a component member of a controlled group (within the meaning of *section 46(a)(6)*) to another corporation which is a component member of the same controlled group, the basis of such property to the lessor.

(2) Special rule for certain short term leases.—

(A) In general.—A person (other than a person referred to in section 46(e)(1)) who is a lessor of property described in paragraph (4) may (at such time, in such manner, and subject to such conditions as are provided by regulations prescribed by the Secretary) elect with respect to such property to treat the lessee as having acquired a portion of such property for the amount determined under subparagraph (B).

(B) Determination of lessee's investment.—The amount for which a lessee of property described in paragraph (4) shall be treated as having acquired a portion of such property is an amount equal to a fraction, the numerator of which is the term of the lease and the denominator of which is the class life of the property leased (determined under section 167(m)), of the amount for which the lessee would be treated as having acquired the property under paragraph (1).

(C) Determination of lessor's qualified investment.—The qualified investment of a lessor of property described in paragraph (4) in any such property with respect to which he has made an election under this paragraph is an amount equal to his qualified investment in such property (as determined under section 46(c)) multiplied by a fraction equal to the excess of one over the fraction used under subparagraph (B) to determine the lessee's investment in such property.

(3) Limitations.—The elections provided by paragraphs (1) and (2) may be made with respect to property which would be new section 38 property if acquired by the lessee. For purposes of the preceding sentence and section 46(c), the useful life of property in the hands of the lessee is the useful life of such property in the hands of the lessor. If a lessor makes the election provided by paragraph (1) with respect to any property, the lessee shall be treated for all purposes of this subpart as having acquired such property. If a lessor makes the election provided by paragraph (2) with respect to any property, the lessee shall be treated for all purposes of this subpart as having acquired a fractional portion of such property equal to the fraction determined under paragraph (2)(B) with respect to such property.

(4) Property to which paragraph (2) applies.—Paragraph (2) shall apply only to property which—

(A) is new section 38 property,

(B) has a class life (determined under section 167(m)) in excess of 14 years,

(C) is leased for a period which is less than 80 percent of its class life, and

(D) is not leased subject to a net lease (within the meaning of *section 57(c)(1)(B)*).

(g) Special Rules for Qualified Rehabilitated Buildings.—For purposes of this subpart—

(1) Qualified rehabilitated building defined.—

(A) In general.—The term "qualified rehabilitated building" means any

building (and its structural components)—

    (i) which has been rehabilitated,

    (ii) which was placed in service before the beginning of the rehabilitation, and

    (iii) 75 percent or more of the existing external walls of which are retained in place as external walls in the rehabilitation process.

    (B) 20 YEARS MUST HAVE ELAPSED SINCE CONSTRUCTION OR PRIOR REHABILITATION.—A building shall not be a qualified rehabilitated building unless there is a period of at least 20 years between—

    (i) the date the physical work on this rehabilitation of the building began, and

    (ii) the later of—

        (I) the date such building was first placed in service, or

        (II) the date such building was placed in service in connection with a prior rehabilitation with respect to which a credit was allowed by reason of subsection (a)(1)(E).

    (C) MAJOR PORTION TREATED AS SEPARTE BUILDING IN CERTAIN CASES.—Where there is a separate rehabilitation of a major portion of a building, such major portion shall be treated as a separate building.

    (D) REHABILITATION INCLUDES RECONSTRUCTION.—Rehabilitation includes reconstruction.

(2) QUALIFIED REHABILITATION EXPENDITURE DEFINED.—

    (A) IN GENERAL.—The term "qualified rehabilitation expenditure" means any amount properly chargeable to capital account which is incurred after October 31, 1978—

    (i) for property (or additions or improvements to property) with a useful life of 5 years or more, and

    (ii) in connection with the rehabilitation of a qualified rehabilitated building.

    (B) CERTAIN EXPENDITURES NOT INCLUDED.—The term "qualified rehabilitation expenditure" does not include—

    (i) PROPERTY OTHERWISE SECTION 38 PROPERTY.—Any expenditure for property which constitutes section 38 property (determined without regard to subsection (a)(1)(E)).

    (ii) COST OF ACQUISITION.—The cost of acquiring any building or any interest therein.

    (iii) ENLARGEMENTS.—Any expenditure attributable to the enlargement of the existing building.

    (iv) CERTIFIED HISTORIC STRUCTURES.—Any expenditure attributable to the rehabilitation of a certified historic structure (within the meaning of section 191(d)(1)), unless the rehabilitation is a certified rehabilitation (within the meaning of section 191(d)(4)).

213

(3) PROPERTY TREATED AS NEW SECTION 38 PROPERTY.—Property which is treated as section 38 property by reason of subsection (a)(1)(E) shall be treated as new section 38 property.

STATE AND LOCAL STATUTES PROVIDING TAX RELIEF FOR HISTORIC PRESERVATION

A number of states and municipalities now offer relief from real property or income taxation for privately owned historically or architecturally significant properties, in addition to the more traditional property tax exemption granted historic properties owned by nonprofit organizations such as historical societies. These measures encompass relief ranging from complete or partial exemption from property taxes to state income tax deductions similar to those found in section 2124 of the Tax Reform Act of 1976.

Property Tax Relief

I. *Exemption from Property Tax*

A. States

Alaska Statutes section 29.53.025(b)(2)(c)(e) (Supp. 1978) provides that municipalities may, by ordinance ratified by popular vote, totally or partially exempt residential property from real property taxes. The exemption may not exceed $10,000 for any one residence and may benefit historic sites, buildings and monuments.

New York General Municipal Law section 96-a (McKinney 1977), which authorizes the creation of local landmarks and historic district commissions and the designation of significant structures, provides that any controls imposed under these local ordinances that constitute a taking of private property must be offset by due compensation, which may include the limitation or remission of taxes.

Puerto Rico Laws Annotated, title 13, section 551 (Supp. 1977) offers a complete exemption from property tax for up to 10 years for structures that have been completely improved or restored and are located in the San Juan historic district. Partial restoration, which includes restoration of the facade, vestibule and main staircase, earns a five-year exemption.

Texas Revised Civil Statutes article 7150(i) (Vernon Supp. 1978), enacted pursuant to a 1977 amendment to the state constitution, authorizes municipalities to exempt from property tax all or part of a historic structure and the land necessary for its access and use, if the structure is (a) designated as a Recorded Texas Historical Landmark by the Texas Historical Commission and by the governing body of the taxing unit, or (b) designated as a historically significant site under an ordinance adopted by the governing body of the taxing unit and is in need of tax relief to encourage its preservation.

B. Municipalities

Oyster Bay, New York, landmark preservation ordinance section 23-9 provides that properties designated by the town board as landmarks, landmark sites or as within a local historic district are eligible for reimbursement of the general town tax; the building, zoning and Memorial Day assistance tax; and the highway tax.

New York City Code chapter 8A, section 207-8.0(b)-(e) authorizes the Board of Estimate, upon the recommendation of the landmarks preservation commission, to grant designated property a full or partial exemption of property taxes when the property's failure to earn a "reasonable rate of return" would otherwise require granting permission to demolish a structure on the property.

II. *Credit Against Property Tax*

Maryland Annotated Code article 81, section 12G (Supp. 1978) authorizes each county to allow as a credit against local real property tax up to 10 percent of owners' maintenance and restoration costs on properties in locally designated historic districts. The law also authorizes a tax credit of up to 5 percent of the expenses incurred in constructing buildings that are architecturally compatible with the district in which they are located. Both credits may be spread over up to a five-year period.

New Mexico Statutes Annotated section 18-6-13 (1978) recognizes as a credit against local city, county and school real property taxes the costs of restoring or maintaining historic buildings that are listed in the state register of historic places with the written consent of the owner and that are available for educational purposes. Continued allowance of the credit rests on approval by a state review board of all restoration, preservation and maintenance plans. Expenses incurred in one year may be carried forward for tax purposes for up to 10 years. If the property is removed from the state register, an unused and accumulated tax credit shall immediately lapse.

III. *Abatement of Property Tax*

A. States

Arizona Revised Statutes section 42-139.01-.03 (Supp. 1978) authorizes, under a schedule of different assessment rates for separate classes of property, the assessment of historic property at 8 percent of its actual cash value for a 15-year renewable term. To qualify for this special rate, property must be listed in the National Register, be available for public visitation at least 12 days a year and must be maintained in accordance with standards of the Arizona State Parks Board. The owner must also agree not to use the property for profit-making purposes or to charge an admission fee greater than is necessary to offset the building's maintenance or restoration expenses. Disqualification subjects the owner to a tax penalty of either half the reduction in taxes obtained or half the property's fair market value, whichever is less.

Connecticut General Statutes Annotated section 12-127a (West 1972) authorizes municipalities to abate, in whole or in part, real property taxes on historically or architecturally significant structures if "the current level of taxation is a material factor which threatens the continued existence of the structure." The determination of significance is to be made by the municipality or by a local private preservation or architectural group selected by the municipality. All abated taxes must be repaid by the owner if the structure subsequently is demolished or remodeled and thereby loses its significance. The Connecticut legislature may reimburse municipalities for property tax revenues lost on account of this abatement.

North Carolina General Statutes section 105-278 (Supp. 1977) provides that property designated as "historic" under local ordinances shall be taxed on the basis of 50 percent of the property's value upon annual application of the owner. Disqualification for this benefit, such as by an incompatible alteration that causes loss of designation, but not by change of ownership or use, requires the owner to pay back all taxes saved for the prior three years plus interest accumulated.

Oregon Revised Statutes sections 358.475 to 358.565 (1979) allow owners of properties listed in the National Register and open to the public at least once a year to receive a freeze on their assessment for 15 consecutive years at the true cash value of the property at the time of initial application. Eligible property owners must agree to maintain their properties according to standards of the state historic preservation officer. Loss of this special assessment triggers the recapture of all tax savings plus a penalty of 15 percent of those savings if the owner is at fault. No applications for special assessment may be made after December 31, 1985.

Tennessee Code Annotated sections 67-519 to 521 (Cum. Supp. 1978) grant an exemption for the value of improvements to or restoration of any structure certified locally or by the state as significant and when the improvement or restoration either is necessitated by a federal or state preservation or redevelopment plan or is done by property owners who agree to restore their properties in accordance with guidelines specified by a local historic properties review board and to refrain from significantly altering or demolishing their buildings during the exemption period. The exemptions last 10 years for partial or exterior restorations and improvements and 15 years for total restorations. The law provides that only counties of 200,000 or more population (Nashville and Memphis) and incorporated municipalities may choose to utilize this exemption by majority vote of their governing bodies.

B. Municipalities

Austin, Texas, City Code sections 32-49 to 32-55, enacted in 1978 pursuant to an amendment to the state constitution, offer a partial abatement from ad valorem taxation for all structures designated historic landmarks under the city's historic zoning ordinance. Qualifying properties used exclusively as residences or owned by nonprofit organizations shall, upon annual application of their owners, be granted exemptions for 100 percent of the assessed value of their structures and for 50 percent of the assessed value of the portion of the surrounding land found reasonably necessary for the structure's access and use. All other qualifying properties shall be granted exemptions for 50 percent of their structures' assessed values and for 25 percent of the surrounding land's assessed value. If the historic property is rezoned by the city, the owner is liable for all taxes saved during the prior three years.

Code of Brookhaven, New York, section 85-63R authorizes taxpayers whose property is situated within a locally designated district or within 500 feet of the district to receive a limitation or remission of their property taxes in an amount calculated to compensate them for any added costs in maintaining their property in accordance with the standards of the historic district.

Petersburg, Virginia, Historic Zoning Regulations, section 4 provides that the city board of equalization may, upon the recommendation of the board of historic review, grant a reduction in the assessment of designated landmark structures. To qualify for this benefit, the owners of such structures must agree, by written contract, to maintain the structures in good condition.

IV. *Assessment Based on Actual Use*

California Government Code sections 50280-50289 (West 1979); *California Revenue and Taxation Code* sections 439-439.4 (West Supp. 1979);

216

and *California Public Resources Code* sections 5031-5033 (West Supp. 1979) were amended in 1977 pursuant to article XIII, section 8 of the state constitution and provide that owners of qualifying historic properties may have their assessments based on their properties' current uses rather than their highest and best uses. A capitalization of income method is used for this valuation. To qualify, properties must be listed either in the National Register, the state historic properties register or in a city or county register. In addition, the property owners must enter into 20-year renewable contracts with their city or county governments. These contracts typically require the properties to be preserved and maintained, restrict their use and require reasonable public access to the property.

District of Columbia Code Encyclopedia sections 47-651 to 47-654 (West Supp. 1978) specify that eligible historic property shall be assessed at its current use value if that value is lower than its fair market value. To qualify for this benefit, the property must be designated by the Joint Committee on Landmarks and the owner must sign a 20-year covenant guaranteeing the property's maintenance and preservation. Failure to abide by this covenant causes the imposition of a sizable tax penalty and recovery of the tax savings.

Louisiana Revised Statutes Annotated section 47-305.14 (West Supp. 1978) grants an actual use assessment to properties 50 years or older that have been designated as landmarks by state or local jurisdictions and whose owners have signed agreements imposing maintenance and use restrictions on the properties. These agreements, which are renewable every four years, require owners at a minimum to forego all commercial uses of the properties and to devote them to their traditional uses or use as museums. The owners must guarantee the properties' architectural character for at least 10 years and may be required to undertake restoration or rehabilitation. Violations of these agreements will trigger the recovery of property taxes saved during the prior four years.

Nevada Revised Statutes sections 361A.170 to 361A.280 (1977) provide that open space property shall be assessed at 35 percent of its full cash value for open space use. For the purposes of this statute, real property used for open space purposes includes lands on which designated historic sites are situated.

217

Oregon Revised Statutes sections 308.740-308.790 (1977) authorize the assessment of open space land at its actual use value in order to reduce economic pressure and prevent the forced conversion of such land to more intensive uses. "Open space" is defined as any land area whose maintenance in its present condition and use will preserve historic sites.

Virginia Code Annotated sections 58-769.4 to 58-769.16 (1974) provide that certain qualifying land shall be assessed as open space in order to counter economic market pressures that might otherwise force its more intensive development. "Real estate devoted to open-space use" is defined to include land used for historical purposes under uniform standards prescribed by the director of the Commission of Outdoor Recreation.

Washington Revised Code Annotated sections 84.34.010 to 84.34.921 (Supp. 1977) authorize procedures for the separate assessment for property tax purposes of open space land, which for this purpose is defined to include any land whose preservation in its present use would preserve historic sites.

V. *Deferral of Increase in Assessment Due to Rehabilitation*

Maryland Annotated Code article 81 authorizes Allegany County (section

9C(b)(8) of article 81), Frederick County (section 9c(j)(3) of article 81) and Washington County (section 9C(o-1)(3) of article 81) (Cum. Supp. 1978) to grant a credit against property tax for improvements to historically and architecturally significant structures. The credit declines over a five-year period from 100 percent of the increase in assessed valuation attributable to the improvements the first year to a 40 percent credit the fifth year. Thereafter, all improvements made during that five-year period are added to the assessed valuation.

VI. *Assessments to Reflect Encumbrances on Property*

A. A number of states that have enacted statutes validating facade and scenic easements for historic preservation purposes have mandated, at the same time, that property tax assessors must take into account the effect of easements in determining property assessments. These states are the following:

California Government Code section 51064 (West Supp. 1979) (open space easements only).

Colorado Revised Statutes section 38-30.5-109 (Supp. 1978).

Connecticut General Statutes Annotated section 7-131b (West 1972) (open space easements only—owner entitled to revaluation).

Georgia Code Annotated section 85-1409 (1978) (owner entitled to revaluation).

Illinois Municipal Code section 11-48.2-6 (Smith-Hurd Supp. 1978) (easements acquired by governmental bodies only).

Oregon Revised Statutes sections 271.710 to 271.750 (1977).

Tennessee Code Annotated section 11-1805 (Supp. 1978) (acquired by governmental bodies only).

Texas Revised Civil Statutes article 7150n (Vernon Supp. 1978).

Virginia Code section 10-155 (1978).

B. State statutes requiring the property tax assessor to consider, for the purposes of tax assessments, the effect of designations by state or local historic preservation commissions and/or the effect of recorded preservation restrictions on such designated properties are the following:

North Carolina General Statutes section 160A-399.5(6) (1976) (local designations only).

South Dakota Codified Laws Annotated section 1-19B-25 (1974).

Virginia Code sections 10-139, 10-140 and 10-142 (1978) (state designations only and restrictions imposed only with owner's consent).

West Virginia Code sections 8-26A-5 (1976) (Supp. 1978) (restrictions only with owner's consent).

C. *Colorado Revised Statutes* section 39-1-104(5) (Supp. 1978) forbids local tax assessors from increasing the assessed valuation of property on the basis of its inclusion in the state register of historic places.

Miscellaneous

South Dakota Codified Laws sections 1-19A-20 and 1-19A-21 (Supp. 1978). Establishes a moratorium on the taxation of real property listed in the state register of historic places and which has been either (1) assisted through a federal preservation grant-in-aid, (2) substantially restored or rehabilitated with a state historic preservation loan or (3) privately restored or rehabilitated and approved by the state board of cultural preservation. The moratorium extends for five years from the year that the property qualifies until the work is completed. To qualify, property owners must also attach a restrictive covenant running with the land that states that the property will be maintained in an appropriate manner.

Income Tax Relief

Maryland Annotated Code article 81, section 281A (Supp. 1978) provides for a tax deduction, amortized over five years, of the expenses incurred in rehabilitating certain owner-occupied historic structures.

Puerto Rico Laws Annotated title 13, section 3022(26) (Supp. 1975) exempts from gross income for income tax purposes all rental income from the lease of buildings in the historic zone of San Juan and in any other historic zone established by the Institute of Puerto Rican Culture.

Property Tax Relief for Renovation or Rehabilitation

Many state statutes now offer tax relief for activities and instances that implicitly, rather than explicitly, benefit historic structures. Listed below are a sampling of these statutes.

I. States

Colorado Revised Statutes section 39-5-105 states that any rehabilitation or modernization commenced on or after July 1, 1976, to a residential structure of three units or less and more than 30 years old shall not be taken into account in determining the assessment of the structure for the five tax years immediately following completion of the work. Rehabilitation and modernization, for the purposes of this statute, do not include room additions; the conversion of patios, porches or garages into living areas; the addition of outbuildings; or a change in the structures' use.

Illinois Revised Statutes chapter 120, section 500.23-3 (Smith-Hurd Supp. 1978), known as the Illinois Homestead Improvement Act, offers a tax exemption for private home improvements limited to $15,000 in actual value, occurring in counties of 1,000,000 or more in population (Cook County only). The exemption is limited to properties owned and used exclusively for residential purposes and requires a showing that the increase in assessed value for which the exemption is claimed is attributable solely to the structural improvements. The exemption may be spread over a four-year period for tax purposes.

1966 Rhode Island Public Laws chapter 15 authorizes the Providence tax assessor to abate, for a period of five years, any increase in tax assessment resulting from alterations and improvements to existing dwellings that are used exclusively for residential purposes. Alterations and improvements must be completed within two years of their commencement. For structures not used exclusively for residential purposes, the increased assessment is apportioned and the abatement benefits only that part used for residential purposes. This statute, which as enacted applied to alterations and improvements commenced between June 1, 1966, and June 1, 1968, has been extended several times and is still in effect, according to the Rhode Island Historical Preservation Commission.

Virginia Code Annotated sections 58-760.2 and 58-760.3 (Supp. 1978) provide that Virginia jurisdictions are authorized to exempt from real property taxation for up to 10 years increases in assessed value resulting from improvements to rehabilitated residential, commercial or industrial structures of 25 years in age or older. To qualify, the assessed value of residential structures must have increased 40 percent and that of commercial and industrial structures 60 percent.

II. Municipalities

Utica, New York, Code section 4.340 grants the planning board the right to permit tax relief not to exceed 20 percent of the assessed value of improvements to a building or structure that is undergoing renovation, remodeling, rehabilitation or new construction.

Inheritance Tax Relief

Maryland House Bill 275, passed by the 1978 session of the Maryland General Assembly, provides that land used for farming purposes at least five years preceding, and five years following, the owner's death shall be taxed for inheritance tax purposes at its current use value, rather than at its fair market value.